STUDIES IN WELSH H

RALPH A. GRIFFITHS   CHRIS WILLIAMS
ERYN M. WHITE

38

THE OPPOSITION TO THE GREAT WAR
IN WALES, 1914–1918

THE OPPOSITION TO THE GREAT WAR IN WALES, 1914–1918

by

ALED EIRUG

CARDIFF
UNIVERSITY OF WALES PRESS
2018

www.uwp.co.uk

British Library CIP Data
A catalogue record for this book is available from the British Library

ISBN 978-1-78683-314-3
eISBN 978-1-78683-315-0

The right of Aled Eirug to be identified as author of this work has been asserted in accordance with sections 77 and 79 of the Copyright, Designs and Patents Act 1988.

MIX
Paper from
responsible sources
FSC
www.fsc.org
FSC® C013604

Typeset by Mark Heslington Ltd, Scarborough, North Yorkshire
Printed by CPI Antony Rowe, Melksham

SERIES EDITORS' FOREWORD

Since the foundation of the series in 1977, the study of Wales's history has attracted growing attention among historians internationally and continues to enjoy a vigorous popularity. Not only are approaches, both traditional and new, to the study of history in general being successfully applied in a Welsh context, but Wales's historical experience is increasingly appreciated by writers on British, European and world history. These advances have been especially marked in the university institutions in Wales itself.

In order to make more widely available the conclusions of original research, much of it of limited accessibility in postgraduate dissertations and theses, in 1977 the History and Law Committee of the Board of Celtic Studies inaugurated this series of monographs, *Studies in Welsh History*. It was anticipated that many of the volumes would originate in research conducted in the University of Wales or under the auspices of the Board of Celtic Studies, and so it proved. Although the Board of Celtic Studies no longer exists, the University of Wales Press continues to sponsor the series. It seeks to publish significant contributions made by researchers in Wales and elsewhere. Its primary aim is to serve historical scholarship and to encourage the study of Welsh history.

CONTENTS

ACKNOWLEDGEMENTS

This book has been in gestation since 1977 and has been inspired by my father, Dewi Eirug Davies, a conscientious objector in the Second World War, and my grandfather Tom Eirug, a conscientious objector in the First World War, who unfortunately I never met. I have tremendous respect and love for both men and they have been at my side on this journey towards publication.

My academic interest in the Opposition to the Great War was inspired by the boundless enthusiasm and ceaseless intellectual curiosity of my history tutor in Aberystwyth University, Deian Hopkin. Although a life and a career in journalism intervened to postpone work on this book until 2010, for thirty years, my interest in Welsh history was sustained by Llafur, the Welsh people's history society, the inspiring example of its founders, including Deian, the miners' leader Dai Francis and his son Hywel, its organiser Sian Williams and the comradeship of its members. It has made a remarkable contribution to political and historical thought in Wales, and has brought thinkers from different traditions together to create history that is relevant to us all.

The key individual who made this book possible is Professor Chris Williams of Cork University, my supervisor, who shepherded an inexperienced, albeit mature, student through the pitfalls and blind alleys of research. Dr Martin Wright was a pillar of strength both as chair of Llafur and as my second supervisor, and Professor Bill Jones has shared his wisdom generously in the preparation of this book.

Numerous archives and libraries have been used for this book and I wish to record my thanks to the staff of the following institutions in Wales: the National Library of Wales, Bangor University Library and Archive, the South Wales Miners' Library and Archive, the West Glamorgan Archive in Swansea, Cardiff University Library and Archive, Merthyr and Aberdare Public libraries, the Glamorgan Archives in Cardiff, and Cardiff Central Library. Beyond our borders, staff were unfailingly courteous and helpful at the British Library of Political and Economic Science in my *alma mater* in the London School of Economics, the National Archives at Kew, the House of Lords Archives, and the Friends House Library, the Bodleian Library in Oxford, the Cumbria Archives in Carlisle and the National Library of Scotland in Edinburgh.

Particular thanks are due to the Studies in Welsh History series editors, and in particular to Professor Chris Williams for his support, and Dr Llion Wigley and the staff of the University of Wales Press for guiding this book through the press. I must, however, take responsibility for any remaining errors.

Finally I owe an enormous debt of gratitude to my family. My wife, Maggie, has had to deal with my obsession with the Great War for the past eight years, and she has been a loving presence, knowing when to cajole, chivvy or sympathise. I owe her a great deal and this book is dedicated to her. I thank my stepchildren, Max and Holly, and my son, Tane, for their crucial love and support, and hope that this book will help them gain an understanding of how our generation stand on the shoulders of those who have gone before them.

LIST OF TABLES

ABBREVIATIONS

Conscientious Objectors	COs
Fellowship of Reconciliation	FoR
Friends Ambulance Unit	FAU
Independent Labour Party	ILP
International Bible Students' Association	IBSA
London School of Economics	LSE
Miners' Federation of Great Britain	MFGB
National Archives	NA
National Council for Civil Liberties	NCCL
National Library of Scotland	NLS
National Library of Wales	NLW
No-Conscription Fellowship	NCF
Non-Combatant Corps	NCC
South Wales Miners' Federation	SWMF
Royal Army Medical Corps	RAMC
Union of Democratic Control	UDC
Unofficial Reform Committee	URC

INTRODUCTION

The commemoration of the hundredth anniversary of the Great War has concentrated on the military aspects of the conflict. Given that over 750,000 British soldiers died during the course of the war, including 35,000 Welshmen, it is inevitable that this terrible legacy has been uppermost in our minds. This war dominated British society for a generation, and its lasting effect was to mobilise civil society in support of the armed forces in 'total war'. But attitudes towards the war were not uniform throughout the country, and those who doubted the wisdom of going to war, and dissented from the rush to arms, were obscured by the public hysteria and the initial enthusiasm that greeted the outbreak of the conflict. This study suggests that our understanding of the impact of the profoundly traumatic experience of the Great War and the effect of this social and economic watershed for Welsh society is incomplete without an appreciation of the diversity of responses to it, including the opposition to the war.

The shock of the onset of war in August 1914, the pro-war enthusiasm of Welsh political leaders, such as Lloyd George, and the patriotic fervour that led thousands to volunteer for the armed forces have tended to dominate our image of Wales's initial response to war. This shock was heightened by the contrast with Wales's pre-war radical Nonconformist tradition of pacifism and its deep suspicion of the armed forces, regarded as social outcasts and unemployable. The army was suspicious towards the Welsh language, and Nonconformist ministers were prohibited from serving as chaplains.[1] This antipathy towards the military was reflected by Wales's status as the leanest recruiting area in Britain

---

[1] John S. Ellis, 'Pacifism, militarism and Welsh identity', in Matthew Cragoe and Chris Williams (eds), *Wales and War: Society, Politics and Religion in the Nineteenth and Twentieth Centuries* (Cardiff: University of Wales Press, 2007), pp. 22–3.

before the war, when Welshmen made up only 1.8 per cent of the regular army.[2]

The pacifist legacy was closely associated with a number of formidable Nonconformist radicals, including Samuel Roberts, Llanbrynmair, who had opposed the Crimean War and campaigned for an international arbitration court, and Henry Richard, the Member of Parliament for Merthyr, known as the 'Member for Wales', the 'Apostle of Peace' and leader of the Peace Society in the nineteenth century. Their spiritual mantle was taken up by the anti-militarism of the first Labour Member of Parliament and spiritual leader of the Independent Labour Party (ILP), Keir Hardie, MP for the Merthyr Boroughs, and even that of Lloyd George's unpopular opposition to the South African War.

Welsh civil society, including the Nonconformist denominations, encouraged by Lloyd George's persuasive pleading, supported the military recruiting campaign for volunteers to come to the defence of the neutrality of Belgium and for Wales to be seen to play its part amongst the nations of the British Empire. A total of over 122,995 men volunteered for the armed forces before January 1916, and 272,924 Welshmen enlisted in the armed forces throughout the war.[3] Welsh society was transformed for the purposes of war, and the state intervened in daily life to an unprecedented extent. Undoubtedly, the majority of Welsh people supported the war effort, but the extent of this support waxed and waned throughout the period 1914–18, as the initial hope that the war would be over within months gave way to a more realistic understanding of the requirements of 'total war' and its human cost.

In spite of the thousands of tomes published to coincide with the commemoration of the hundredth anniversary of the Great War, little of this archive material as it reflects the opposition to the Great War in Wales has been explored hitherto. This book provides the first comprehensive study of the breadth and depth of the opposition to the Great War in Wales, and is primarily based on my fuller doctoral thesis on

---

[2] Robin Barlow, *Wales and World War One* (Llandysul: Gomer, 2014), p. 22.

[3] Chris Williams, 'Taffs in the trenches: Welsh national identity and military service 1914–1918', in Cragoe and Williams (eds), *Wales and War*, p. 126.

the subject of 'Opposition to the Great War in Wales', and also on a number of articles that have analysed aspects of the anti-war movement.[4] This study is largely based on a number of archive collections that include material relevant to the anti-war movement, but have not been researched previously in the Welsh context. They include the collections of the No-Conscription Fellowship (NCF) in Cumbria Archives and the Friends House Library, the papers of the Fellowship of Reconciliation (FoR) and the Independent Labour Party in the London School of Economics, and the South Wales Miners' Library in Swansea University for archive material and tapes of interviews with union activists and conscientious objectors. A number of personal archive collections have been especially valuable, including the E. K. Jones collection in the National Library of Wales, the Thomas Jones papers in Bangor University and the National Library of Wales, and the Emrys Hughes collection in the National Library of Scotland. I am indebted to a number of families of conscientious objectors for entrusting me with their private papers, including those of Percy Ogwen Jones, Albert Davies and D. J. Davies (Rhondda). A small number of newspapers have been an indispensable resource for plotting the course of the opposition to the war in Wales, and those include the *Pioneer*, published by the ILP in Merthyr and mainly circulating in the south Wales coalfield, *Y Deyrnas*, which between October 1916 and the summer of 1919 was the only dedicated anti-war newspaper in Wales, and the NCF's newspaper, the *Tribunal.*

The opposition to the war in Britain has been described and assessed, with greatly varying degrees of thoroughness and detail, in scattered histories of the labour movement,

---

[4] Aled Eirug, 'Opposition to the First World War in Wales 1914–1918' (unpublished PhD thesis, Cardiff University, 2017); Aled Eirug, 'Agweddau ar y Gwrthwynebiad i'r Rhyfel Byd Cyntaf yng Nghymru (Aspects of the Opposition to the First World War in Wales)', *Llafur*, 4/4 (1987), 58–68; Aled Eirug, 'Gwrthwynebu'r Rhyfel Mawr yng Nghwm Tawe', *Llafur*, 12/1 (2016), 25–42; Aled Eirug, 'Spies and Troublemakers in South Wales: How British intelligence targeted peace and labour activists in south Wales at the height of the Great War', *Llafur*, 12/1 (2016), 103–15; Aled Eirug, 'Rhaff ac iddi amryw geinciau: Gwrthwynebiad i'r Rhyfel Mawr yng Nghymru', in Gethin Matthews (ed.), *Creithiau* (Cardiff: University of Wales Press, 2016), pp. 141–62; Aled Eirug, 'The Security Services in South Wales during the First World War', *Welsh History Review*, 28/4 (2017), 753–84.

religion, the security services, the peace movement and pacifism, and that of conscientious objectors. The range and
significance of opposition to the war in Wales has rarely been
discussed in any depth in these histories, and within the
British context, attempts to measure and assess the activities
of anti-war organisations on a local or regional level have
been rare. This book sets out to address this omission, to
describe the extent of political and religious opposition to
the Great War in Wales and to assess how influential it
became as a coherent political movement.

Recent general histories of Wales have been characterised
as influenced by either a labour or political/cultural nationalist tradition. As Johnes points out in relation to the growth
of labour history, both traditions occasionally overlap and
have contributed to a greater sense of Welsh identity,[5]
although that writing has often been done to 'safeguard, or
justify a particular standpoint in the historian's present'.[6] He
highlights the 'heroic undertone' of some labour history,[7]
and Davies warns of 'idolising the heroes of the long march
of labour',[8] but the subject of opposition to the war has not
fitted comfortably into either a labour or nationalist narrative. This book's aim is to consider the full range of anti-war
activity in its own right, rather than as an incomplete part of
another narrative of Welsh history.

This study considers the active opposition to the war
beyond the portrayal of the travails of the individual conscientious objector, by placing anti-war activists within a
religious, social and political context, and within those
geographical, political and industrial communities that gave
them succour. Even though the Great War was one of the
major transformational historical periods for Wales, it is
remarkable that only recently have comprehensive and more
nuanced treatments of the impact of the war on Wales been

[5] Martin Johnes, 'For Class and Nation: Dominant Trends in the Historiography
of Twentieth Century Wales', in *History Compass*, 8/11 (2010), 1257–74.
[6] Russell Davies, *Hope and Heartbreak: A Social History of Wales and the Welsh, 1776–1871* (Cardiff: University of Wales Press, 2005), p. 11.
[7] Johnes, 'For Class and Nation', 1258.
[8] Russell Davies, *People, Places and Passions: 'Pain and Pleasure': A Social History of Wales and the Welsh 1870–1945* (Cardiff: University of Wales Press, 2015), p. 13.

published.[9] In contrast, the Great War experiences of both Scotland and Ireland have been the subject of substantial studies, most notably in Jeffery's military histories of Ireland, and Spiers, Crang and Strickland's military history of Scotland.[10]

The promisingly titled *Wales and the Quest for Peace* highlights Wales's peace tradition in the nineteenth century but falters in its consideration of the war, and whilst suggesting that the 'Socialist movement' was in a state of disarray,[11] fails to explore the extent of the influence of the anti-war movement.[12] The two full-length general histories of the Great War in Wales are Jenkins's richly visual evocation of the war on the home front and the front line, and Barlow's wide-ranging study of all aspects of the war. Both provide an accessible, popular and episodic account of aspects of the war, both on the home front and in the trenches, through the eyes of ordinary Welshmen and women. Barlow recognises that there is little agreement amongst historians about the efficacy of the opposition to the war, yet doubts whether there was a 'coherent and unified anti-war movement'.[13] He describes the opposition as 'localised, limited and largely *ad hoc*',[14] and concentrates on the individual fate of eight prominent conscientious objectors, ranging from the socialist Emrys Hughes and the Marxist Arthur Horner to the Christian pacifist views of George M. Ll. Davies. He contends that 'the torch of pacifism was kept alight in Wales by a number of prominent individuals'[15] rather than by a wider movement. However, whilst it may be argued that the

---

[9] Barlow, *Wales and World War One*; Gwyn Jenkins, *Cymry'r Rhyfel Byd Cyntaf* (Talybont: Y Lolfa, 2014).

[10] Keith Jeffery, *Ireland and the Great War* (Cambridge University Press, 2000); Thomas Bartlett and Keith Jeffery (eds), *A Military History of Ireland* (Cambridge University Press, 1996); Catriona M. M. Macdonald and E. W. McFarland (eds), *Scotland and the Great War* (Edinburgh: John Donald, 2014); Edward M. Spiers, Jeremy Crang and Matthew Strickland (eds), *A Military History of Scotland* (Edinburgh University Press, 2012).

[11] Goronwy J. Jones, *The Quest for Peace* (Cardiff: University of Wales Press, 1969), p. 90.

[12] Jones, *The Quest for Peace*, pp. 91–2.

[13] Barlow, *Wales and World War One*, p. 132.

[14] Barlow, *Wales and World War One*, p. 118.

[15] Barlow, *Wales and World War One*, p. 124.

anti-war movement was disparate in nature, this should not imply that there was no effective organisation or that on occasion, such as in the summer and autumn of 1917, it caused the government concern for the dangers of serious social, industrial and political discontent in the south Wales mining valleys in particular.

Barlow himself refers to two meetings that reflect the full force of the disagreement over the war in south Wales. A peace meeting of over 400 delegates, organised in Cardiff in November 1916 to oppose conscription, was violently disrupted by an angry crowd of 'patriots', but he only briefly mentions the rescheduled rally held in Merthyr the following month, described as 'the most remarkable meeting of the war', which attracted a supportive anti-war crowd of 3,000 people.[16]

Professor Kenneth O. Morgan, who has created the intellectual framework for much of the development of Welsh history in the second half of the twentieth century,[17] describes the impact of the war as the final blow to the 'radical idealism' of the Welsh national movement that had been sustained by the Liberal Nonconformity political hegemony. His most recent discussion of the Great War reflects Braybon's view that the multidimensional nature of war and the 'complexity of its impact on different societies and social groups emphasises there is no one war experience'.[18] He recognises that the portrayal of Wales as enthusiastically pro-war is 'a deceptive, incomplete picture', and describes 'important areas of dissent hidden by the public hysteria of wartime'. He instances the growth of 'humane Liberal dissent' against the war, argues that the government's growing attacks on civil liberties caused many Liberals to desert Lloyd George,[19] and describes 'powerful and aggressive anti-war dissent' amongst 'workers in the Valleys', especially after the introduction of military conscription in January 1916, and the growth of

[16] Barlow, *Wales and World War One*, p. 30.
[17] Neil Evans, 'Writing the Social History of Modern Wales: Approaches, Achievements and Problems', *Social History*, 17/3 (1992), 481.
[18] Gail Braybon, *Evidence, History and the Great War* (New York, Oxford: Berghahn Books, 2003), p. 5.
[19] K. O. Morgan, *Revolution to Devolution; Reflections on Welsh Democracy* (Cardiff: University of Wales Press, 2014), pp. 158–9.

syndicalism and pressure for workers' control in the mining industry in the latter half of the war.[20]

Yet his general portrayal of Wales is primarily one of enthusiasm for the war, and he illustrates this in the readiness of miners' agents to participate in the recruiting campaigns, the defeat of the ILP in the Merthyr by-election in 1915, held after Hardie's death, and greater support for the war effort encouraged by Lloyd George's accession to the premiership in December 1916.[21] His case is built primarily on the basis of military enlistment figures drawn from Nicholson's and Williams's propagandist publication, *Wales: Its Part in the War*,[22] commissioned by the War Office, to suggest that Wales had the largest percentage of recruits of the four nations of the British Isles. Their statistics stated that in Scotland 13.02 per cent of men, as a percentage of the total population, were recruited to the armed forces; in England the figure was 13.3 per cent, and in Wales 13.82 per cent.

However, these recruiting figures used to illustrate Wales's greater enthusiasm for the war were based on an erroneous interpretation of the statistics, derived from a speech by Sir Auckland Geddes, the Director of Recruiting, to the House of Commons on 14 January 1919.[23] The official statistics reveal that 11.57 per cent of England's total population enlisted, compared with 11.5 per cent of Scotland's total population and 10.96 per cent of Wales's population.[24] Morgan's continuing use of these mistaken figures over the past fifty years, although he now concedes that they are 'strongly contested',[25] has contributed to the myth of Wales's greater enthusiasm to such an extent that it has skewed and oversimplified the interpretation of the response to war by

---

[20] Morgan, *Revolution to Devolution*, p. 164.

[21] K. O. Morgan, *Wales in British Politics 1868–1922* (Cardiff: University of Wales Press, 1970), p. 283.

[22] Ivor Nicholson and Lloyd Williams, *Wales: Its Part in the War* (Hodder and Stoughton, 1919), p. 29.

[23] Barlow, *Wales and World War One*, p. 21; Clive Hughes, *I'r Fyddin Fechgyn Gwalia; Recriwtio i'r Fyddin yng Ngogledd-Orllewin Cymru 1914–1916* (Llanrwst: Gwasg Carreg Gwalch, 2014), p. 277.

[24] *Statistics of the Military Effort of the British Empire during the Great War* (HMSO, 1922), p. 364; Chris Williams, 'Taffs in the trenches: Welsh national identity and military service 1914–1918', in Cragoe and Williams (eds), *Wales and War*, p. 126.

[25] Morgan, *Revolution to Devolution*, p. 152.

other historians, such as Gareth Elwyn Jones, J. Graham Jones and Philip Jenkins.[26]

David Williams's groundbreaking synthesis of modern Welsh history, whilst recognising that 'life in Wales in the quarter of a century after 1914 was entirely dominated by the First World War and its consequences', did not pursue the implications of his statement,[27] whilst Davies's voluminous *Hanes Cymru* takes a similar view to Morgan, in contrasting Wales's pre-war peace tradition with Wales's initial enthusiasm for military adventure and acceptance of the justification for the war.[28] Gwyn Alf Williams's combative and iconoclastic *When Was Wales?* characterises the war as an 'unhingeing shock of the first order, above all to the pacifist and small-nation pieties of Welsh Liberalism',[29] and portrays attitudes towards the war as split between the majority that 'rallied to the War' and the 'resistance', which was comprised of a fusion of Christian pacifism, revolutionary socialism and Marxism. But studies such as Barlow's highlight the general dearth of Welsh historiography that addresses the subject of opposition to the Great War in Wales.

Whilst the significance of the anti-war movement has not been pursued in any detail by generalist Welsh historians, there have been a number of significant contributions to our understanding of the range of religious opposition towards the war. The writing of the history of the opposition to the Great War in Wales has been heavily influenced by the active Christian peace movement that emerged in Wales during the first half of the Second World War, especially in the Welsh language. A series of pamphlets was published under the banner of 'Cymdeithas Heddychwyr Cymru' (Society of Welsh Pacifists), an active Welsh-language version of the Peace Pledge Union, with Gwynfor Evans, later to become President of the Welsh Nationalist party in 1945, as its main

[26] Gareth Elwyn Jones, *Modern Wales, A Concise History, 1485–1979* (Cambridge University Press, 1984); J. Graham Jones, *The History of Wales* (Cardiff: University of Wales Press, 1990); Philip Jenkins, *The History of Modern Wales 1536–1990* (Longmans, 1992); Barlow, *Wales and World War One*, p. 20.

[27] David Williams, *The History of Modern Wales* (John Murray, 1950), p. 286.

[28] John Davies, *Hanes Cymru* (Allen Lane, 1990), pp. 494–6.

[29] Gwyn A. Williams, *When Was Wales?* (Penguin Books, 1985, repr. 1991), p. 249.

organiser in Wales.[30] Mainly written by nationalists who were also pacifist, they reflected the tendency within the Welsh nationalist party to eschew armed force and to support a neutral stance during the Second World War. This literature placed pacifism and opposition to war solidly within the Liberal Nonconformist tradition associated with Henry Richard and Samuel Roberts, Llanbrynmair, and gave little attention to the socialist or Marxist opponents of the Great War. Evans, the secretary of the Peace Pledge Union in Wales, was instrumental in ensuring that pacifism remained a core belief of Plaid Cymru until he relinquished the presidency of the party thirty-eight years later.[31]

The most comprehensive description of the anti-war religious movement is Dewi Eirug Davies's *Byddin y Brenin*,[32] which reviews the attitudes of church and chapel through the prism of the Welsh religious press, and celebrates the stories of a number of conscientious objectors. It analyses the mainly pro-war religious press of the time and the response of key religious figures, such as Revd John Williams, Brynsiencyn, who recruited enthusiastically for the army and became chaplain to the Welsh Army Corps, and highlights those ministers who gave the anti-war movement and the ILP moral succour and practical support in their strongholds.[33] A further collection of hagiographical essays that celebrate leading conscientious objectors and others active in the peace movement during the two world wars, produced by Rees on behalf of the Fellowship of Reconciliation, reflects this uncritical tradition in *Herio'r Byd* (Challenging the World) and *Dal i Herio'r Byd* (Still Challenging the World).[34]

Histories of the Nonconformist denominations in Wales have given scant attention to the impact of the war, and even less to the religious opposition to the war. Whilst a number of valuable biographies have focused on prominent anti-war individuals, such as the Fellowship of Reconciliation's

[30] *Pamffledi Heddychwyr Cymru* (Denbigh: Gwasg Gee, 1943).

[31] Rhys Evans, *Gwynfor Evans: Rhag Pob Brad* (Talybont: Y Lolfa, 2005).

[32] Dewi Eirug Davies, *Byddin y Brenin: Cymru a'i Chrefydd yn yn Rhyfel Mawr* (Swansea: Tŷ John Penry, 1988).

[33] Davies, *Byddin y Brenin*, pp. 151–76.

[34] D. Ben Rees, *Herio'r Byd* (Liverpool: Cyhoeddiadau Modern Cymreig, 1980); D. Ben Rees, *Dal i Herio'r Byd* (Liverpool: Cyhoeddiadau Modern Cymreig, 1983).

assistant secretary, George M. Ll. Davies,[35] little attention has been paid to the views of the anti-war millenarian sects, such as the Christadelphians, Jehovah's Witnesses and Plymouth Brethren, who constituted a substantial proportion of the conscientious objectors who opposed the war.

Wallis's history of the Fellowship of Reconciliation focuses mainly on the founders of the organisation centrally and gives very little detail about the FoR's development in Wales,[36] while Evans's history of the Society of Friends in Wales emphasises that it had very little presence in Wales beyond Colwyn Bay, Radnorshire, Swansea and Cardiff.[37] Pope suggests that the 'Nonconformist predilection for pacifism' was brought to a shuddering end by the introduction of military conscription in 1916, and marked 'the end of both political Nonconformity and the Liberal party'.[38] His primary interest is in the impact of war on the Nonconformist denominations and, in common with a number of other studies, concentrates on the attitudes of certain key individuals, such as Principal Thomas Rees, Revd John Puleston Jones and George M. Ll. Davies. He is dismissive of the naivety of pacifists and contends that they 'had drunk deeply from the wells of Hegelian idealism and Kantian moralism' in the belief that mankind was on a revolutionary path towards perfection, but that war was a temporary regression. Pope summarises the conflicting attitudes towards the war within Nonconformity as between those who accepted the case that the state had justified the decision to go to war, and those opposed to the war who believed that force should not be an option in resolving international disputes.[39] Morgan similarly portrays a gloomy picture of the war as marking the fault-line between religious and post-religious Wales, and defines the

[35] Jen Llywelyn, *Pilgrim of Peace: A Life of George M. Ll. Davies, Pacifist, Conscientious Objector, and Peacemaker* (Talybont: Y Lolfa, 2016).
[36] Jill Wallis, *Valiant for Peace: A History of the Fellowship of Reconciliation 1914 to 1989* (Fellowship of Reconciliation, 1991)
[37] Owain Gethin Evans, *Benign Neglect: Quakers and Wales circa 1860–1918* (Wrexham: Bridge Books, 2014).
[38] Robert Pope, 'Christ and Caesar? Welsh Nonconformists and the State', in Cragoe and Williams (eds), *Wales and War*, pp. 4–5.
[39] Robert Pope, 'Welsh Nonconformists and the State 1914–1918', in Cragoe and Williams, *Wales and War*, p. 174.

principal intellectual weaknesses of Welsh pacifism in this period as:

> an inability to face the implications of corporate morality and explicitly social ethics and idealism which had scant appreciation for the depths of human malignancy and evil … Lacking an adequate doctrine of structural sin and corporate redemption, no matter how vigorously pacifist Dissenters protested at the undoubted horrors of war, they failed to provide a sufficiently realistic philosophy whereby conflict could be overcome and abolished.[40]

In contrast to Davies's *Byddin y Brenin*, Morgan's emphasis is on the individualistic pacifism of those opposed to the war, and he does not place it within either a social, geographical or political context.

The other major motivation for the anti-war movement was the political opposition to the war. The importance of the members of the Independent Labour Party to the anti-war movement is recognised by Dowse's *Left in the Centre*,[41] in which he traces the party's developing response to the war from August 1914 onwards, although he does not analyse the ILP's activity on a regional level. He highlights the different emphases given by various socialist anti-war activists, such as David Thomas, the organiser of the ILP in north Wales, who argued against the war on moral and religious principles, and Mark Starr, the miner and lecturer on Marxist economics, who viewed the needs of capitalism and imperialism as the causes of the war. Lewis's brief analysis of the growth of the Labour Party in Wales recognises growing scepticism towards the war effort, and the growth of the revolutionary anti-capitalist movement, but contends that hostility towards an anti-war stance remained strong.[42] Tanner's study of the growth of the Labour Party between 1900 and 1918 identifies the war as the crucial event that changed the political and ideological climate of the time and cemented the 'symbiotic

---

[40] D. Densil Morgan, *The Span of the Cross: Christian Religion and Society in Wales 1914–2000* (Cardiff: University of Wales Press, 1999), p. 46.

[41] R. E. Dowse, *Left in the Centre* (Longmans, 1966).

[42] Richard Lewis, 'Political Culture and Ideology, 1900–1918', in Duncan Tanner, Chris Williams and Deian Hopkin (eds), *The Labour Party in Wales 1900–2000* (Cardiff: University of Wales Press, 2000), pp. 103–5.

link' between the miners and the Labour Party. His central argument, that the growth of Labour cannot be understood in this period without studying the regional and local context, is also relevant for a more localised study of anti-war activity during the war.[43]

Although it was the ILP that was the most significant political force against the war, Francis and Smith suggest that the two Russian revolutions in 1917 inspired the hugely influential miners to take a more explicitly anti-war position and to refuse to cooperate in the recruitment of colliery workers into the army.[44] Studies of the syndicalist movement within the South Wales Miners' Federation in Wales during the war, by Davies and May,[45] have described the opposition to war as a secondary but intertwined theme within the demand for workers' control in the mining industry during the war, and beyond.

Local studies have provided a more nuanced description of attitudes towards the war. Adams's studies in the Briton Ferry and Port Talbot areas illustrate how the local anti-war movement was an integral part of the wider community, consisting as it did of the ILP, local trade unions and Labour councillors, with the involvement of a supportive local chapel and minister.[46] Other valuable studies of localised opposition to the war include Cyril Pearce's influential history of anti-war activity in Huddersfield,[47] Duncan's account of the anti-war movement in Dundee[48] and Weller's description of

---

[43] Duncan Tanner, *Political Change and the Labour Party 1900–1918* (Cambridge University Press, 1990), p. 226.

[44] Hywel Francis and Dai Smith, *The Fed, A History of the South Wales Miners in the Twentieth Century* (Lawrence and Wishart, 1980), p. 22.

[45] David Keith Davies, 'The Influence of Syndicalism and Industrial Unionism on the South Wales Coalfield 1898–1921: A Study in Ideology and Practice' (unpublished PhD thesis, Cardiff University, 1991); Edward May, 'A Question of Control: Social and Industrial Relations in the South Wales Coalfield and the Crisis of Post-War Reconstruction' (unpublished PhD thesis, Cardiff University, 1994); Susan E. Demont, 'Tredegar and Aneurin Bevan: A Society and its Political Articulation' (unpublished PhD thesis, Cardiff University, 1990).

[46] Philip Adams, *Not in Our Name: War Dissent in a Welsh Town* (Ludlow: Briton Ferry Books, 2015); Philip Adams, *Daring to Defy: Port Talbot's War Resistance 1914–1918* (Ludlow: Briton Ferry Books, 2016).

[47] Cyril Pearce, *Comrades and Conscience* (Francis Boutle Publishers, 2001).

[48] Robert Duncan, *Objectors and Resisters* (Glasgow: Common Print, 2015).

the anti-war movement in north London.[49] These local studies emphasise the value of examining diverse geographical, social and political differences in attitudes towards the war, and suggest that they can only be understood by a more granular view of local circumstances. This study builds on this work to consider the extent to which opposition to the war was not only an individual matter of conscience, but also part of a broader social and political response within rooted communities.

The narrative of opposition to the Great War has focused primarily on the perceived heroism of the conscientious objectors. The tone was set by the NCF's own published history[50] and Graham's *Conscription and Conscience: A History 1916–1919*, which took a religious pacifist standpoint, and gave an unabashed partisan account of the heroism of the objectors.[51] This publication was followed forty-five years later by David Boulton's *Objection Overruled*,[52] which lionised socialist conscientious objectors in particular,[53] but the main body of work to have reflected the experiences of conscientious objectors in the period up until the 1970s was the numerous biographies and autobiographies of those war resisters and objectors who were prominent in the anti-war movement, such as the NCF's leaders, Clifford Allen and Fenner Brockway. The main academic analyses of the conscription debate and conscientious objection, by Rae, Robbins and Swartz,[54] have captured how government responded to the anti-war movement, but all suffer from a metropolitan focus and fail to give a more localised picture of its complexity.

[49] Ken Weller, *Don't Be a Soldier: The Radical Anti-War Movement in North London 1914–1918* (Journeyman Press, 1985).

[50] The No-Conscription Fellowship, *The No-Conscription Fellowship: A Souvenir of its Work During the Years 1914–1919* (London: No-Conscription Fellowship, 1919).

[51] John W. Graham, *Conscription and Conscience* (Allen and Unwin, 1922).

[52] David Boulton, *Objection Overruled* (MacGibbon and Kee, 1967).

[53] Thomas C. Kennedy, *The Hound of Conscience* (Lafayette: University of Arkansas, 1981), p. 312.

[54] John Rae, *Conscience and Politics* (Oxford University Press, 1970); Keith Robbins, *The Abolition of War* (Cardiff: University of Wales Press, 1976); Marvin Swartz, *The Union of Democratic Control in British Politics During the First World War* (Oxford: Clarendon Press, 1971).

Robbins, for example, whilst complimented for describing the government's attempts to deal with conscientious objectors as a 'complex pattern of conflicting events and personalities', has been criticised for concentrating on 'drawing-room (i.e. middle-class) pacifism', and ignoring working-class anti-war activity.[55] Whilst these authors have tended to take a more academically astringent and dispassionate view of the anti-war movement, those such as Boulton and Graham have championed the anti-war movement and concentrated on the plight of the conscientious objectors, in particular.

The most original contribution to our understanding of conscientious objectors during the war is Lois Bibbings's *Telling Tales about Men*,[56] which deploys gender theory to examine the way conscientious objectors were portrayed and treated, and to consider how they were made to be 'outsiders' and demonised. She selects six main categories to typify the differing 'histories' of conscientious objectors, ranging from the negative portrayal of them in the press of the time as deviants, cowards, shirkers, a national danger and as 'unmen' or 'unmanly', in which the objector was the very antithesis of the brave soldier, to the more positive image of them as brave and honourable martyrs who followed the dictates of their beliefs. The conscientious objector was seen by the pro-war press as 'Shirking, lazy, spineless, un-Christian, unpatriotic and un-English/unBritish. Moreover, sometimes he was perceived of as womanly and sexually undesirable to women or was suspected of sexual inversion.'[57]

Much of the history of anti-war activity during the Great War in Britain has concentrated either on the individual tales of sacrifice suffered by conscientious objectors, or on an analysis of government provision for conscientious objection provided for in the first Military Service Act, 1916. The local and regional analysis of the anti-war movement is significant as an indication of how attitudes towards the war and

---

[55] A. J. A. Morris, 'Review of Robbins's *Abolition of War*', *Welsh History Review*, 9/1–4 (1978–9), 112.

[56] Lois B. Bibbings, *Telling Tales about Men: Conceptions of Conscientious Objectors to Military Service During the First World War* (Manchester University Press, 2009).

[57] Bibbings, *Telling Tales about Men*, p. 89.

objection to the war could vary substantially in relation to both location and the period of the war, as attitudes shifted from initial support in the early autumn of 1914 to growing war-weariness and support for the anti-war movement by the summer of 1917. The history of the opposition to the Great War in Wales has frequently been written in the context of other subject areas, and no substantial study has dealt solely and exclusively with the subject of the extent of opposition to the war in Wales. This book addresses this historical omission.

This study takes a thematic approach towards the opposition to the war in Wales and considers the two main categories of religious and political opposition. Although there was a strong degree of fusion between these two elements, which expressed itself in a moral objection to war, these broad categories help to define the nature and extent of the anti-war movement. Chapter 1 describes the opposition to the war on religious grounds and, within the context of the churches' general support for the war, considers the activity of the most significant anti-war religious organisation, the Fellowship of Reconciliation, and its newspaper, *Y Deyrnas*.

Chapter 2 describes the influence of the Independent Labour Party (ILP) and the Unofficial Reform Movement (UCM), the syndicalist movement within the South Wales Miners' Federation. The Independent Labour Party was the most significant political organisation opposed to the war, and included a wide range of anti-war views, but ameliorated its policy with a defence of the interests of soldiers and their dependants.[58] This chapter assesses the role of the ILP in sustaining and developing anti-war activity throughout the war in Wales, and focuses on two of those geographical areas where the ILP was strongest in south Wales, in Briton Ferry and Merthyr Tydfil. This chapter also examines the anti-war grouping of 'advanced men', those syndicalist activists within the South Wales Miners' Federation, and considers the significance of the coalfield ballot over conscription within the mining industry in Wales, and the extent to which it was a proxy for the wider conflict between those who supported

---

[58] Dowse, *Left in the Centre*, pp. 21–4.

the war wholeheartedly and those who opposed the war passionately.

Chapter 3 considers the organisation of the National Council for Civil Liberties (NCCL) and the No-Conscription Fellowship (NCF), whose members and leadership in Wales were closely intertwined with each other and with the ILP. The NCF represented the interests of conscientious objectors and their families but was dominated organisationally by members of the ILP, and the NCCL, although ostensibly created to oppose the extension of conscription into the civilian sphere, was again dominated by anti-war activists. Chapter 4 analyses the most obvious manifestation of the opposition to the war, namely the conscientious objectors. They were a remarkably diverse group from a variety of social backgrounds and views, and this chapter examines their different responses to the range of options granted to them by the government and the military. Whilst the Military Service Act of January 1916 allowed for freedom of conscience, the manner by which tribunals interpreted this provision caused confusion for many tribunal members and resentment within the anti-war movement and beyond. This study quantifies and identifies the known conscientious objectors in Wales, and considers the range of categories they adopted, either as uncompromising absolutists or as 'alternativists', who accepted alternative service in civilian employment or in the Non-Combatant Corps under military control. This chapter also considers those substantial numbers of conscientious objectors who were members of those millenarian sects and were opposed to the state's intervention through the introduction of military conscription. The conscientious objectors were characterised by a wide diversity of political and religious views, which made it more difficult for them to become an effective and united movement to oppose the war.

1

RELIGIOUS OPPOSITION TO THE WAR IN WALES

INTRODUCTION

The opposition to the war in Wales on religious grounds
was initially muted and cowed by the shock of the onset of
war, and the rapidity with which the treasured traditional
nineteenth-century ideals of pacifism were jettisoned. This
opposition to the war on religious grounds was conducted
primarily by millenarian sects, whose fundamental beliefs
prohibited their members from swearing allegiance to
a temporal power represented by military conscription,
for instance, and also by those individuals within the
Nonconformist denominations who held the fundamental
belief that killing was an absolute sin. These individuals were
organised mainly through the No-Conscription Fellowship
(NCF), but in particular by the Fellowship of Reconciliation
(FoR), established in Wales in June 1915, and the monthly
magazine *Y Deyrnas*, first published in October 1916. These
gave the pacifist movement its unique Welsh voice and gave
succour to those individuals within the Nonconformist
denominations in particular, who disagreed with the war on
the grounds of their Christian faith. The leaders of the anti-
war pacifist movement, such as Dr Thomas Rees, Principal of
the Bala-Bangor Congregationalist theological college, gave
their moral and practical support to conscientious objectors
and made the notion of 'peace by negotiation' more acceptable to members of Nonconformist denominations by the
summer of 1917, at a time when the Prime Minister, Lloyd
George, was calling for a 'knock-out blow' against Germany.
In addition, amongst a comparatively small number of
chapels throughout Wales, no more than about fifty ministers
of religion upheld a pacifist stance and proselytised against
the war, but their moral stance gave succour to conscientious
objectors and those who were actively anti-war.

The significance of religion to the anti-war movement is reflected in the professed allegiance of the majority of those conscientious objectors in Wales, who cited religious grounds for their stance and are studied in greater detail in chapter 4. Whereas the literature of conscientious objection in the war has been dominated by accounts which have emphasised the contribution of Quakers and socialists associated with the ILP,[1] these constitute only approximately three per cent and eleven per cent respectively of those conscientious objectors in Wales who professed an organisational allegiance.[2]

This opposition was conducted primarily by individuals within the Nonconformist denominations who held the fundamental belief that war was a 'negation of the plain teaching of Jesus Christ that we should forgive, help and love even our enemies'.[3] They felt themselves to be inheritors of Wales's pacifist tradition within Nonconformity that had commenced with the example of the Protestant martyrs, such as John Penry, and the persecution of the Quakers by the state in the seventeenth century. The overwhelming motivation for opposition to the war amongst conscientious objectors (COs) in Wales was their religious pacifism and their total opposition to the taking of life.

Morgan attributes Nonconformity's general support for the war primarily to the influence of the Chancellor of the Exchequer, the Liberal David Lloyd George. Though the initial response to the outbreak of war was one of sober regret and reluctant recruiting in strongly Nonconformist areas such as north-west Wales, this gave way to 'widespread anger and revulsion' which was supplemented by propaganda concerning German atrocities during the invasion of Belgium, the Zeppelin raids over the east coast of England, the sinking of the *Lusitania* and the execution of Edith Cavell in October 1915.[4] Not only the Anglican Church, but the main Nonconformist denominations 'endorsed the war

---

[1] John W. Graham, *Conscription and Conscience: A History 1916–1919* (Allen and Unwin, 1922); David Boulton, *Objection Overruled* (MacGibbon and Kee, 1967).

[2] Cyril Pearce, *Pearce Register of Anti-War Activists in Wales* (Wales for Peace, 2016). Available at *http://www.wcia.org.uk/wfp/pearceregister.html*. Accessed November 2016.

[3] Jen Llywelyn, *Pilgrim of Peace* (Talybont: Y Lolfa, 2016), p. 90.

[4] D. Densil Morgan, *The Span of the Cross: Christian Religion and Society in Wales 1914–2000* (Cardiff: University of Wales Press, 1999), p. 42.

effort wholeheartedly' and were thought 'to have discarded all that was distinctive in the Christian faith and ethic according to the demands of the moment … institutional Christianity appeared to have become a function of the imperial cause'.[5]

Lloyd George's speech to a congregation of Free Church people and London Welshmen in the City Temple, Westminster, in November 1914 emphasised that the country was at war to defend the weak, and that Belgium was like Wales, a small nation, 'a poor little neighbour whose home was broken into by a hulking bully'. However regrettable, therefore, the war was both inevitable and just: 'We are all looking forward to the time when swords shall be beaten into ploughshares', but in the meantime there was no alternative but to fight.[6] Biblical rhetoric and allusions to divine righteousness and God's protection of the weak were used to dispel pacifist concerns and to justify the decision to go to war. According to the prominent Calvinistic Methodist minister Revd Thomas Charles Williams, 'It has become our sacred calling to take up arms, he that hath no sword, let him sell his garment and buy one.'[7]

Lloyd George's success in persuading Nonconformist ministers as well as Anglican prelates to become recruiting officers was key to the flow of young men from Wales into the army from the autumn of 1914 onwards.[8] A number of the leaders of the Calvinistic Methodists, such as Revd John Williams, Brynsiencyn, and Thomas Charles Williams, Menai Bridge, were close friends of Lloyd George and became leading recruiters. Even the most radical of Nonconformists, such as W. Llewelyn Williams, the Liberal Member of Parliament for Carmarthen Boroughs and a prominent barrister, was persuaded of the force of the pro-war argument;

> Diolchaf, er trymed fy nghalon wrth feddwl am echryslonrwydd rhyfel, i mi gael byw i weled cenhedloedd yr Ymerodraeth brydeinig yn sefyll i fyny, galon wrth galon, fel un gwr yn y rhyfel ysbrydol hon: rhyfel yw yn

[5] Morgan, *The Span of the Cross*, p. 46.
[6] Morgan, *The Span of the Cross*, p. 43.
[7] *Y Goleuad*, 11 September 1914.
[8] John Davies, *Hanes Cymru* (London: Allen Lane, 1990), p. 492.

erbyn rhyfel; rhyfel i roddi pen bythol ar ryfel. Ni cherais ryfel erioed ond dywedaf fod y rhyfel hwn yn gyfiawn ac anocheladwy.[9]

(I give thanks, in spite of my heavy heart at the horror of war, that I have lived to see the nations of the British Empire standing up, heart by heart, as one man in this spiritual war: it is a war against war: a war to end all war. I never loved war but I say that this war is just and inevitable.)

The Calvinistic Methodists' leading preacher, Dr John Williams, Brynsiencyn, known as 'the idol of the preaching meetings',[10] was persuaded by Lloyd George of the righteousness of the Allied cause and made honorary chaplain with the rank of Lieutenant-Colonel in the new Welsh Army Corps:[11]

Yr oedd yn gyfeillgar iawn a Mr Lloyd George, a derbyniodd ei dystiolaeth ef, a thystiolaeth Mr Asquith a'r Arglwydd Grey, fod y rhyfel yn annichonadwy. Os bu petruster yn ei feddwl o gwbl, diflannodd hwnnw yn llwyr pan dorrodd yr Ellmyn eu cytuneb ac y croesasant Belgium, a sawdl haernaidd, er mwyn cyrraedd Ffrainc.[12]

(He was very friendly with Mr Lloyd George, and he accepted his evidence and that of Mr Asquith and Lord Grey, that the war was inevitable. If there was any hesitation in his mind at all, it disappeared totally when the Germans broke their promise and they crossed Belgium with their iron heels, in order to reach France.)

A photograph of Revd John Williams, Brynsiencyn, resplendent in his clerical collar and the uniform of the 38th Welsh Division, standing in the garden of 11 Downing Street, is testament to Lloyd George's power of persuasion. The 38th Division was created in order to use Welsh national sentiment as a recruiting tool and to attract Nonconformist Welshmen into the army. The appointment of an Anglesey Congregationalist, Brigadier General Owen Thomas, as the only Nonconformist and Welsh speaker in such a senior role within the British Army, recognised Nonconformity and

---

[9] *Y Beirniad* (October 1914), 162. All translations from Welsh to English are mine.
[10] Morgan, *Span of the Cross*, p. 43.
[11] Clive Hughes, *I'r Fyddin Fechgyn Gwalia: Recriwtio I'r Fyddin yng ngogled-Orllewin Cymru 1914–1916* (Llanrwst: Gwasg Carreg Gwalch, 2014), p. 243.
[12] R. R. Hughes, *John Williams, Brynsiencyn* (Caernarfon: Llyfrfa'r Cyfundeb, 1929), p. 246.

the Welsh language officially for the first time, within the Welsh Army Corps.[13] His biographer's belief that if Williams had decided to oppose the war, Nonconformist north-west Wales might have taken a very different attitude towards the war may be speculative, but the slowness of the response to the call to arms in the first months of the war in the area generated a great deal of anxiety that was alleviated only by local recruiting efforts led by Williams and Thomas Charles Williams. In Anglesey, within the Calvinistic Methodist congregations, John Williams's leadership was unquestioned, and in the quarrying town of Bethesda, for instance, a total of 200 quarrymen were recruited in the first year, but from the middle of 1915, 'recruiting became a more difficult business'. Both the Ogwen Rural District Council and Bethesda Urban District Council refused to undertake recruiting, and when in November 1915, Bethesda UDC eventually attempted to persuade every church and chapel in the area to appoint recruitment canvassers, only the Anglican Church did so, and then only to canvass their own members. By the autumn of 1915, the task of recruiting in the area was 'practically hopeless' because, it was alleged, there was 'not enough sufficient public spirit among the leading inhabitants'.[14]

THE ATTITUDE OF THE CHURCHES

The Established Church in Wales had almost 200,000 members, or thirteen per cent of the population of Wales in 1905.[15] In keeping with its role as the State Church, it shared a total commitment to the war effort, but was a politically and socially divisive organisation in Wales, and regarded by the Nonconformist establishment as politically Conservative, anglicised and associated with landed interests. The most popular religious institutions in Wales at this time were the Nonconformist churches, and the combined numerical

---

[13] Hughes, *John Williams, Brynsiencyn*, p. 227; David Pretty, *Rhyfelwr Môn* (Denbigh: Gwasg Gee, 1989), p. 69.

[14] Bangor University Archive, Thomas Jones Papers, f. 3192, 'Recruiting during the War, and the Attitude of Ministers and Leaders of Religious Thought towards the War'.

[15] L. J. Williams, *Digest of Historical Statistics*, 'Communicants, by county and denomination, 1905', vol. 2 (Cardiff: Welsh Office, 1985), p. 353.

strength of Welsh Protestant Nonconformity in 1914 was approximately 535,000 out of a total population of some 2,450,000, representing nearly one in five who were baptised or were communicants. In a survey undertaken in 1905, the main Nonconformist denominations were the Baptists, with 142,551 communicants, the more politically conservative Calvinistic Methodists with 170,343, the Congregationalists with 175,097, the Wesleyans with 43,358, and other smaller denominations and sects with 21,876. As half a million people attended Sunday schools but may not have been members, the total numbers of people associated with churches or chapels made Nonconformity the 'single significant institution which Wales possessed'.[16]

Even the Congregationalists and Baptists who had been associated with the Peace Society and the pacifistic movement of the nineteenth century were overwhelmingly supportive of the rush to war. Koss suggests that the support of the leading Free Churchmen in England to the war was an atonement 'for their earlier pacifism and to compensate for centuries of outsideness',[17] but this view underestimates the brittleness of Nonconformity's anti-war sentiment in the nineteenth century. The doctrine of non-resistance in the Peace Society, for instance, was shattered by the war and its own newspaper lamented this change: 'Even the most foremost pacifist leaders of the churches have surrendered. As for the rank and file of the ministers, they too are recruiting agents and their churches and schools recruiting stations.'[18] Although before 1914 the denominations had consistently declared war to be a barbarous act, they were largely unwavering in their support for the war. Although as late as 1913, the Union of Welsh Independents stated that 'every war was contrary to the spirit of Christ',[19] in its first annual conference after the outbreak of war in 1915, it expressed its joy

---

[16] Morgan, *The Span of the Cross*, p. 23.

[17] Stephen Koss, *Nonconformity in Modern British Politics* (London: B. T. Batsford, 1975), p. 127.

[18] *Herald of Peace*, 1 October 1914.

[19] R. Tudur Jones, *Hanes Annibynwyr Cymru* (Swansea: Welsh Union of Independents, 1966), p. 278, citing the *Annual Conference Report of the Union of Welsh Independents, Rhyl Meeting* (1913), p. 636.

that so many young men had joined the armed forces.[20] Its 1916 conference condemned the harmful influence of the cinema and the trade in alcoholic spirits, delighted in the creation of the Welsh Army under the command of the Nonconformist and Welsh-speaking Brigadier Owen Thomas, and admired the heroism of those who had joined the army. The sole suggestion of any alternative view of the war was the conference's recognition that the conscience clause in the Military Service Act was not always respected by the authorities:

> Gofidir am fod unrhyw swyddog gweinyddol o'r ddeddf yn ymddwyn, fel yr ymddengys i ni, yn annheg tuag at y cyfryw bersonau. Hyderwn y gwna'r Llywodraeth bopeth yn ei gallu i atal pob camwri o'r fath.[21]

> (it is regretted that any administrative officer under the act, behaves unfairly towards such people, as it seems to us. We hope that the Government does everything within its power to prevent any such injustice.)

In the 1915 annual conference, the jingoistic mood was reflected in the sermon given by the son of Samuel Roberts, Llanbrynmair, also Samuel, who compared the war to a battle between the Kingdom of God and his enemies. However, the denomination's annual conference in 1917 was cancelled in the hope that the country's circumstances would have improved,[22] and the next annual conference was not held until the summer of 1919.

Of the Nonconformist denominations however, it was the Independents, also known as Congregationalists, who proved most active in the anti-war movement, primarily through the involvement of a number of their ministers in the FoR, and through the leadership of Principal Thomas Rees and the group of theological lecturers and students based in the Congregationalist Bala-Bangor theological college in Bangor. A social and economic study of Wales in 1922, funded by the Carnegie Trust and commissioned by Thomas Jones,

---

[20] *Annual Conference Report of the Union of Welsh Independents*, Merthyr Tydfil, 19–22 July 1915 (Merthyr: Williams and Son, 1915), p. 1036.
[21] *Annual Conference Report of the Union of Welsh Independents*, Brynaman, 13–16 June 1916 (Swansea: Y Llyfrfa, 1916), p. 101.
[22] R. Tudur Jones, *Yr Undeb* (Swansea: John Penry Press, 1975), p. 392.

formerly secretary to Lloyd George, included an analysis by the ILP organiser and former CO David Thomas of the nature of the anti-war movement in Wales, which he described as 'Pacifist'. He described the movement as mainly religious in north Wales and political in south Wales, and assessed Nonconformity's response towards the war:

> Some of them were loud in their support of the war, and travelled the country addressing recruiting meetings: others were emphatic in their denunciation of the war. Probably the majority of the ministers kept quiet, preferring not to take any side, some from sheer pusillanimity, others from a consciousness of their ignorance and lack of vision, and others because they believed that they could preserve the unity of their churches only by refraining from taking sides in any controversial matter.[23]

Only a minuscule number of members of the small denomination of Methodist churches opposed the war. The denomination was part of the larger England and Wales organisation, and supported the war wholeheartedly. The few pacifists included the prominent novelist Revd Tegla Davies, Oswestry, Revd D. Gwynfryn Jones, Flint, and Revd Conwy Pritchard in the Llŷn peninsula, and lay members including David Thomas. In the larger Calvinistic Methodist denomination, the anti-war element was led by the blind minister for Penmount, Pwllheli, Dr J. Puleston Jones, whose first class in modern history at Balliol College, Oxford, reflected his academic brilliance, and who propagandised passionately in favour of peace throughout the war.[24] In a meeting of the North Wales Association of the denomination in August 1917 in Caernarfon, he successfully proposed a resolution that called for an immediate peace settlement:

> Fod y Gymdeithasfa yn llawenychu o blaid heddwch, ac o'r farn y dylai y llywodraeth gymeryd mantais ar bob cyfleustra i gario ymlaen drafodaeth er sicrhau heddwch.[25]

---

[23] Bangor University Archive, Thomas Jones Papers, f. 19885, David Thomas, 'The Pacifist Movement'.

[24] D. Ben Rees, *Herio'r Byd* (Liverpool: Cyhoeddiadau Modern Cymreig, 1980), pp. 93–103.

[25] Simon B. Jones and E. Lewis Evans, *Ffordd Tangnefedd: Pregethau a Barddoniaeth* (Llandysul: Gwasg Gomer, 1943), p. 27.

(that the Methodist Association rejoices in favour of peace, and is of the opinion that the government should take advantage of every opportunity to carry on the discussion in order to secure peace.)

Remarkably, this was the first time during the war that any of the Welsh Nonconformist denominations had passed a motion in favour of peace. Other Methodist ministers involved in the anti-war movement were Peter Hughes Griffiths, Llewelyn Williams and D. Francis Roberts, but perhaps the most active was Revd John Morgan Jones, Hope Methodist chapel, Merthyr Tydfil, whose pervasive influence in south Wales was comparable to J. Puleston Jones's inspiration of pacifists in north Wales.[26] However, even in Merthyr Tydfil, where there was an active anti-war tradition that drew on Henry Richard's opposition to the Crimean War, most chapels and churches were silent on the question of the war. In February 1916, the Merthyr branch of the NCF sent forms to seventy local chapels and churches asking them to protest against the 'ethical vandalism' of conscription and calling upon the government to repeal military conscription. Thirteen replies were received, and in the three places of worship where this request was presented, the resolution was supported. In another ten cases the officials of the church refused to submit the resolution, on the grounds that it was not 'wise to lay this matter before the congregations'.[27] Thus, even in one of the most active districts in south Wales for the anti-war movement, this response showed a general reluctance to create conflict within congregations, and reflected deep divisions over war policy.

Whilst most religious leaders in south Wales supported the war, David Thomas considered that in north Wales the pacifists, although in a minority, were 'powerful and influential in the churches'.[28] The Welsh Baptists was one of the largest denominations, with over 150,000 adherents, and faced the war with 'no settled point of view'. Until August 1914 Baptists had been opposed alike to militarism and the social

[26] E. H. Griffiths, *Heddychwr Mawr Cymru: George M. Ll. Davies* (Caernarfon: Llyfrfa'r Methodistiaid Calfinaidd, 1967), p. 28.

[27] *Pioneer*, 4 March 1916.

[28] *Pioneer*, 4 March 1916.

establishment,[29] but the denomination's attitude to war now was that when 'the horizon was clear, it tended to emphasise the pacific message of Christianity but when the clouds of war gathered, it spoke with many voices'.[30] The war seems to have taken the denomination by surprise, and official explanations for its outbreak were accepted. In the autumn of 1914, Welsh Baptists refuted Anglican claims that most of the recruits were coming from the Established Church and pointed proudly to the numbers of Nonconformists who were enlisting. The editor of the denomination's newspaper, *Seren Gomer*, D. Wyre Lewis, provided a platform for pacifism and pleaded against fomenting hatred against the German people, whilst the leading figure of the anti-war element in the denomination was Revd E. K. Jones, Cefnmawr, who became a key member of the FoR and the NCF in north Wales. The veteran minister Dr Cernyw Williams was a renowned pacifist who prayed for an early end to the conflict and adjured all to pray for forgiveness. Both ministers collaborated with Revd Herbert Morgan (who was to become the unsuccessful Labour candidate for Neath in 1918) and George M. Ll. Davies in FoR meetings, such as one held in Aberdare in February 1918.[31] Other prominent anti-war ministers included Revd Morgan Jones, Whitland, and Revd Gilbert Jones, Llangloffan, Pembrokeshire, who supported local COs.

Of the four main Nonconformist newspapers, the strongest supporter of the war was the Congregationalist/Independent *Y Tyst*, and its editor, Dr H. Michael Hughes, Cardiff, became a chaplain in the army. The Calvinistic Methodists' *Y Goleuad* generally supported the war, but its columns were open to dissenting views, and Revd J. Puleston Jones, in his weekly column, deprecated those churches who had become part of the recruiting campaign. A correspondent replying to him said that he believed that every minister should tell the young men of his church that if they rejected the appeal to enlist, they were in peril of the destruction of their souls. Jones

[29] Alan Wilkinson, *The Church of England and the First World War* (SPCK, 1978), p. 30.

[30] T. M. Bassett, *The Welsh Baptists* (Swansea: Ty Ilston, 1977), p. 386.

[31] Bassett, *The Welsh Baptists*, pp. 388–91.

retorted that this was 'very much like what our brothers the Tories used to call "sgriw'r saint" and that he should prefer the screw of the State to that'.[32] The pacifist nature of a number of the leading articles of *Y Goleuad* led to a disagreement between the editor, the respected journalist and author E. Morgan Humphreys, and the managing committee. His criticism of Lloyd George's support for conscription brought matters to a head and led to letters of complaint sent by Revd John Williams, Brynsiencyn, who was also the chairman of the editorial committee.

Williams 'protested vigorously' against the tone of the editor's comments, and stated that Lloyd George himself was taking a great interest in the paper's comments. In October 1917 Humphreys published a letter that was critical of Lloyd George, and received another missive from Revd John Williams:

> Rwyf wedi protestio o'r blaen yn erbyn tôn y Goleuad ynglyn a'r Prif Weinidog (Lloyd George). Gofyn oeddwn am ddistawrwydd hyd y gellid. Yn awr wele 'the unkindest cut of all'.

> (I have protested before against the Goleuad's tone regarding Lloyd George. I was asking for as much silence as possible. Now see 'the unkindest cut of all'.)

Thereafter, the editorial committee, which Williams chaired, decided to reduce Humphreys's salary, and within the year, in December 1918, he was replaced as editor.[33]

Both the Wesleyan *Gwyliedydd Newydd*, edited by the future Labour candidate for Flintshire, Revd Gwynfryn Jones, and the Baptist *Seren Cymru*, edited by the peace activist, Revd D. Wyre Lewis, were sympathetic towards the anti-war movement, and although these papers were official organs of their denominations, the attitude of each paper depended on the individual editor's personal views and did not always represent the broader pro-war view of the membership.

A small number of prominent literary figures found their voice against the war. W. J. Gruffydd, 'whose mind was

---

[32] Bangor University Archive, Thomas Jones Papers, f. 19885, David Thomas, 'The Pacifist Movement'.

[33] Bangor University Archive, Morgan Humphreys Papers, fos 15970–1; Harri Parri, *Gwn Glân a Beibl Budr* (Caernarfon: Gwasg y Bwthyn, 2014), pp. 167–71.

especially tortured', translated into Welsh an anti-war sermon by the pacifist Maude Royden. The most public outlet for these individuals was the student paper *Y Wawr*, published in the University of Wales, Aberystwyth, which was closed down by the authorities in 1918 because of its radicalism and its articles in support of conscientious objectors as well as for the Easter Rising in Ireland. In this magazine, T. Gwynn Jones, T. H. Parry-Williams and others spoke of their sense of moral outrage at the brutality of war, and although Morgan suggests it was a 'powerful antidote to the war fever',[34] it had little influence. A more significant newspaper was the weekly *Y Darian*, originally known as *Tarian y Gweithiwr*, published in Merthyr until its office was moved to Aberdare in 1916, funded by the newspaper magnate Henry Seymour Berry and edited by Revd J. Tywi Jones, a Baptist minister in Glais in the Swansea Valley. A Nationalist, a supporter of the Welsh language, and a pacifist, he published strongly worded anti-war editorials throughout the war, and, whilst he recognised that advertising was lost as a result of his views, the newspaper's circulation increased from 2,000 before the war to 3,500 in 1921:

> *Y Darian* oedd yr unig bapur yng Nghymru a barhaodd i ddweud y gwir am bethau yn ystod y rhyfel fawr, ac oherwydd hynny y bu rhai o weithwyr Aberdar yn bygwth 'smasho'r' swyddfa, a dichon mai hynny a wnaethent onibae iddynt gael allan nad Cwmni'r Darian a berchenogai'r *Darian*.[35]

> (*Y Darian* was the only paper in Wales that kept telling the truth about things during the Great War, and because of that a few Aberdare workers threatened to 'smash' the office, and that would have happened if they had not understood that *Y Darian* company did not own *Y Darian*.)

In south Wales, the secular Merthyr *Pioneer*, published by the ILP, was the only other standard-bearer opposed to the war, and in north Wales, the only daily or weekly newspaper that opposed the war was *Y Dinesydd Cymreig*, the Labour

---

[34] Kenneth O. Morgan, *Wales in British Politics* (Cardiff: University of Wales Press, 1970), p. 164.

[35] *Y Darian*, 28 June 1934, cited in Noel Gibbard, *Tarian Tywi* (Caernarfon: Gwasg y Bwthyn, 2011), p. 123.

paper which had been established in 1912 by three striking Caernarfon printers and was described by David Thomas as 'consistently pacifist and religious in tone'.[36]

Y Gwyliedydd Newydd and *Seren Cymru* were readier than the majority of mainstream newspapers in Wales, such as the *South Wales Daily News* and the *Western Mail*, to give a voice to pacifist arguments against the war. This in part was due to the character of the editors involved, but also reflected unease with the challenge to traditional Liberal Nonconformity of the introduction of conscription and the growth of the state. This tension is captured in the disagreement between Humphreys and the editorial board of *Y Goleuad*, and in the revulsion shown by relatives of fallen soldiers to John Williams, Brynsiencyn, after the end of the war.[37]

THE QUAKERS AND THE MILLENARIAN SECTS

Amongst the smaller religious sects, the attitude towards war was ostensibly clearer. The Quakers had traditionally opposed the taking up of arms, but were split on the issue of the war, and as a denomination on 'the margins of Welsh Nonconformity' had very little influence or impact in Wales.[38] The popular assumption that members of the Society of Friends automatically became conscientious objectors was based on a misunderstanding of the Quaker position, for members were inspired by a belief in the authority of the inner light rather than an adherence to a pacifist tenet. Traditionally this inspiration had led Quakers to reject 'all outward wars and strife and fighting with outward weapons',[39] but fewer than half of its members of military age became conscientious objectors during the war, whilst a third enlisted in the armed forces.[40] In Wales, its membership was comprised of eight Welsh Quaker congregations, composed

---

[36] Bangor University Archive, Thomas Jones Papers, f. 19885, David Thomas, 'The Pacifist Movement'.

[37] Parri, *Gwn Glân a Beibl Budr*, pp. 179–82.

[38] Owen Gethin Evans, 'Quakers in Wales and the First World War', *Quaker Studies* (2014), 20.

[39] *Peace among the Nations* (September 1915) (Friends House Library).

[40] *Minute and Proceedings of the London Yearly Meeting of Friends* (Friends House Library, 1923), pp. 231–2.

of some 250 attendant members, with another forty members scattered abroad. Four of the meetings were in mid Wales, at Aberystwyth and Llandrindod, Penybont and Llanbadarn in Radnorshire; there were three in south Wales, at Swansea, Neath and Cardiff, and one in north Wales, at Colwyn Bay.[41]

An important Quaker initiative was the creation of the Friends Ambulance Unit (FAU), established in 1915, which attracted men who wished to provide practical support for soldiers in the front line, but did not wish to carry arms. These men were not officially conscientious objectors because they had joined the FAU before conscription was introduced, but were 'in the most part composed of those who were prepared to make a definite stand on the question of military service'.[42] Most did not return to Britain to obtain individual exemption from a tribunal, and the remainder were exempted by a special agreement between the Unit's committee and the Army Council.[43] Even so, of the twenty-nine men who enlisted from Wales in the FAU, only twelve were Quakers; the rest were seven Congregationalists, four Presbyterians, two Baptists, one Wesleyan and one Plymouth Brethren, and two who were not categorised. There was a total of 750 Quaker conscientious objectors, of whom there were only thirteen Quaker conscientious objectors from Wales. Of these, only four were absolutists, namely Bernard Cudbird and his brother Horace, who attended the Cardiff Meeting and had been Congregationalists, Samuel Broomfield of Newport, who notably refused to take off his hat before the tribunal,[44] and Harold Watkins, from Llanfyllin, who appeared before the Ledbury tribunal in Herefordshire, where he taught at Colwall Quaker school near Malvern, and was imprisoned for four terms in all.[45]

Other religious sects that emphasised group rather than individual conscience produced high numbers of

---

[41] Morgan, *The Span of the Cross*, p. 10.

[42] M. Tatham and J. E. Miles, *The Friends Ambulance Unit 1914–1919* (Swarthmore Press, 1920), pp. 186–7.

[43] Friends House Library, Arnold Rowntree Papers, Box 1, letter to the members of the FAU, 17 May 1916.

[44] Owain Gethin Evans, *Benign Neglect: Quakers and Wales circa 1860–1918* (Wrexham: Bridge Books, 2014), p. 89.

[45] Harold Watkins, *Life Has Kept Me Young* (Watts and Co., 1952), pp. 71–92.

conscientious objectors compared with their comparatively small size. The most important of these were the Christadelphians, the Plymouth Brethren and the Jehovah's Witnesses. Their beliefs differed radically from the conventional eschatology of the majority of Christians and centred upon the expectation of the early return of Jesus Christ to the world. The Kingdom of God was one to be established on earth after the forces of evil had been defeated at Armageddon, and as citizens of this future Kingdom the members of the sects were not permitted to owe allegiance to any earthly ruler, nor could they become involved in the affairs of the world through which they were passing. Their rejection of military service in the armies of this world was, like their disinclination to exercise the franchise, a logical consequence of their apocalyptic beliefs.

There were no fewer than 1,716 Christadelphian conscientious objectors, representing approximately ten per cent of the total number of COs in Britain, of whom at least 155 came from Wales. The Christadelphians' successful petition to Parliament in 1915 sought exemption from military service on the grounds that they were 'conscientiously opposed to bearing arms, on the ground that the Bible, which they believe to be the word of God, commands them not to kill'.[46] Most Christadelphians were absolutists and opposed non-combatant service because of their objection to military authority, which involved oaths of loyalty to the Crown. Even in the case of the medical service of the Royal Army Medical Corps (RAMC), Christadelphians believed that it was part of an organisation which was maintained for the special purpose of fighting, and that medical personnel would have to carry arms to defend the sick and wounded and for their own protection.[47] The Army Council eventually agreed to grant a unique dispensation and gave a certificate of exemption from military service to all registered Christadelphians who were liable as conscripts under the Military Service Act, so that from August 1916 onwards, all Christadelphian cases were referred to the Pelham

---

[46] Frank G. Jannaway, *Without the Camp* (London: F. G. Jannaway, 1917), p. 32.

[47] John Botten, *The Captive Conscience* (Birmingham: Christadelphian Military Service Committee, 2002), p. 38.

Committee on Work of National Importance. The Christadelphians were adamant that they were not opposed to others engaging in war, and indeed went to great pains to stress that they did not oppose conscription for others. The sect's leader, Frank Jannaway, stressed that the duty of a Briton was to join the army and fight for his country, but that Christadelphians, however, were 'not of this world' and were neutrals, never voted and, as such, should not be liable to fight.[48] In all other respects, he accepted they were subject to the laws of the land, and thus, whilst not permitted by their beliefs to fight, would 'do his best in civil life to help the land of his birth in its hour of distress'.[49] This conscientious objection to military service hardly constituted opposition to war itself.

The Pelham Committee on Work of National Importance operated as an employment exchange, bringing together those conscientious objectors who had been referred by the tribunals with employers who required labour.[50] Three-quarters of the cases from Wales before the Committee – 155 out of 207 – were Christadelphians, who were all allocated work of national importance. These appeals were from seventy-one individuals in Glamorgan, fifty-eight in Monmouthshire, twenty-four in Carmarthenshire, mainly in Pont-yates, Llanelli and Ammanford, and two in Pembrokeshire.[51] Whilst little is known of the work and the size of membership of the Christadelphians in Wales during the war, an indication of their strength is that twenty-seven of their Welsh churches, known as ecclesias, sponsored the publication of Jannaway's history of their struggle to gain exemption from military service.[52]

---

[48] Jannaway, *Without the Camp*, p. 199.
[49] Jannaway, *Without the Camp*, p. iv.
[50] Rae, *Conscience and Politics*, p. 195.
[51] Rob Phillips, 'Gorfodaeth Filwrol yn Sir Gaerfyrddin' (unpublished MPhil thesis, University of Wales, Lampeter, 1992), p. 93; Friends House Library, T. E. Harvey Papers, Box 9, Draft of the Report of the Pelham Committee on Work of National Importance.
[52] Jannaway, *Without the Camp*, pp. v–vi; the ecclesias named are Aberaman, Aberdare, Abergavenny, Abertillery, Ammanford, Bridgend, Cardiff, Ferndale, Haverfordwest, Hengoed, Llanelli, Merthyr Tydfil, Mumbles, Neath, New Tredegar, Pont-yates, Pontycwmmer, Pontypool, Pontypridd, Porth, Port Talbot, Swansea, Tredegar and Ystrad.

The Plymouth Brethren's position was more complex, because the sect consisted of two main groups, the Open Brethren and the Exclusive Brethren, formed after the sect had split in 1849. Whilst some members of the Open Brethren joined the armed forces, their strictest branch, the Churches of God, or the Exclusive Brethren, believed that fighting was incompatible with the teaching of Christ,[53] and refused to be 'unequally unyoked with unbelievers' in the army.[54] At least nineteen of the COs in Wales described themselves as Plymouth Brethren.[55]

The Jehovah's Witnesses' objection to the war differed in one important respect from that of the Christadelphians and the Brethren. Known as the International Bible Students' Association (IBSA), their objection to war was based on their interpretation of Scripture, although their neutrality in respect of the war meant that they were 'neither pacifist or patriot'.[56] The first IBSA branches had only appeared in Wales in 1911, amongst a group of miners in Clydach in the Swansea Valley, and by 1914 they had established a number of classes in the area, in Morriston, Abercrave, Ystalyfera and the centre of Swansea.[60] Most IBSA conscientious objectors refused to accept military service in the Non-Combatant Corps and were imprisoned, but were prepared to accept work of national importance under the Home Office Scheme. One hundred and forty-five throughout Britain were registered under the Pelham Committee, and only ten members from Wales are known to have registered as conscientious objectors.[57] Whilst IBSA members found work of national importance acceptable, the refusal of members of the apocalyptic sects to participate in the running of work centres or to take part in political agitation was an irritant to other politically committed COs.

[53] *Report of the Conference of Representative Overseers of the Churches of God in the British Isles and Overseas* (Plymouth Brethren, 1935), p. 24.
[54] Rae, *Conscience and Politics*, p. 75.
[55] *Pearce Register*.
[56] Russell Grigg, 'Jehovah's Witnesses', in Richard Allen, David Ceri Jones and Trystan Hughes (eds), *The Religious History of Wales* (Cardiff: Welsh Academic Press, 2014), p. 178.
[57] *Pearce Register*.

Of the other small religious denominations, only the Seventh Day Adventists and the Pentecostal churches produced comparatively small numbers of conscientious objectors. Both groups expressed their unswerving loyalty to the government and were anxious that their refusal of combatant service should not be misinterpreted. In this they differed radically from those COs who emphatically rejected loyalty of this nature for political or eschatological reasons. The Seventh Day Adventists based their objection to combatant service on the literal interpretation of the Bible, and believed in the 'undiminished authority and perpetuity of the moral law, given by God himself in the Ten Commandments', and that their members were 'forbidden to take part in combatant service in time of war'.[58] This funda-mental tenet meant that very few joined the armed forces, whilst in the various Pentecostal churches rejection of combatant service was a logical consequence of membership, but the decision was left to the individual. In the Assemblies of God and the Apostolic Church, refusal of military service was encouraged, and in all Pentecostal bodies, literal bibli-cism and sectarian withdrawal from the conflicts of society provided a general, but not universally accepted, basis for conscientious objection.[59]

THE RELIGIOUS ANTI-WAR MOVEMENT IN WALES

Key individual chapels, whose congregations included ILP members, became well known as havens for anti-war activists. These included Jerusalem English Baptist chapel in Briton Ferry, Hope English Presbyterian chapel, Merthyr Tydfil, Seion Baptist chapel in Cwmafon, Carmel, Pont-y-Rhyl (near Pontycymmer), Revd E. K. Jones's Welsh Baptist chapel in Cefnmawr, Wrexham, and a number of chapels in the Swansea Valley, including Beulah, Cwmtwrch, Bryn Seion, Craig-cefn-parc, and the two Congregationalist chapels in Alltwen, near Pontardawe, where two prominent supporters

---

[58] F. McL. Wilcox, *Seventh Day Adventists in Time of War* (Washington, DC: Review and Herald Publishing Association, 1936), p. 256.

[59] Rae, *Conscience and Politics*, p. 76.

of the ILP officiated, Revds W. J. Rees and Llywelyn Bowyer.[60] These ministers were rare public supporters of the anti-war movement and were heavily involved in the organisation of the NCF and the FoR, producing and translating pamphlets into the Welsh language, distributing propaganda and providing practical and moral support for conscientious objectors and their families.[61] A number of them became the NCF's official visitors to conscientious objectors in either prison or military camps, and the link between the objectors and the NCF's central information bureau. In north Wales, for instance, the main visitor to Caernarfon prison and the five main army camps, such as Kinmel Park and Park Hall, near Oswestry, was the Baptist minister Revd E. K. Jones, who was supported in his work by Revd John Clifford, Colwyn Bay, and Principal Thomas Rees. In south Wales, the visitors included Revd John Morgan Jones, Merthyr Tydfil, the NCF and ILP organiser Minnie Pallister, Agnes Hughes, sister of Emrys Hughes, and a prominent peace activist, and Revd Gilbert Jones, Llangloffan in Pembrokeshire. These served as visitors to conscientious objectors in prisons and army camps, acted as a defendant's friend and witness in military tribunals and court martials, and provided intelligence on their movements within the army and the prison system to the NCF.[62]

One of the most renowned opponents of the war was T. E. Nicholas, known as 'Niclas y Glais', born in 1879 at Llanfyrnach in Pembrokeshire, who became a Congregation-alist minister of religion in Glais, in the Swansea Valley, before moving to the rural hamlet of Llangybi, near Tregaron in Cardiganshire, in 1914. A remarkably proficient writer, poet and propagandist in the Welsh language, his poetry was infused with an uncompromising belief in Christian Socialism, and was renowned for his unorthodox muscular brand of anti-militarism and socialist internationalism. His Christian Socialism bridged the religious sphere of radical

---

[60] Dewi Eirug Davies, *Byddin y Brenin* (Swansea: Tŷ John Penry, 1988), pp. 156, 167.

[61] Albert Davies, *Wanderings* (unpublished autobiography in private hands), p. 20.

[62] National Library of Wales, E. K. Jones Papers, Box 2, list of NCF visitors, 27 October 1916.

Nonconformity and the political sphere of the ILP. He joined the ILP in 1905 and his influences included R. J. Campbell's *New Theology*, with its liberal interpretation of the Bible and its call for a radical social policy, and R. J. Derfel and Robert Owen's beliefs in the brotherhood of man, peace and righteousness.[63] He wrote the Welsh-language column in Keir Hardie's paper, the Merthyr-based *Pioneer*, and was the main speaker at Hardie's memorial service in Merthyr on 10 October 1915. As secretary of the NCF in Cardiganshire he encouraged young men to become conscientious objectors, travelled widely and spoke incessantly in anti-war meetings under the aegis of the NCF, ILP and the FoR. Nicholas was followed constantly by the police, who took detailed notes of many of his speeches, and whose Chief Constable in Glamorgan, Lionel Lindsay, obsessively persecuted him but failed in multiple attempts to prosecute him for his anti-war activity. His correspondence was constantly intercepted because he 'openly preaches sedition at his chapel, abuses the King, and does all in his power to stop recruiting, and upholds the conscientious Objectors'.[64] He was recorded as having delivered 'a most disloyal speech' at Keir Hardie's memorial service, and a local member of the Cardiganshire gentry, Mrs Drummond, wrote to warn Lindsay that Nicholas had been involved in 'dangerous activities', that he had taken up the cause of conscientious objectors and that he encouraged 'pacifist and pro-German propaganda'. Police officers reported his speeches in ILP meetings in Aberaman and Mountain Ash, in which he excoriated the government and its religious apologists and stated that if this was a religious war, it was those religious men who should fight these battles:

> Our means of worshipping God is very sinful, we ask Him to save us here and destroy our enemies, but we are all God's children. We ask God to do things we would not ask a mother in Aberaman to do. If two boys in Aberaman went to fight each other, we would not ask the

---

[63] Ivor Thomas Rees, 'Thomas Evan Nicholas 1879–1971', *National Library of Wales Journal*, 35/1 (2010), 1–15.

[64] National Archives, Security Services Papers, KV2/1750, f. 23970, T. E. Nicholas file.

mothers to save one and destroy the other, but that is just what we are asking God to do.[65]

Nicholas was arguably the most prominent anti-war propagandist in Wales in this period. However, the undoubted main centre of organised opposition to the war was the Congregationalist Bala-Bangor theological college in Bangor and its principal, Thomas Rees. Born ten years earlier than Nicholas, and within yards of his birthplace in Llanfyrnach in north Pembrokeshire, he was the fulcrum for a group of theologically liberal anti-war professors, lecturers, ministers and students who were radicalised and alienated from Liberalism by their opposition to the war. As Congregationalists, their activities were bolstered by the denomination's historical suspicion of the state, and they argued that since Nonconformists had spent the best part of two centuries trying to win liberties for the individual believer in the face of hostile state oppression, it was hardly surprising that they should be deeply wary of the encroaching state and military conscription. Rees, the most significant leader of the anti-war movement on religious grounds in Wales, was an early voice of opposition at the beginning of the war, and as Principal of Bala-Bangor theological college inspired a generation of his students to oppose the war. His letter in *Y Tyst* on 30 September 1914 was the first anti-war broadside in Wales and he appealed to the Congregationalists' heroes and to its tradition of peace:

> Mae gennym fel enwad draddodiadau Henry Richard, S.R. a Gwilym Hiraethog i'w cadw'n lân. Mae gennym Efengyl y Groes a'r cariad i'w phregethu; a bydd yn union fwy o angen nag erioed am bregethu tangnefedd. Ond nid hawdd fydd pregethu tangnefedd yn fuan ar ol gyrru pobl i ryfela.[66]

> (We have as a denomination, the tradition of Henry Richard, S.R. and Gwilym Hiraethog to uphold, we have the gospel of the Cross and Love to preach, and there is greater need today than ever before to preach peace. It will not be easy to preach peace after driving people to war.)

---

[65] National Archives, Home Office papers, HO45/263275, f. 428, Report of ILP meeting in Aberaman.
[66] *Y Tyst*, 30 September 1914.

Rees condemned crude anti-Germanism and the propaganda that alleged German atrocities in Belgium, and his appeal to Wales's pacifist tradition aroused widespread anger and hostility. The Anglican magazine *Y Llan* charged him with treason, and the *Western Mail* accused him of performing 'a gross and unpardonable act of disloyalty' in suggesting that Britain was not guiltless in the present conflict, and of using 'baseless and inexcusable' arguments:

> These ridiculous perversities would not claim a moment's attention but for the fact that they appear over the signature of a leader of Welsh Nonconformity and a burning and shining light among Welsh Congregationalists. If his statements are not publicly repudiated by those who can speak in the name of Welsh Nonconformity serious harm may be done to the national and patriotic movement in Wales initiated by Mr Lloyd George and Mr Asquith ... The need for official action to counteract the pernicious effects of the Rev. T. Rees letter is the greater seeing that in Wales ... the popular leaders are the religious leaders.[67]

The *Western Mail* commenced a vitriolic campaign against Rees during the following months which started with an imaginative cartoon by Staniforth showing the Kaiser complimenting him: 'Well done, Principal Rees! Continue, my dear fellow, to pooh-pooh German atrocities, and do all you can to prevent Welsh men enlisting and later on my soldiers shall come to Wales and treat your university as they did at Louvain.'[68] The editor accused Rees of the 'foul slander' that British soldiers were as guilty as German soldiers of massacres, burnings and looting, and called on him to cease using his influence 'as a religious leader in Wales in way which would deter recruiting on an occasion of national emergency'.[69] Rees's trenchant reply accepted the government's right to wage war, but protested against the pressure being put on the churches to support the recruiting drive:

> I note that the Cardiff Tory paper, as if it were the Czar and the Kaiser rolled into one, calls upon the leaders of Nonconformity and the Congregational authorities to put me in the stocks for presuming

---

[67]   *Western Mail*, 7 October 1914.
[68]   *Western Mail*, 10 October 1914.
[69]   *Western Mail*, 16 October 1914.

to request newspapers to be more truthful and politicians to be honest, and for asking that religious people should have liberty. This is precisely the spirit against which I protested. The newspapers and the Government made the war without consulting the Church, and now they call upon the Church to carry it on, while the *Western Mail* commands the Nonconformist denominations to penalize whomsoever will not kneel before its idol[.][70]

Further letter-writers to the *Western Mail*, such as a Congregationalist minister from Llanboidy in Carmarthenshire, threatened to stop funding Bala-Bangor theological college,[71] and a number of chapels did withdraw support from the college, but other organisations, including the ILP, were moved to send money to the college. Following the report of one Aberdare chapel withdrawing funding, the Garw branch of the ILP wrote of its admiration:

the unselfish, courageous and noble stand which the Revd. Thomas Rees has made, in spite of misrepresentation and abuse, on behalf of the principles of peace and International Brotherhood, and its deep regret at the evidence of religious persecution and want of Christian charity displayed by the recent action of an Aberdare church in withholding its financial support from the College of which he is Principal. It further considers that such action is vindictive and utterly unworthy of a religious community and inimical to the highest interests of a clear political social and religious life and the interests of truth.[72]

Further criticism steeled Rees's resolve, and he expressed his wish to create a greater pacifist movement in Wales:

You see I am in open revolt ... I will join any rebellion that will come along ... I mean ... to make the anti-war position recognized and of some authority in North Wales politics and religion, but it will take some time.[73]

Surprisingly, the college did not suffer financially as a result of Rees's views, and the college's annual collections in chapels throughout Wales increased throughout the war, but in the wake of this controversy Rees reached 'the pinnacle of his unpopularity':

---

[70] *Western Mail*, 16 October 1914.
[71] *Western Mail*, 20 October 1914.
[72] *Pioneer*, 6 July 1918.
[73] Bangor University Archive, Thomas Rees Papers, MS 17773, letter to Revd J. T. Rhys, 3 April 1915.

> Yn yr unigrwydd oer hwnnw y ceir ef yn broffwyd gwrthodedig. Melltithiwyd ei enw yn y cudd a'r cyhoedd. Di-arddelwyd ef o'i aelodaeth gan Glwb Golff Bangor, cyfyngwyd i raddau ar ei gyfleusterau pregethu, amheuwyd ei addasrwydd fel Pennaeth coleg, ac edrychid arno'n wir megis un i'w osgoi ymysg dynion.[74]

> (In this cold loneliness he was a spurned prophet. His name was reviled publicly and privately. He was expelled as a member of Bangor Golf Club, his preaching opportunities were curtailed, his suitability as a Principal was questioned, and he was viewed as someone to avoid in company.)

Farcically, the proposer of the attempt to strike him off the membership roll of Bangor Golf Club himself resigned when the executive committee refused to take the matter further, after Rees had repudiated the views ascribed to him.[75] He was subsequently excluded from his club, but his response was phlegmatic:

> The whole thing is too idiotically absurd. One would scarcely know that we are living in a 'free country' if we hadn't a daily press that tells us so. Well, it's glorious weather and even the Huns, local and universal, can't spoil the joy of it.[76]

Rees's militant pacifism arose from his profound conviction that war under any circumstances was inconsistent with the teaching and spirit of Jesus, and he suffered great vituperation for his anti-war views, but his influence on the development of the pacifist anti-war movement was profound, and never more so than in his involvement with the FoR in Wales.[77]

THE FELLOWSHIP OF RECONCILIATION

The opposition to the war on religious grounds in Wales was mainly organised through the FoR, which was established at a conference in Cambridge in September 1914. Among those present were a number of prominent personalities, including

---

[74] Thomas Eirug Davies, *Prifathro Thomas Rees* (Llandysul: Gomer Press, 1939), pp. 70, 139.
[75] Bangor University Archive, Bangor Golf Club Papers, Executive minutes, November 1914–January 1915.
[76] Bangor University Archive, Bala-Bangor Papers, MS 17782, letter to J. T. Rhys, 29 April 1916.
[77] Miall Edwards, 'Obituary of Thomas Rees', *Welsh Outlook* (July 1926), 185.

Henry Hodgkin, an English Quaker and missionary doctor, the ILP Member of Parliament, George Lansbury, and George Maitland Ll. Davies. Those present were drawn from the 'professional middle classes', and the individuals present shared a 'sense of deep unease and the germs of a subjective interpretation of the Christian ethic which left each largely out of step with the "official" line taken by his Church'.[78] The conference produced a five-point statement that included express opposition to the war:

> that, as Christians, we are forbidden to wage war, and that our loyalty to our country, to humanity, to the Church Universal, and to Jesus Christ, our Lord and Master, calls us instead to a life service for the enthronement of love in personal, social commercial and national life.[79]

For those present it was a relief that others shared their conviction that war and Christianity were not compatible, but the ILP Member of Parliament, George Lansbury, highlighted the Fellowship's otherworldliness and was critical of its 'indefiniteness': 'We talked a lot about Christian witness, but few amongst us were willing to say "war was murder".'[80] By February 1915, 170 people had joined the FoR and attempts were being made to set up local groups, but a profound reflection of its upper-middle-class sensibilities was its executive committee's suggestion that:

> Drawing Room classes were suggested for the upper class circles, but with regard to the other end of the social spectrum, members were warned that they should attend Independent Labour Party meetings in order to familiarise themselves with the atmosphere before speaking at working-class gatherings on the subject of peace.[81]

There were strong personalities within its ranks who agreed with each other on little except that war was always wrong. The Fellowship was to prove a difficult ship to steer for the chair, Henry Hodgkin, and reconciliation within its own ranks was embarrassingly hard to achieve in practice during its early years: 'what leading members had most in common

[78] Jill Wallis, *Valiant for Peace* (Fellowship of Reconciliation, 1991), p. 6.
[79] Wallis, *Valiant for Peace*, p. 7.
[80] Wallis, *Valiant for Peace*, p. 7.
[81] Wallis, *Valiant for Peace*, p. 10.

was confidence in their own spiritual intuition and the courage to stand by it even to the detriment of their own careers'.[82] Its tone was quietist, it tended to take the view that pacifism was essentially for the individual conscience, and it was mainly supported by clergy and intellectuals in search of a 'rigorous theological and spiritual basis for pacifism'. Even by the end of the war, it had not worked out a coherent Christian pacifist philosophy and had generally been content to reassure members, rather than attempt to mobilise them as part of the anti-war movement.[83]

The Fellowship's first administrator was Revd Richard Roberts, born in 1874 in Blaenau Ffestiniog, who studied at Bala theological college and ministered in south Wales before becoming Presbyterian minister in Crouch End, London, in 1910. He had worked with Keir Hardie to oppose the Boer War, but after the outbreak of war in 1914 he found difficulties with his congregation because of his anti-war views. He chose temporarily to leave the ministry to take up the post of general secretary of the FoR and left in December 1915 to take up a pastorate in New York, by which time the FoR's membership had reached 2,000 and was growing at 200 a month. It was to grow to an organisation of approximately 5,000 members, distributed amongst 165 branches and groups in Britain, by the end of the war. With Roberts's departure, Revd Leyton Richards, a Presbyterian minister from Cheshire, was appointed to succeed him as general secretary in December 1915. Up until Roberts's departure, another Welsh Presbyterian, George M. Ll. Davies, who had left his prestigious post as secretary to three housing associations in the Welsh Town Planning and Housing Trust, worked as his unpaid assistant secretary and became the first editor of its quarterly magazine, *The Venturer*, which sold approximately 2,270 copies per month throughout Britain and Ireland. He had already rejected an offer from the Trust's President, David Davies, by then a Colonel with the Royal Welsh Fusiliers and later Lloyd George's parliamentary private secretary, to become editor of the prestigious monthly

---

[82] Martin Ceadel, *Pacifism in Britain 1914–1945: The Defining of a Faith* (Oxford, 1980), p. 37.
[83] Ceadel, *Pacifism in Britain 1914–1945*, p. 36.

magazine *Welsh Outlook*. Based in the FoR's office in Red Lion Square in London, Davies travelled around the country, establishing branches, and writing leaflets, articles and propaganda. A frequent speaker throughout Wales, the largest anti-war meeting he addressed was a public meeting in the Rink at Merthyr Tydfil at the end of 1915 with over 2,000 people present.

In Wales the growth of the FoR took on a strikingly distinctive and less quietist character of its own and was developed primarily by key individuals, mostly Welsh-speaking, Nonconformist ministers of religion, although not exclusively so, and concentrated in north Wales. Whilst the proportion of the Welsh population who spoke Welsh was approximately forty-three per cent, and in Gwynedd the proportion of monoglot Welsh speakers was thirty-six per cent,[84] nevertheless it is remarkable that the evidence of FoR activity through the medium of English is very slight and extremely limited in south Wales. The founding meeting of the FoR in Wales was held in Bangor on 31 May and 1 June 1915, and was addressed by the Fellowship's administrator, Revd Richard Roberts, Revd Peter Hughes Griffiths and E. Llywelyn Williams, all from the FoR in London. A service was held in the English-language Presbyterian church in Princes Road, addressed by Revd Hywel Harris Hughes, minister of the local Tabernacle chapel, and Principal Thomas Rees, both of whom became key figures in the development of the opposition movement. The congregation included scores of students, and many of those theological students present would become conscientious objectors. In a subsequent meeting at Thomas Rees's home, it was decided to create an organisational division for Caernarfonshire, and four branches were created – Bangor/Bethesda; Caernarfon/ Penygroes, Blaenau Ffestiniog, and Pwllheli.[85] The second regional division was created in the Wrexham area on 2 June, when a group mostly of ministers of religion met and held a number of peace meetings in Ponciau and Rhosllanner-chrugog, which were addressed by G. M. Ll. Davies, Herbert

[84] Davies, *Hanes Cymru*, p. 478.
[85] Rees, *Dal i Herio'r Byd*, p. 116.

Dunnico, secretary of the Peace Society and Revds D. Wyre Lewis and Revd E. K. Jones, Cefnmawr, near Wrexham. A number of smaller branches were then established in the locality, but the membership was small. Revd Tegla Davies's small branch in Oswestry was ineffectual and received little public sympathy:

> Pan gychwynasom ar y gwaith, caem groeso i ystafell bur dymunol, ond pan ddaeth chwaon o amheuaeth heibio ynghylch ein hamcanion, gwthiwyd ni i ystafell fwy dirywiedig, ac felly ymlaen nes o'r diwedd gyrraedd y seler.[86]

> (When we started on our work, we were welcomed to a quite desirable room, but when our aims caused draughts of doubt, we were pushed to a more unsuitable room, and then onwards until we reached the cellar.)

In Merthyr Tydfil, the FoR joined an alliance of anti-war bodies, including the ILP, the NCF, the UDC and trade union lodges, to form the Merthyr Stop the War and Peace Council, which attracted crowds of up to 3,000 people to its meetings,[87] but comparatively few branches were formally established in other parts of Wales. By January 1918, the FoR had only eleven branches, scattered throughout Wales. In north Wales the branches were clustered near Bangor, Caernarfon and Penygroes, in the Nantlle Valley, and the Wrexham area, with branches in Corwen and Oswestry. In south Wales, they were distributed more widely, in Cardiff, Swansea, Merthyr Tydfil, Nelson in the Rhymney Valley, and in Aberystwyth in mid-Wales, whilst Cardiff boasted an associated students' group.[88] Six of the eleven branch secretaries were ministers of religion. The extent to which these groups were organised coherently and in a disciplined manner is doubtful. It may be significant that areas in which there was substantial anti-war activity by FoR members, such as the Swansea Valley and Briton Ferry, did not boast their own branches, but worked through local peace councils with other organisations, such as the ILP and the NCF. In November 1918, sympathy towards

---

[86] E. Tegla Davies, 'Yr Eglwys Fethodistaidd', in Jones and Evans, *Ffordd Tangnefedd*, p. 22.

[87] *Pioneer*, 22 April 1916.

[88] *The News Sheet of the FoR* (Peace Pledge Union, 1918).

the plight of conscientious objectors was the motivation for the establishing of another branch in Trawsfynydd, with about fifty members,[89] but this proved an exception, and the energy of active FoR members was mostly directed towards sustaining local peace organisations and building a relationship with local anti-war organisations, such as the ILP. The FoR organisation in Wales seems to have been autonomous of the formal central structures of the FoR, and very few members from Wales attended its General Council,[90] whilst the relationship between the FoR in Wales and London was a very direct personal one between G. M. Ll. Davies, Richard Roberts and Principal Thomas Rees, in particular.

The FoR centrally funded the translation and printing of pamphlets into Welsh, such as 2,500 copies of 'Faith for the New Age' and 2,500 copies of the pamphlet 'How to Check the Spirit of Militarism'.[91] The most crucial initiative taken by the organisation in Wales in the aftermath of the introduction of conscription was its decision to create a Welsh-language newspaper to oppose the war. In January 1916, Principal Thomas Rees notified the FoR's Literature Committee that the Bangor and Wrexham groups had considered creating a new anti-war magazine, as 'the only means of getting at the public in Wales was by a distinctively Welsh journal', and Rees was assured of the FoR's support and given a financial guarantee of twenty pounds against a loss on the new venture for the first twelve months.[92]

In March 1916, the conference to consider the FoR's approach to the 'peculiar social and religious problems of Wales and to consider the creation of a newspaper to advocate pacifist views' was held at Hendre Hall, Bont Ddu, near Dolgellau. Its convening circular was signed by the FoR's

---

[89] National Library of Wales, E. K. Jones Papers, Box 6, letters from Owen Owen, Trawsfynydd, to Jones, 8 February 1918, 4 November 1918, 22 December 1918.

[90] British Library of Political and Economic Science, Fellowship of Reconciliation Papers, Coll. Misc. 0456/2/1, General Council Minutes; of the seven meetings between April 1915 and September 1919, at which an average seventy were present, only six Welsh delegates attended.

[91] British Library of Political and Economic Science, Fellowship of Reconciliation Papers, Coll. Misc. 0456/4/1, Literature Committee Minutes, 13 January 1916.

[92] British Library of Political and Economic Science, Fellowship of Reconciliation Papers, Coll. Misc. 0456/5/1, Minutes of Business Committee, 3 May 1916.

chairman, Dr Richard Roberts, and its general secretary, George M. Ll. Davies, together with the leadership of the FoR in Wales, including Thomas Rees and his fellow Bala-Bangor lecturer Revd John Morgan Jones. They informed the invitees that:

> In view of the extreme seriousness of the present political situation, and the need for expression of the growing dissatisfaction in Wales with the existing order in the political and religious world, it is felt that the Conference may be an event of very great significance.

The agenda for the two days reflected a combination of religious devotion and practical politics, and included discussions on a Welsh journal and the role of the FoR in Wales.

The prominent poet T. Gwynn Jones led a discussion on 'national affairs', and the Flintshire minister and prominent ILP-er Revd D. Gwynfryn Jones led on international affairs.[93] The twenty-eight people present were mostly ministers of religion, with a sole woman, Eluned Morgan, a well-known literary figure from the Welsh colony of Patagonia, Argentina. The party included Revd J. Puleston Jones, Pwllheli, the minister of Hope chapel in Merthyr, Revd J. Morgan Jones, four Bala-Bangor students, the Students' Christian Movement secretary, and three of the most prominent Welsh-language literary figures of the day, Revd Tegla Davies, T. Gwynn Jones and T. H. Parry-Williams.[94] The decision to establish the journal was the most momentous of the conference and it became the link for the Christian pacifist movement throughout Wales, although its geographical reach and its Welsh-language content also marked its limitations.

This monthly journal, *Y Deyrnas*, published its first edition in October 1916. It consisted at first of twelve pages but in December 1917 was reduced to eight pages, and it had a monthly circulation average extending throughout Wales of 2,750 until the end of the war, although after the Armistice it dropped to 2,600, and it suffered a small financial loss on the last editions published.

---

[93] Bangor University Archive, E. K. Jones Papers, circular from H. Harris Hughes, Box 39, February 1916.
[94] Griffith, *Heddychwr Mawr Cymru*, p. 61.

The chairman and editor of its board of management was Principal Thomas Rees, the 'dynamic power behind this crusade'.[95] Its secretary was Revd H. Harris Hughes, the minister of Tabernacle chapel in Bangor and a former printer, and the treasurer was Professor John Morgan Jones, also of Bala-Bangor college. The printer and publisher Evan Thomas, Gwalia Printing Works, Sackville Road, Bangor, proved a willing and enthusiastic collaborator in the venture.[96] In its first edition, Rees stated that the magazine would examine the relevance of the principles of Christ to every department of human life, including religion, politics, commerce and labour, and explained that the journal's mission arose from a sense of shame at Christianity's failure:

> am na fu Cristnogaeth Ewrob yn wrthglawdd digonol yn erbyn y rhyfer-thwy dinistriol. Ond o ystyried, gwelwn mai un yn unig o effeithiau ysbryd Anghrist yw y gyflafan hon; i'r un achos y rhaid olrhain drygau cymdeithasol, cenedlaethol a rhyng-genedlaethol ein hoes. Yn wyneb hyn oll, rhaid fod rhywbeth i'w dystiolaethu yn enw Teyrnas Dduw.[97]

> (Christian Europe had not been a sufficient bulwark against the destructive flood. But we see now that the present disaster is only one of the effects of the Spirit of Anti-Christ; all social, national and inter-national evils of the age must be traced to the same cause. In the face of all this, there must be some message to be delivered in the name of the Kingdom of God.)

Rees wrote a third of its content and other ministers of religion wrote the bulk of the articles, while a monthly column on conscientious objectors by Revd E. K. Jones exposed their ill-treatment. A number of the younger and most prominent poets, including T. Gwynn Jones and T. H. Parry Williams, both recently crowned bards, published poetry in *Y Deyrnas*, as well as prominent writers such as T. E. Nicholas and David Thomas, Talysarn, the north Wales organiser of the ILP and member of the FoR.

Three Liberal Members of Parliament also contributed individual articles to the magazine, Ellis Davies, the Member for Eifionnydd, E. T. John, East Denbighshire, and W.

[95] Davies, *Prifathro Thomas Rees*, p. 143.
[96] Rees, *Dal i Herio'r Byd*, p. 113.
[97] *Y Deyrnas*, October 1916.

Llewelyn Williams, Carmarthen Boroughs, which reflected the growing unease at conscription and the developing gulf between Lloyd George and traditional Liberals. None could be said to be opponents of the war, but they focused on the dangers of increasing militarism and were sympathetic to the plight of COs, and both Davies and John were ready to be used by the Fellowship to put down parliamentary questions about the ill-treatment of conscientious objectors and the prospects of an early peace settlement by the summer of 1917.[98] Most of the other contributors, however, were undoubtedly 'out and out' pacifists.

The print run of *Y Deyrnas* varied from 2,500 in December 1916 to 3,000 in November 1917, before declining to 2,750 by September 1918. This impressive level of sales was similar to the *Venturer*'s circulation throughout Britain, and it was distributed openly to 219 outlets, including forty shops and newsagents. The agents included only three ministers of religion, and the distribution was limited primarily to the counties of north Wales, Carmarthenshire and Glamorgan (see Table 1).

Glamorgan	915
Denbigh and Flintshire	381
Caernarfonshire	371
Carmarthenshire	332
Merionethshire	278
Cardiganshire	117
Pembrokeshire	89
Anglesey	71
Montgomeryshire	60
Breconshire	6
London	26
Total	**2,646**

Table 1: Monthly distribution of *Y Deyrnas* to shops and agents in 1917[99]

[98] Bangor University Archive, Bala-Bangor Papers, MSS 234, letter from Ellis Davies MP to Revd J. Morgan Jones, Bangor, 6 July 1917.
[99] Bangor University Archive, Bala-Bangor Papers MSS 258, circulation of *Y Deyrnas*.

Whilst it may not be surprising that no copies of *Y Deyrnas* were sold in such a heavily anglicised county as Radnorshire, the lack of sales in the western valleys of Monmouthshire suggests a lack of penetration and influence east of the Rhondda valleys and Cardiff, and that its influence was felt mainly in north Wales, Carmarthenshire and the western half of the south Wales coalfield. In north Wales, circulation was highest in the Wrexham area (124 copies), Trawsfynydd (72) and Blaenau Ffestiniog (73), with Caernarfon and the slate-quarrying centres of the Nantlle and Ogwen Valleys and Caernarfon (74), and Bangor (30). In Pembrokeshire, there was a cluster around the northern villages of Clunderwen, Boncath, Y Glôg and Llanfyrnach (76 copies), possibly related to the influence of a local minister, Revd Gilbert Jones, Llangloffan, and Thomas Rees's and T. E. Nicholas's influence locally, given that both were from the area. The Amman Valley had a circulation of 254 copies, ranging from Llandybie in the west through Ammanford to Brynamman and Cwmtwrch in the east. In Glamorgan, the main centres were Swansea (63), Swansea Valley (59), Merthyr and district (51) and Aberdare (36). But the densest area of circulation in Glamorgan was undoubtedly the Rhondda, with its large population, with 123 copies sold, ranging from Pontypridd upwards to Tonypandy, Treherbert, Treorchy, Tylorstown and Clydach Vale.

Given the nature of its content, including trenchant criticism of government policy, it is remarkable that *Y Deyrnas* did not fall foul of the Defence of the Realm Act and the censor, but the authorities were very slow to respond to the appearance of the paper, and even then did not pursue the journal. It was only in February 1918 that the military intelligence officer responsible for north Wales, based in the army headquarters in Chester, identified that the magazine might be controversial.[100] The influence of *Y Deyrnas* was broadened in 1917–18 by those who had originally accepted the necessity for war but were increasingly alienated by the government's illiberal support for conscription and pursuit of COs.[101]

[100] National Archives, Air Ministry papers, AIR 1/560/15/59, Weekly Intelligence Summary, General Headquarters, Great Britain, Report of Military Intelligence Officer, Chester Barracks, February 1918.

[101] Morgan, *The Span of the Cross*, p. 61.

The onset of conscription in January 1916 proved one of the most significant watersheds for the anti-war movement, and although there was provision for a 'conscience' clause in the Military Service Act, the lack of clarity of this provision meant that much of its 'intended generosity' would be frustrated. The FoR's attitude was that it was for the individual to decide what his conscience should do, although they urged members to consider taking alternative service of a non-military nature.[102] In Wales, an indication of Thomas Rees's influence was his college's response to the introduction of conscription in February 1916 and its impact on the college and its students. Although seven of its theological students had enlisted voluntarily in the army, in February 1916, eighteen of its students sought exemption on grounds of conscientious objection before the Bangor military tribunal. They had the support of the college's executive committee and these Bala-Bangor students appeared with another eleven students from the local Baptists' college, and six from Bangor University. The tribunal's members received a circular from Bala-Bangor college, which stated that the grounds on which the applicants based their claims were firstly on grounds of conscience, that a man being educated or trained for any work should continue to be so educated and trained, and that the Christian ministry had been expressly recognised by Parliament as a work of sufficient importance to exempt those who perform it from military service.[103] The tribunal was informed that about one half of the Congregationalist students in the Welsh theological colleges had enlisted and there was a danger of a shortage of ministers if theological students were not exempted. The tribunal proved sympathetic despite the hectoring presence of one of its members, the member of the Bangor Golf Club who had sought Rees's expulsion, and it gave absolute exemption to six of the Bala-Bangor students, and conditional exemption to the others. Rees spoke at the tribunal on behalf of the students, and it became apparent that Thomas Rees had also aided fifteen students of the Bangor Baptist

---

[102] Wallis, *Valiant for Peace*, pp. 17–18.
[103] Bangor University Archive, Bala-Bangor Papers, f. 3169, newspaper cutting; Henry Lewis papers, MS 5278.

college to apply for exemption, which included instructions on how to fill the relevant forms.[104] Of the twenty-one Bala-Bangor students, eight gained absolute exemption on the grounds of their vocation as theological students, whilst only one was rejected.[105]

Other colleges' authorities showed little tolerance towards war resisters, and the Cardiff Baptist college, for instance, encouraged its students to enlist, even though a sizeable minority of them opposed conscription.[106] Other colleges, such as Carmarthen Presbyterian College, attempted to secure exemption, and its principal successfully appealed on behalf of three of his students who were about to enter the ministry, but a fourth was refused exemption because of the gap of sixteen months he had to wait to qualify fully as a minister.[107] Brecon Memorial Congregationalist College's students included at least ten conscientious objectors. Whilst the majority of theological students gained exemption there were isolated exceptions. In the case of Ben Meyrick, a Baptist minister in Anglesey and a member of the FoR, exemption was refused on grounds of conscience, and despite a series of appeals and campaigns led by Revd E. K. Jones and others, he was sentenced in October 1917 to two years' imprisonment with hard labour.[108]

From November 1917 onwards, the intelligence agencies pursued the FoR with vigour. Its London headquarters was raided in November 1917 and its journal, *The Venturer*, prosecuted for the publication of a critical letter by George M. Ll. Davies to his wife criticising prison conditions.[109] Wales was reported to be receptive to the FoR message, 'a combination of recent religious revival and acute industrial problems' thought to make the Valleys entirely congenial for the

---

[104] National Library of Wales, E. K. Jones Papers, Box 39, letter from Dan Jones, February 1916.
[105] Bangor University Archive, Bala-Bangor Papers, f. 3169, notes by Thomas Rees.
[106] National Library of Wales, E. K. Jones Papers, Box 29, letter from S. J. Leeke, secretary, students' body, Baptist College, Cardiff, 31 December 1915.
[107] *Carmarthen Journal*, 10 March 1916.
[108] National Library of Wales, E. K. Jones Papers, Box 2, letters 24 February 1916.
[109] Wallis, *Valiant for Peace*, p. 30.

deliverance of FoR's evangelism.[110] But this rose-tinted view of the FoR's potential in Wales was undermined by the organisation's quietist tone and reluctance to offer political guidance.

The first national Welsh conference to be organised by the FoR was held in September 1917 in the Friends' Meeting House in Llandrindod. Seventy people were present, with Dr Thomas Rees presiding and Revd D. Wyre Lewis as secretary, but attempts to persuade two of the most sympathetic Members of Parliament, E. H. John and Ellis W. Davies, who had written for *Y Deyrnas* and had opposed conscription, to attend the conference, were rebuffed. Davies responded that although he sympathised with the aim of the conference, he felt that:

> nothing would be gained from the intervention of MPs in such a conference where possibly extreme speeches might be delivered and which would in no way contribute to focusing public opinion on what must be the basis of an European peace. I mentioned the matter to Mr. E. T. John the other day and he agrees with me in thinking that it would be better in the first instance that a small number – from six to ten – should meet in private and ascertain the points on which they are agreed.[111]

This caution did Davies little good, for although he had been careful to be an ultra-loyalist to Lloyd George it failed to save him from challenge by a Coalition Liberal candidate in December 1918 and the loss of his parliamentary seat.[112] John in turn deserted the Liberal Party for the Labour Party in the 1918 election, and also lost his seat. In Llandrindod, resolutions called for immediate peace by negotiation, and an appeal was made to the Prime Minister to investigate how the Military Service Acts led to the ill-treatment of COs:

> We are convinced that all measures of persecution cause grievous harm to the country at large, and would call your attention to the fact that many of the most loyal citizens and noblest characters are now imprisoned not for any crime, but for reasons of loyalty to conscience only.

[110] Wallis, *Valiant for Peace*, p. 31.

[111] Bangor University Archive, Bala-Bangor Papers, MSS 234, letter from Ellis Davies to Revd John Morgan Jones, 6 July 1917.

[112] J. Graham Jones, *David Lloyd George and Welsh Liberalism* (Aberystwyth: Welsh Political Archive, 2010), pp. 184–5.

In particular we would call your attention to the practice of sentencing men to several terms of imprisonment for what is practically but one act of disobedience. We appeal to you with confidence, remembering your many fights for freedom of speech and liberty of conscience, and also knowing that you can at pleasure put an end to what is now a stain upon the character of this country.[113]

A public meeting on the second evening of the conference was broken up after the opening speaker, John Davies, a prominent ILP member and miners' agent for Dowlais, struck a truculent tone in his speech which was out of step with the emollient calm of the meeting during that day.[114] The initial prayers offered by Revd John Morgan Jones, Bangor, included supplication for the men at the front, but Davies's criticism of shipowners for profiteering from the war led to heckling and howls of protest from a part of the audience, and the meeting was brought to an end by the church minister and his deacons.[115] It is evident that the organisers received prior warning of the interruption of the meeting earlier that day, and a feature of the conference was the debate between the labour and miners' federation activists and the ministers of religion on the forthcoming 'war after the war' to come between Capital and Labour.[116]

The conference resolved to continue its work and to organise further local conferences and set up committees for north and south Wales, to take on the responsibility of organising further similar conferences. Thomas Rees was elected President, Professor John Morgan Jones, Bangor, elected as treasurer, and two secretaries elected – Revd Wyre Lewis for north Wales and Revd W. J. Rees, Alltwen, for south Wales.[117] The local committees organised public meetings, mostly in south-west Wales, in Ystalyfera, Cwmtwrch, Trimsaran, Cefneithin, Tycroes, Briton Ferry and the Tumble, where the police attempted but failed to stop the meeting addressed by four pacifist ministers of religion, Gwynfryn Jones, Flint, J.

[113] Y Deyrnas, October 1917.
[114] Evans, Benign Neglect, p. 277.
[115] Brecon and Radnor Express, 13 September 1917.
[116] Y Deyrnas, October 1917.
[117] Y Deyrnas, October 1917.

Morgan Jones, Bangor, Llywelyn Bowyer and W. J. Rees.[118] Another two conferences and three public meetings were arranged on 23–25 January 1918, in Briton Ferry, Glanaman and Cwmtwrch, with Wyre Lewis and E. K. Jones as the main speakers.[119] *Y Deyrnas* reported meetings in March in Corwen, and peace meetings in Cwmaman and Gwaun-cae-Gurwen were addressed by T. E. Nicholas on the subject of the peace legacy of Samuel Roberts, Llanbrynmair. Two more peace meetings held in Briton Ferry and Pontardawe were addressed by the minister of Jerusalem Baptist chapel in Briton Ferry, Revd Rees Powell, together with Principal Thomas Rees and H. Harris Hughes, Bangor.[120]

From the autumn of 1917 onwards, there was a rapid increase in the numbers of Nonconformist organisations locally and nationally who passed resolutions in favour of peace by negotiation and protested against the treatment of conscientious objectors. In December 1917, for instance, the Bethesda Free Church Council protested against the withdrawal of the right to vote from conscientious objectors, and pacifist meetings were held in Holywell, Cwmtwrch, Pontardawe and Llanrwst against the war.[121] In January 1918, motions protesting against the ill-treatment of conscientious objectors were passed by the Free Church Councils for south-west Wales and Bangor Free Church Council, the Anglesey and Conwy Valley Monthly Meeting, the Welsh Wesleyan circuits in Manchester, Tregarth and Beaumaris, and Corwen's group of Nonconformist ministers.[122]

But the first conference in south Wales to follow on from the Llandrindod conference was held fully six months later, in March 1918, in the Ebeneser Independent chapel in Trecynon, Aberdare, where fifty delegates came to discuss how 'the spirit of reconciliation could be enacted by securing peace' and to protest against the treatment of conscientious objectors. Both Thomas Rees and Harris Hughes from Bangor spoke, and a number of prominent local ILP

---

[118] Jones and Evans, *Ffordd Tangnefedd*, p. 17.
[119] *Y Deyrnas*, February 1918.
[120] *Y Deyrnas*, April 1918.
[121] *Y Deyrnas*, December 1917.
[122] *Y Deyrnas*, January 1918.

members, including Rose Davies and Councillors Edwin
Stonelake and Idris Thomas, took part. That evening a
'numerous' anti-war public meeting was held in the local
Baptist chapel, which was monitored by two local policemen.[123] A similar 'Peace Conference' held in Penygroes, near
Ammanford, in May 1918, was addressed by J. Puleston Jones,
Llewelyn Bowyer and Wyre Lewis.[124] In June 1918 the North
Wales League of Free Churches passed a motion that called
for a quick end to the war and for the creation of a supra-
national institution to create worldwide peace so as to make
war impossible, rejoiced because the ideal of a League of
Nations was gaining ground, and expressed confidence in
the nations' desire to unite and agree on general
disarmament.[125]

In July 1918, two further conferences were organised in
Llandudno and Wrexham in north Wales to protest against
the introduction of militarism in schools. These were organised by the NCCL and its Welsh organiser, Ivor H. Thomas,
and the prominent ILP activist J. E. Thomas, Penygroes.
These conferences reflected the NCCL's success and the
FoR's contribution in harnessing the anti-war movement
with those who, whilst supporting the war, opposed militarism and conscription. The Llandudno conference was
presided over by Thomas Rees, and addresses were given by
Principal Graham, the headmaster of the Quaker college in
Manchester, and Noel Langdon-Davis, representing the
NCCL. These two conferences were particularly successful,
with 326 delegates representing a large number of the
chapels of Anglesey, Caernarfonshire and Meirion, including
250 churches and Free Church councils, and thirty-one trade
unions, with a total membership of 110,000. Letters of
support were also received by sixty other churches, who
regretted their inability to send delegates. David Thomas
emphasised that there were many ministers and others who
had supported the war who attended, but wished to oppose

[123] *Y Deyrnas*, April 1918.
[124] *Y Deyrnas*, June 1918.
[125] *Y Deyrnas*, June 1918.

local militarism as much as German militarism.[126] The
following meeting in Wrexham, presided over by E. T. John,
MP, was a similar delegates' conference which resolved that
the 'militarisation of the rising generations [is] a menace to
the industrial freedom, the safety of the democracy, and the
future good relations of the peoples of the world'.[127]

In preparation for these conferences, a list of the 'anti-war
religious leaders' in north Wales had been sent by the
National Council for Civil Liberties' Welsh organiser, Ivor
Thomas, to Ethel Snowden in June 1918, but was seized by
MI5 officers during a raid of the NCCL's London offices.
The list confirms that these key anti-war activists in north
Wales were associated with the group of activists involved
with *Y Deyrnas*. Of the nineteen listed, eight were founders
or involved in producing the journal; also included were
J. Huw Williams, the influential editor of the Caernarfon
labour paper *Y Dinesydd*, the editor of the Congregationalist
theological magazine, *Y Dysgedydd*, Revd Pari Huws, and a
prominent local schoolteacher and ILP leader from the
quarrying Nantlle Valley, J. E. Thomas. Seven of these
names, namely Huw Williams, J. E. Thomas, Revd J. H
Howard, Revd R. Bell, Revd Cernyw Williams, H. Parri-
Roberts and Frederick Pane, were considered by MI5 to be
'very active', but it is a reflection of the security services' poor
grasp of the nature of the movement that David Thomas, the
ILP organiser for north Wales, for example, was not
included.[128]

'A WELSHMAN'S DREAM IN BORROWED CLOTHES'[129]

The military authorities' concern for the likelihood that
many theological students would become conscientious
objectors explains why the army leadership in north Wales

---

[126] Bangor University Archive, Thomas Jones papers, David Thomas, 'The Pacifist Movement'.

[127] *Llangollen Advertiser*, 26 July 1918.

[128] National Archives, Security Service Papers, KV2/666, NCCL documents and note from Major Mathews, 6 June 1918.

[129] R. R. Williams, *Breuddwyd Cymro mewn Dillad Benthyg* (Liverpool: Gwasg y Brython, 1964), tells the story of the Welsh company of the Royal Army Medical Corps, set up for would-be conscientious objectors in January 1916.

felt the need to create an alternative opportunity for those young men. In January 1916, a company of the Royal Army Medical Corps was formed, in connection with the Welsh Army Division, by the army's chief recruiting officer in north Wales, the Congregationalist Brigadier Owen Thomas, in Rhyl, and consecrated by Revd John Williams, Brynsiencyn. The company was nicknamed 'God's Own' and initially comprised of 187 men, drawn mainly from the Welsh theological colleges.[130] The circular sent to prospective recruits informed them that the War Office had consented to the formation of an RAMC unit, connected to the Welsh Army Division.[131]

These men were not thought by the army to be in the same category as the conscientious objectors, but its members' understanding was that the company had been specifically created in order to accommodate those who might otherwise have become conscientious objectors. One of its members, the poet Revd A. E. Jones (Cynan), explained the character of the new company:

> cwmni o efrydwyr Cymreig oeddem, yn wir cwmni o efrydwyr yn siarad Cymraeg gan mwyaf, ar wahan i ychydig athrawon, rhai myfyrwyr Wesleyaidd o Golegau Handsworth a Didsbury ac eraill. Ag eithrio nifer bychan iawn a oedd eisoes yn ordeiniedig, ymgeiswyr ar gyfer y weinidogaeth gyda gwahanol enwadau Cymru oedd y rhelyw mawr ohonom, ac ar gyfer gwŷr ifainc o'r fath y llwyddodd Prif Gaplan y Milwyr Cymreig, y Dr. John Williams, Brynsiencyn, gael gan y Swyddfa Ryfel gytuno i ffurfio'r cwmni arbennig hwn o'r RAMC. *Rhan o'r cytundeb sylfaenol oedd na throsglwyddid yr un aelod o'r cwmni tan unrhyw amgylchiadau o'r RAMC i unrhyw adran ymladdol o'r fyddin.* [my emphasis]

> (we were a company of Welsh students, mostly Welsh speaking, apart from a number of teachers, some Wesleyan students from Handsworth and Didsbury Colleges and others. Apart from a small number who had already been ordained in a number of Wales's denominations, the majority of us were candidates for the ministry, and it was for such young men that the main Chaplain of the Welsh Army, Dr. John Williams, Brynsiencyn, won an agreement with the War Office to form a special company of the RAMC. *Part of the fundamental agreement was*

---

[130] Williams, *Breuddwyd Cymro mewn Dillad Benthyg*, p. vii.
[131] Williams, *Breuddwyd Milwr mewn Dillad Benthyg*, p. 2.

that not one member of the company would in any circumstances be transferred
from the RAMC to any fighting unit of the Army.[my emphasis])[132]

The company included 129 theological students, and seventy-
three of the company's number came from Welsh theological
colleges, including fifteen Anglican students from St David's
Lampeter, thirty-two students from the Calvinist Methodist
colleges in Aberystwyth, Bala and Clynnog preparatory
college, eleven students from Cardiff Baptist college, three
students from Brecon Congregationalist college, and four
from Bala-Bangor Congregationist college. It also included
twenty-six theological students from the Wesleyan colleges at
Didsbury and Headingley in Leeds, thirty-one students and
teachers from the Normal teacher training college in Bangor,
eleven ordained ministers and preachers, and seven medical
students.[133] These young men felt they could join without
violating their consciences, but considered themselves to be
pacifists:

> mi ddwedwn i mai cwmni o basiffistiaid oeddem ni, yn yr ystyr fod
> gennym wrthwynebiad cydwybodol i ladd ac ymladd, ond ein bod yn
> barod i gymryd ein hanfon i rywle a cario'r clwyfedigion i ddiogelwch
> a'u hymgeleddu, neu i weini ar y cleifion, a hynny tan yr un amodau o
> galedi a disgyblaeth â milwyr eraill.[134]

> (I would say that we were a company of pacifists, in the sense that we
> had conscientious objection to killing and to fighting, but that we
> were ready to be sent somewhere to carry the injured to safety and to
> protect them, or to serve the wounded, and to do so under the same
> conditions of hardship and discipline as other soldiers.)

Following its period of training in Llandrindod and
Sheffield, in September 1916 approximately 150 members of
the company were sent to Salonika, forty to work on hospital
ships and others to France and Egypt.[135] More sceptical
commentators have described the creation of this company
as a propaganda masterstroke to prevent motivated young
and idealistic intellectuals amongst those trainee ministers

---

[132] Williams, *Breuddwyd Milwr mewn Dillad Benthyg*, p. vii.
[133] Williams, *Breuddwyd Milwr mewn Dillad Benthyg*, pp. 4–7.
[134] Williams, *Breuddwyd Milwr mewn Dillad Benthyg*, pp. ix–x.
[135] Williams, *Breuddwyd Milwr mewn Dillad Benthyg*, p. 14.

from becoming COs,[136] but in spite of their understanding that they would not be required to bear arms, the company's exemption from combatant duties did not last. Rumours which spread in 1918 that the 'strong and the able' in the company were likely to be transferred to other regiments were confirmed when an Army Order was published on 14 June 1918, stating that the War Office had no opposition to transferring men from this company to other companies and regiments. It is thought that this volte-face was made in order to enable three members of the company to win army commissions. The three were Cynan and David Morris Jones, who were made chaplains, and Tom Jenkins of Llanelli, who was made an officer.[137] There is only one example of a man forced to leave the unit because of his objection to carrying arms, namely Herbert Lewis of Carmarthen, who was transferred to the Non-Combatant Corps and subsequently died of a local disease.[138] This change of policy apparently caused difficulty for those in the army charged with dealing with conscientious objectors. In June 1918, the War Office announced there would be no 'objection' to the transfer to the infantry of the Welsh theological students specially enlisted,[139] but the change in policy does not seem to have caused a major exodus from the ranks of the Welsh unit, and for almost 200 men who might otherwise well have become conscientious objectors, it proved to be a satisfactory compromise between the requirements of the state and the call of conscience.

Indeed, they found themselves in a similar position to other recruits who had joined other companies, such as the Royal Army Medical Corps or Non-Combatant Corps, on the basis that they would not be required to bear arms. For example, Wilfred Knott was a member of an RAMC Field Ambulance Unit in Salonika in June 1918 and described how men who considered themselves 'conscientious objectors' had joined the RAMC, but were forced to participate in road-making alongside Turkish prisoners of war, which they

---

[136] Gareth Miles, 'Review of "Cofiant David Elis"', in *Taliesin*, 81(1993), 106–10.
[137] Williams, *Breuddwyd Milwr mewn Dillad Benthyg*, p. 55.
[138] Williams, *Breuddwyd Milwr mewn Dillad Benthyg*, p. 55.
[139] Williams, *Breuddwyd Milwr mewn Dillad Benthyg*, p. 55.

regarded as reneging on their understanding of their roles. This group of so-called 'conscientious objectors' appeared before a military tribunal in July 1918, in which sixteen men had their objections to joining the infantry upheld but thirty-seven had their objections disallowed and were transferred to the infantry. Knott was transferred to the 1/3rd Welsh Field Ambulance along with five others in August 1918, and some of the other men, including the 'St John's Men' and other volunteers, were sent to France as ambulancemen, leaving Knott to muse about 'what the boys will think who have been duped and sent into the infantry when they hear the remainder have been sent as ambulancemen to France'.[140] The 'God's Own' Welsh company provided to be an effective compromise for those theological students and ministers whose consciences were torn between their belief in the sanctity of life and their passion to aid their fellow man in their suffering.

It is striking that in the pages of Y Deyrnas the plethora of anti-war public meetings in 1917 and the momentum of the Llandrindod Wells conference of September 1917 had ground to a halt by July 1918, but the journal continued to be published until the autumn of 1919, with a comparatively small drop in circulation. Much of the discussion in Y Deyrnas from the autumn of 1918 onwards focused on the fate of those conscientious objectors who were still imprisoned, and the peace conditions to be imposed on the German nation and its allies in the Paris discussions that led to the Treaty of Versailles and the seeds of another war. Its edition of February 1919 was hopeful of the attempt to establish peace and permanent justice between the nations of the world, but in September 1919 it traced the current industrial and social discontent to Lloyd George's wish to prolong the war unnecessarily for two years.[141]

Morgan considers that the fundamental weakness of Welsh pacifism in this period was its failure to appreciate the 'depths of human malignancy and evil';

> No matter how vigorously pacifist Dissenters protested at the undoubted horrors of war, they failed to provide a sufficiently realistic philosophy

---

[140] Imperial War Museum, Wilfred Knott Diary, Document 7987, 24 June 1918.
[141] Y Deyrnas, September 1919.

whereby conflict could be overcome and abolished. Whereas pacifism became a potent individual witness, it remained unconvincing as a political strategy.[142]

He rightly argues that anti-militarism was chosen by very few indeed and suggests that the most substantial contribution made by the opposition to war on religious grounds may have been to prepare the ground for the creation of a consensus for an idealistic peace movement after the war. But this perspective underestimates the gradual development of anti-war activity, including the religious pacifist movement, from 1916 onwards, as disillusionment with the war effort and the jettisoning of the traditional tenets of liberalism was marked most dramatically by the introduction of military conscription. At the end of the war, David Thomas's cool assessment of the pacifist movement from his experience as a conscientious objector, a member of the FoR and a prominent leader of the ILP in north Wales was that within the religious anti-war movement, occasionally there was an element of being 'agin the Government' and of self-righteousness in thinking that 'we were not as other men'. While most pacifists believed that the immediate responsibility for the war lay mainly upon Germany, in trying to correct the patriotic bias of the majority, there was the danger of acquiring the opposite bias. Thomas believed that he and his fellow-pacifists' fundamental belief in non-violence was their outstanding legacy: 'the appeal to force of any kind is futile in the long run, and [that] only moral suasion and education can really overcome the evil forces in the world that are destroying men's happiness, and crippling their personalities'.[143]

The religious anti-war movement in Wales gained its leadership and impetus from key individuals such as Principal Thomas Rees and Revd T. E. Nicholas, who influenced a comparatively small number of activists and groups of mainly Nonconformist ministers and students, primarily based in north Wales. The Fellowship of Reconciliation was the

---

[142] Morgan, *Span of the Cross*, p. 63.
[143] Bangor University Archives, Thomas Jones papers, David Thomas, 'The Pacifist Movement'.

vehicle for its campaigning, and its success was marked by the extent that it took possession of the Nonconformist radical tradition associated with Henry Richard and Samuel Roberts and made it its own during the war. The Welsh language was an inherent characteristic of the Welsh anti-war religious movement's unique character, suggesting that the movement did not extend effectively to many English-language churches and more anglicised parts of Wales. This was reflected in the circulation of the most significant anti-war publication, *Y Deyrnas*, which underpinned the philosophical basis for the movement, and provided the leadership and the link for the organisation. The journal reflected the activity of a key group of Welsh-speaking activists, mainly ministers of religion and Welsh-language literary figures, organised primarily through the Fellowship of Reconciliation, who also collaborated with other anti-war organisations, such as the ILP and NCCL.

The contrast between this grouping of anti-war activists and the religious conscientious objectors is striking. Most of those conscientious objectors who professed an allegiance did so to a religious organisation, and almost half of this number were members of millenarian sects, such as the Christadelphians, the Plymouth Brethren and the Jehovah's Witnesses. This factor suggests strongly that a substantial proportion of the millenarian conscientious objectors did not necessarily wish to be seen to be part of a wider anti-war movement, and that, as in the case of a number of Christadelphian objectors who worked in munitions, there was no automatic correlation between conscientious objection and opposition to the war.[144] But other alternatives to conscientious objection, such as the opportunity to join the Welsh Students Company of the RAMC, ensured that the numbers of conscientious objectors in Wales were not swelled by over 150 theological students which were, to all intent and purpose, pacifist in their belief.

---

[144] Rae, *Conscience and Politics*, p. 113.

2

POLITICAL OPPOSITION TO THE WAR IN WALES – THE INDEPENDENT LABOUR PARTY, THE RUSSIAN REVOLUTION AND THE 'ADVANCED MEN'

INTRODUCTION

The Independent Labour Party (ILP) was the main political organisation to lead opposition to the war and worked closely with other anti-war bodies, such as the National Council for Civil Liberties (NCCL) and the No-Conscription Fellowship (NCF). An important element of the spectrum of political opposition to the war in Wales was the influence of the revived Unofficial Reform Committee (URC) which increasingly permeated and affected the policy of the South Wales Miners' Federation (SWMF) during the second half of the war. Before the war, the views of these activists in the SWMF were encapsulated in *The Miners' Next Step* (1912), which advocated industrial unionism and syndicalism. These men were organised in the URC, which had been formed to create 'a party for the purpose of propagating advance thought',[1] although Egan describes them as a loosely organised, essentially propagandist body until the summer of 1917.[2] These 'advanced men' very often held no official rank, but often exercised great influence among their fellows and advocated Industrial Unionism.

They were inspired by the two Russian revolutions of 1917, and the delay in the introduction of conscription to the mining industry throughout Britain, between February and December 1917, is attributable to the influence of the anti-war movement within the SWMF in south Wales. The 'comb-out' ballot in November 1917, which eventually

---

[1] Hywel Francis and Dai Smith, *The Fed: A History of the South Wales in the Twentieth Century* (Lawrence and Wishart, 1980), p. 14.

[2] Dave Egan, 'The Swansea Conference of the British Council of Soldiers and Workers Delegates, July, 1917: Reactions to the Russian Revolution of February, 1917, and the Anti-War Movement in South Wales', *Llafur*, 1/4 (1975), 36.

agreed to conscription within the industry, nevertheless, whilst marking the high point of the influence of the 'advanced men', also showed its limitations.

Opposition to the war was limited and not uniform throughout Wales, but was strongest in those areas where the ILP had substantial memberships and was most influential. The localised study of the operation of the anti-war movement in Briton Ferry and Merthyr Tydfil exemplifies how the various organised political elements of the anti-war movement combined together to greater effect, and the main organisations who combined together in this fashion were the No-Conscription Fellowship (NCF), the National Campaign against Conscription (renamed the National Council for Civil Liberties in 1916), and the ILP.

There was an undoubted correlation between anti-war activity and a strong ILP presence, and this study focuses on two of the ILP's strongest areas in south Wales, Briton Ferry and Merthyr Tydfil. Before 1918, membership of the Labour Party was only possible through an affiliated socialist society or trade union, and for those who wished to join on an individual basis, the ILP was often the only way in which to join and participate in the party.[3] The ILP was notably influential in the main south Wales towns of Swansea, Cardiff and Newport, the Swansea Valley and the Rhymney Valley, but was strongest in the town of Briton Ferry in south-west Wales, which had the largest concentration of ILP members in Wales, and the Merthyr Boroughs parliamentary constituency, the 'crucible and matrix of working-class political tradition',[4] which included the towns of Merthyr Tydfil and Aberdare, and which had been the first constituency in Britain to elect a Labour Member of Parliament, Keir Hardie, in 1900. The Merthyr area also had a high ILP membership, whilst both areas also produced a comparatively high level of conscientious objectors, had effective trades and labour

[3] Edward May, 'The Mosaic of Labour Politics, 1900–1918', in Tanner, Williams and Hopkin (eds), *The Labour Party in Wales 1900–2000* (Cardiff: University of Wales Press, 2000), p. 68.

[4] Glanmor Williams (ed.), 'Foreword', *Merthyr Politics: The Making of a Working Class Tradition* (Cardiff: University of Wales Press, 1966); R. E. Dowse, *Left in the Centre* (Longmans, 1966), p. 5.

councils and trade unions on a local level, and were amongst the earliest adopters of the principle of independent labour representation. A study of these two localities suggests that anti-war campaigning was a key element, rather than a marginal activity, for the ILP and labour movement in this period, and that the anti-war movement and the ILP's political and campaigning activities were inextricably linked.

This chapter therefore considers the development of the ILP and its relationship with anti-war activity in Wales throughout the First World War. It charts the initial impact of the war on the ILP, which suffered a rapid decline during the first half of the war, but experienced a gradual increase in membership and income from the spring of 1917 onwards, and assesses how attitudes changed towards the ILP throughout the war. It then considers the impact of the Russian revolutions on the anti-war movement in Wales before analysing the impact of the 1917 'comb-out' ballot.

ATTITUDES TOWARDS THE WAR WITHIN
THE INDEPENDENT LABOUR PARTY

In common with the rest of Britain, political opposition to the war in Wales was led primarily by the ILP on the basis that war could not be justified on moral grounds, a belief held by many of the key leaders of other anti-war organisations in Wales, such as the National Council against Conscription, later renamed the National Council for Civil Liberties (NCCL), and the NCF. Many of those activists within the SWMF who opposed the introduction of conscription into the mining industry in 1917 were also anti-war members of the ILP and were instrumental in postponing conscription in the British mining industry for eleven months, until the 'comb-out' ballot held in south Wales in November 1917, which finally agreed to introduce conscription to the mining industry. The war was also opposed on political grounds by a number of other left-wing political organisations in which ILP members were involved, including the South Wales Socialist Society, the Plebs League, and many of the members and lecturers of the workers' education classes organised by the Central Labour College in south Wales.

Egan asserts that the ILP's role was to hold the central ground of the anti-war movement, which he describes as 'alloying the fundamental religious humanitarianism of the pacifist section to the overt political analysis of the Marxist position'.[1] As soon as Germany invaded Belgium, the bulk of the Labour Party supported the government, and on 7 August 1914, J. Ramsay MacDonald resigned his chairmanship of the parliamentary Labour Party, and the ILP became the most important party in opposition to the government's war policy. On 13 August 1914 the ILP issued a manifesto condemning the war, and five of the seven ILP members of Parliament upheld the party's anti-war stance.

Dowse contends that four main themes could be discerned in the ILP's broad anti-war policy. Both MacDonald's and Keir Hardie's first objective was to maintain at least a limited arena for calm and rational discussion, so that when an opportunity for negotiated peace presented itself it would not be neglected. Their analysis of the causes of the war was that it had been caused by diplomatic blundering, and whilst they felt they should support the troops and their families, they should not support recruiting.

The response of a second group, including George Lansbury and Philip Snowden, was on Christian pacifist rather than socialist grounds, and claimed that for Christians the taking of life was impermissible. A third group, including Fenner Brockway, Clifford Allen and Bruce Glasier, held to the socialist view, claiming that war was simply an extension of the capitalist market economy, and that both sides were equally to blame. However, they did not advocate, as did Lenin at the time, the corollary of this theory, that socialists should endeavour to turn an imperialist struggle into a domestic revolution. The final viewpoint, maintained by the Scottish ILP and a number of prominent activists in south Wales, such as the 'advanced men' Arthur Horner, Nun Nicholas and Mark Starr, was a compromise between Lenin's 'revolutionary defeatism' and that of Brockway. This view accepted that war was a product of capitalism but held that they were only willing to go to war in defence of socialism.

---

[1] Egan, 'The Swansea Conference', 12–37.

Throughout the war, the ILP concentrated its attention on both remaining within the Labour Party and furthering the anti-war crusade. The first impulse of the ILP was to oppose the war by every means, but that could have led to the complete isolation of the ILP from the Labour Party and the trade union movement. To prevent this, the ruling body of the ILP, the National Administrative Council, combined the anti-war policy with a defence of workers' conditions and a fostering of the interests of combatants and their dependants. It was inevitable that whilst the ILP proved unpopular to many in organised labour, such a policy did make antagonisms less sharp.[2]

The ILP did not formally declare its opposition to the war until 1916, but in the meantime, it refused to take part in recruiting campaigns. It was initially uncertain and ambivalent, being both against the war, although wishing Britain to win it, and supporting the troops, whilst opposing military action.[3] So discomfited were Hardie and MacDonald by the barrage of criticism they endured because of their anti-war views that for a time both adjusted their views publicly to support soldiers at the front, in spite of their opposition to the war, and MacDonald notoriously appeared at a recruiting meeting in his constituency of Leicester in 1915 to allay accusations that he was anti-war. Hardie's 'Gethsemane-like' experience of his public meeting, disrupted by C. B. Stanton and his followers, in Aberdare at the beginning of the war, affected him deeply, and he continuously strived to separate his criticism of the war from his support for the individual soldier.

Hardie was profoundly disappointed by the Labour Party's decision to take part in recruiting for the army, and, in an emotional speech in Merthyr, he stated his belief that he could not become a recruiting agent because it would violate his 'dearest and treasured principles', based on Christ's teachings:

> If I did so, an outraged conscience would torture me for the rest of my life. I cannot do it. I shall abide the consequences cheerfully and

[2] Dowse, *Left in the Centre*, p. 23.
[3] Keith Laybourn and David James (eds), 'Philip Snowden', in *The Centennial History of the I.L.P.* (Bradford Libraries and Archive Service, 1987), p. 40.

gladly. If I go under at the next election, I shall not complain but accept it as a crowning glory of my old age.[4]

In meetings of ILP branches in Swansea and Cardiff that autumn, he explained the ILP National Council's continued opposition to the war, and carried the audience with him.[5] He warned that in the present mood of the country, a big anti-war campaign was impossible, and his speech reflected how shaken he had been by the breaking up of his meeting in Aberdare at the beginning of the war. He believed that, unlike the Boer War:

> It was hopeless to appeal to the reason of the people until war hysteria and passion had died down. We must not give the impression that we were supporting German militarism or doing anything to make things difficult for British soldiers at the front. But we must watch carefully for the first opportunity to press for peace negotiations which would bring an end to the war.[6]

By the end of 1914, Hardie had recovered some of his equilibrium, and wrote to his future son-in-law and prominent ILP-er Emrys Hughes that there was greater doubt amongst the general population about the wisdom of going to war than in the first month of the war, and that a saner spirit was beginning to prevail.[7] Hardie's death and funeral in Scotland in September 1915 were followed by numerous memorial meetings in south Wales which were converted into demonstrations against the war and the threat of conscription.[8]

The ILP's Annual Conference in April 1916 for the first time formally agreed a policy of full opposition to the war and called on the socialist parties in Europe to refuse to support every war entered into by any government, whatever its ostensible object.[9] Even so, the ILP also included a substantial proportion of members who joined the armed forces and supported the war, and a split was averted by the

---

[4] *Pioneer*, 21 November 1914.
[5] National Library of Scotland, Keir Hardie and Emrys Hughes Papers, Dep. 176, Box 8/1, 'Welsh Rebel'.
[6] Emrys Hughes, *Keir Hardie* (Allen and Unwin, 1956), p. 233.
[7] National Library of Scotland, Hardie and Hughes Papers, 'Welsh Rebel', p. 241.
[8] National Library of Scotland, Hardie and Hughes Papers, 'Welsh Rebel', p. 76.
[9] Arthur Marwick, 'The Independent Labour Party 1918–1932' (unpublished BLitt thesis, Oxford University, 1962), p. 11.

National Administrative Council's decision to recognise the principle of individual military enlistment as a matter of conscience, but to instruct branches not to take part in recruiting.[10] This policy ensured that the ILP was not riven internally, and this tentative approach to the question of war also ensured that no fatal split occurred within the labour movement during the war.

From January 1916 onwards, inevitably the opposition to the war crystallised around the introduction of compulsory military service. The NCF's statistics for conscientious objectors at the end of the war gave a figure of 1,191 'socialists', of whom 805 were members of the ILP, who represented approximately five per cent of the total of between 16,100 and 16,500 conscientious objectors in Britain,[11] and in Wales the proportion was similar. But their influence was greater than their numerical strength. The ILP leadership adopted the mantle of the campaign against conscription and the war in large parts of south Wales in particular, and they led these campaigns with other related organisations, such as individual lodges of the SWMF, trades councils and branches of the NCCL throughout Wales.

Whilst the ILP suffered in the first two years of the war because of its perceived anti-war stance, its support increased markedly from spring 1917 onwards, and its unpopular views won new supporters. In Marwick's view, the war martyred and glorified the ILP, highlighted the uniqueness of its attitude towards war, and brought in hosts of new supporters, mainly from the ranks of Liberals disillusioned by the inconsistent, immoral and undignified postures they felt their party had assumed.[12]

The consequent vehemence with which the ILP was assaulted, both within and outside the labour movement, united the party, partly from a 'sense of persecution, and partly as a result of missionary zeal'.[13] Virtually alone among

---

[10] Cardiff University Library Special Collections, Independent Labour Party Papers, 'Report of the Annual Conference, April 1916' (Harvester Microfilms), p. 11.

[11] *The No-Conscription Fellowship: A Souvenir of its Work During the Years 1914–1919* (No-Conscription Fellowship, 1919), p. 38.

[12] Marwick, 'The Independent Labour Party 1918–1932', p. 11.

[13] Dowse, *Left in the Centre*, p. 21.

the socialist and Labour parties of the warring countries, the
ILP stood out against war. By 1918, many of its policies on
war and armaments had been accepted by the labour movement, and the anti-war leaders of the ILP were amongst the
most influential in the party. Even throughout the war, the
ILP also retained the loyalty of members who were out of
sympathy with its anti-war policy. Prominent members such
as the president of the SWMF, James Winstone, who fought
the Merthyr by-election in 1915, supported the war but
opposed the introduction of military conscription, on the
basis that it was the precursor to civil conscription, and by
1917 he was calling for a negotiated peace settlement.

THE ILP'S ORGANISATION IN WALES, 1914–1918

The ILP drew much of its ideological and ethical socialist roots
in Wales, as elsewhere, from a 'radicalised Nonconformity'[14]
that was associated with an ethical and moral political belief
that developed into a nebulous and sometimes ill-defined
'religion of socialism'.[15] Its communitarian ethos was derived
from the co-dependent relationships nurtured by the traditions of the chapel and workplace, and led to the pre-war
growth of trade unions, trades and labour councils, and the
cooperative movement, which was accelerated by the war.
But the ILP developed very differently in different communities, largely because of the divergent cultural characteristics
and economic nature of those communities. Egan emphasises that the growth of the ILP before the war was in older
industrial areas like 'Merthyr Tydfil, Aberdare, Briton Ferry
and Swansea' and on the 'fringes' of the coalfield 'with a
different community and political tradition to the relatively
new communities of the coalfield itself'.[16]

A well-organised ILP branch provided its members with a
vibrant social, cultural and educational life as well as a political one. In Merthyr, the ILP had a shop in the centre of

[14] Duncan Tanner, *Political Change and the Labour Party 1900–1918* (Cambridge
University Press, 1990), p. 214.
[15] David Howell, *British Workers and the Independent Labour Party 1900–1918*
(Cambridge University Press, 1990), p. 392.
[16] David Egan, 'Noah Ablett 1883–1935', *Llafur*, 4/3 (1986), 27.

town, named 'Our Shop', run by a local member and close friend of Hardie, John Barr.[17] Hopkin illustrates the extent to which the ILP in Aberdare at the turn of the century, for instance, could be said to be represent an alternative community:

> with its own institute, the party offered weekly meetings, regular concerts, and an ILP Band of Hope, its own football team, annual teas, a children's Christmas party, education classes, numerous committee meetings ... The ILP in Merthyr even had its own tobacconist and newsagent, whilst the Swansea Socialist Society ran a shop and boot club.[18]

Their earnest, improving moralism could set them apart from the rest of the community. In south Wales, W. J. Edwards complained that to be an ILP or Labour activist was to belong to a sect, and a rigidly defined section, rather than to belong to a more open group which fed into a 'wider consensus'. In these circumstances, some activists found 'great compensation' in the ILP's associational life. Entire branches became 'insular bulwarks' against the opinion of the broader community, and whilst some remained determined to preach socialism, they received limited support from the electorate.[19] But this jaundiced view underestimates the contribution of ILP members as the active core of the Labour Party in many communities, and that in peacetime the ILP branches had provided the active core of the Labour Party, both inside and outside the unions. In many areas the militancy and animation of the local party depended on the influence of the socialists of the ILP.

The influence of the ILP was also seen in the growth of trades and labour councils throughout Wales that helped to extend labour organisation on a local level, and grew from forty, representing 133,000 workers, on the eve of war, to sixty-eight, representing 237,000, in 1919. These were a

[17] Swansea University Archive, South Wales Coalfield Collection, George Protheroe interview, Aud. 309.

[18] Deian Hopkin, 'The rise of Labour in Wales, 1890–1914', in Glanmor Williams (ed.), *Politics and Society in Wales 1840–1922* (Cardiff: University of Wales Press, 1988), p. 132.

[19] W. J. Edwards, *From the Valley I Came* (Angus and Robertson, 1956), p. 103.

necessary precursor to the development of independent labour politics and were a crucial focus for the ILP.[20] In the ten years up to 1916 it was estimated that the party had organised 20,000 meetings in the coalfield alone. The ILP's message in north Wales was propagated by *Y Dinesydd Cymreig*, launched in 1912 by striking printers, and in south Wales by the Merthyr-based *Pioneer*, with a readership of at least 10,000. On the eve of the war, at the level of town and borough council representation, Labour's most notable strongholds were Merthyr Tydfil and Swansea, with some success in Newport and Llanelli, but even in north and west Wales it had set up sixteen branches by 1910 owing to the efforts of local ILP organisers, such as David Thomas and Tom Platt. Its success there in scattered farming districts, the slate-quarrying areas, and in Wrexham and Colwyn Bay was partly due to the party's ability to spread the word through the Welsh language, and was helped by its ability to attract a number of Nonconformist ministers to the cause and to counter accusations that socialism was ungodly and alien to Wales. Between 1914 and 1918, the membership grew from 6.9 per cent of the British total to 11.1 per cent,[21] a growth of 70 per cent in membership in Wales in this period. This was in the context of a corresponding growth in total ILP membership across Britain for the same period of 78 per cent,[22] but this also masked a decline in membership in the first thirty months of the war which only recovered from April 1917 onwards.[23]

The organisational development of the ILP in the war period throughout Britain was characterised by initial decline in branches and members from 1914 until the spring of 1917, when there was a rapid growth that continued to the end of the war and beyond.[24] In the war period, membership

[20] Edward May, 'The Mosaic of Labour Politics', in Tanner, Williams and Hopkin (eds), *The Labour Party in Wales 1900–2000* (Cardiff, University of Wales Press, 2000), p. 74.

[21] British Library of Political and Economic Science, Independent Labour Party Papers, ILP 3/59.

[22] British Library of Political and Economic Science, Independent Labour Party Papers, ILP 10/4/3.

[23] Marwick, 'The Independent Labour Party 1914–1932', p. 11.

[24] Cardiff University Library Special Collections, Independent Labour Party Papers, 'Reports of Annual Conferences, 1914–1919' (Harvester Microfilms).

of the ILP in Britain declined up to March 1917, then increased – from 21,088 in November 1916 it dipped to 17,793 in March 1917, but then increased to 23,948 by September 1917 and 35,717 by February 1918. In the same period, membership in Wales also fell up to March 1917, but increased gradually to 4,201 by February 1918.

Affiliation membership fees in Wales 1913–20					
1913–14	1915–16	1916–17	1917–18	1918–19	1919–20
£79	£61	£67	£104 9s.	£147 19s. 7d	£158
Membership of the Independent Labour Party in Wales 1916–18					
Nov. 1916	May 1917	Sept. 1917	Oct. 1917	Jan. 1918	Feb. 1918
2,355	1,745	1,988	2,769	3,499	4,201
Number of branches					
Feb. 1915	Feb. 1916	March 1916	Jan. 1917	March 1917	Feb. 1918
75	58	59	60	70	70

Table 2: The Independent Labour Party in Wales[25]

The initial decline in the number of branches in the first half of the war partly reflects the growing unpopularity of the ILP because of its attitude towards the war. But the economic and industrial impact of war also caused an inevitable degree of 'churn' in the branches in the period between January and August 1915. In the six months prior to February 1915, three new branches were formed, in Neath, Ammanford and the Rhondda, but eleven branches were discontinued, including Brynamman, Clydach Vale, Cwmgwrach, Llandybie, Maesycwmmer, Melyn, New Tredegar and Treherbert. The reason for their fate is not given, but at least three other branches in Caernarfonshire – Caesarea, Rhosgadfan and Waunfawr – reported that the decline of the slate industry had forced members to leave the district to seek work. The most dramatic drop in the numbers of branches happened in the six months before August 1915, when another seventeen branches closed, including three

Table 2 provides a breakdown of membership affiliation fees (1913–20), number of branches and membership numbers for the ILP in Wales from 1914–18.

[25] Cardiff University Library Special Collections, Independent Labour Party Papers, 'Reports of Annual Conferences, 1914–1919' (Harvester Microfilms).

branches in the Caernarfonshire slate-quarrying areas of Port Dinorwic, Deiniolen and Blaenau Ffestiniog, owing to the collapse of the slate trade, where 'all members had left the district'. The party's organiser in north Wales, David Thomas, who was also the organiser for the NCF for the region, explained that these branches were swept out of existence in the early months of the war, not because members ceased to support the ILP, but because, owing to the severe depression in the slate industry, many had left the area, either to join the army or to seek work elsewhere.[26]

In Ammanford, the branch's collapse was ascribed to the secretary's decision to enlist, and the collapse of the Llanelli branch in 1915 was because it was considered to be a 'centre of impossibilism'.[27] In assessing the impact of the war on Llanelli, Hopkin ascribes the growth in Labour support throughout the war partly to improved Labour organisation, but primarily to the psychological and political impact of the war. The latter stages of the war introduced a 'sense of profound change, a new level of political optimism', which Hopkin attributes partly to the impact of the Russian Revolution, but also to a sense of greater power for trade unions in the workplace and the 'growing impact' of anti-war dissent, in which pacifists and socialists seemed to engender as much fear and hatred for the government as the German enemy.[28]

The ILP's Welsh Divisional Council of about fifty representatives, meeting in February 1915, in Cardiff, was solely preoccupied with the war. The meeting unanimously opposed the war, and called for an international peace conference, a reduction in armaments, the nationalisation of the manufacture of armaments and the control of exports of armaments.[29] On a tour of ILP branches in south Wales, the MP Bruce Glasier described meetings in Barry with 100 present, Aberdare with a crowd of 200 present, and Cwmavon,

---

[26] David Thomas, 'The Pacifist Movement', Thomas Jones Papers, Bangor University.

[27] British Library of Political and Economic Science, Independent Labour Party Papers, ILP 3/59, 'Summaries of new and lapsed branches 1914–1918'.

[28] Hopkin, 'The rise of Labour in Wales, 1890–1914', p. 171.

[29] *Pioneer*, 6 February 1915.

accompanied by T. E. Nicholas, with 600 to 700 present, including many working women, as 'most successful'.[30]

> The meetings were well attended, some of them more so than for several years, and in no instance was there any hostile demonstration. I found too the branches in good condition – those at Gorseinon, Neath and Cwmavon especially, and I feel more my going round them will do good.[31]

By the following annual ILP Welsh divisional conference in January 1916, the number of delegates had increased from forty-seven to eighty, and the branches had increased from thirty-five to fifty. Its chairman, Councillor Morgan Jones, celebrated what he termed the ILP's outstanding achievement in withstanding 'all calumny, abuse, and vilification', but warned against the state's growing encroachment on the rights of the citizen:

> What measure of freedom we now enjoy must not – should not – be sacrificed at the bidding of a bastard patriotism. The fair flower of liberty cannot live in the vitiated atmosphere of militarism. The crushing of Prussian militarism may be a good thing, and even a desirable thing, though an operation best left to Prussians, but the destruction of British liberties is not desirable, is not permissible, is not tolerable.[32]

By February 1916, branches had been revived or reinstated in Blackwood, Nantyglo, Llanelli and Tumble, but had 'entirely collapsed' in Penarth, and had closed in the mining village of Penrhiwceiber and the slate-quarrying village of Llanberis. The nadir was reached in March 1916 with fifty-nine branches; the branch was revived in Ammanford, and others created in Aberbeeg, Pengam, Caerau, Blaenavon, Oakdale and Blaina, but others lapsed in Abergwynfi, Coytraherne, Bedlinog, Builth Wells, Cwmaman and Nantlle Vale. The report to the National Advisory Council described the difficulties that the war and changing industrial conditions had caused the party in Wales, especially in the larger

---

[30] Liverpool University Archive, J. Bruce Glasier Papers, GP/1/1/1399, Glasier to Francis Johnson, general secretary ILP.
[31] Liverpool University Archive, J. Bruce Glasier Papers, GP/1/1/1419, Glasier to Francis Johnson.
[32] *Pioneer*, 29 January 1916.

towns, including continued overtime, lighting regulations
and continued military or police restrictions. but the report
also highlighted the new members attracted by the ILP's anti-
war stance:

> The diminution of membership caused by economic voluntary or
> compulsory enlistment has, however, been made good by the acces-
> sion of new members who have joined not only because they believe
> in the attitude of the party towards the war but because they see in the
> Socialist principles held by the Party the only hope for the future.[33]

For the period April 1917–March 1918, thirteen new
branches were opened during the year, and the membership
increased almost fifty per cent year on year.[34] An additional
seventeen branches were created after June 1917, including
Hirwaun Camp near Aberdare, a work camp for COs, the
other branches being mainly in mining areas, including
Bedlinog, Clydach, Aberbargoed, Garw Valley, Taffs Well,
Felinfoel, Merthyr Vale, Kenfig Hill, Ynysybwl, Garnswllt,
Crumlin and Penygraig. Llanelli's branch was revived, and
two branches were formed outside industrial south Wales, in
Pembroke Dock and Colwyn Bay.[35]

For the year April 1917–March 1918, seventy-one branches
paid affiliation fees of £111 11s. 3d. The level of membership
reflected by the level of paid affiliation fees was under-
reported, but the ILP centrally estimated that the number of
members was double the declared number of members, and
put the Welsh membership at about 8,000.[36] The strongest
branches, on the basis of their level of paid affiliation fees
(see Table 2) were Briton Ferry, Aberdare, Merthyr, Cwmavon
and Newport. These branches also raised the most money in
response to the appeal for the 'Special Fund'. This fund was
divided into two portions – that from friends and sympa-
thisers for Head Office expenses, and that from the branches
for election expenses. Briton Ferry's astounding total of £54

[33] British Library of Political and Economic Science, Independent Labour Party
Papers, 3/59, 'Summaries of new and lapsed branches 1914–1918'.

[34] *Pioneer*, 8 June 1918.

[35] British Library of Political and Economic Science, Independent Labour Party
Papers, 3/59, 'Summaries of new and lapsed branches 1914–1918'.

[36] Cardiff University Library Special Collections, Independent Labour Party
Papers, 'Annual Conference report, April 1919' (Harvester Microfilms), p. 51.

7s. 3d raised for this fund was second only to Leicester, whose total of £84 14s. 6d reflected a remarkable degree of local energy and commitment.[37]

The largest branches in south Wales included the towns of Cardiff and Newport, and branches adjoining Aberdare and Merthyr, including Mountain Ash and Dowlais. But in north Wales, in contrast with the early war period, where ten branches had existed, only one branch survived, in Wrexham. The thirty delegates from Wales at the national ILP conference in April 1917 were considered 'a healthy sign of the progression of ILP-ism during the year that has passed considering the number of members arrested as conscientious objectors'[38] and this close connection with the anti-war movement was exemplified in the person of Morgan Jones. During the war he was chairman of the ILP in Wales, the Welsh member of the national committee of the NCF, the chairman of the Anti-Conscription Council in Wales, and a conscientious objector, who subsequently became organising secretary to the Welsh division of the ILP at the end of the war. In a report written in 1920, he analysed the contribution of the ILP to the labour movement generally in Wales, and stated that ILP members were the chief officials and speakers of most of the Labour Party and trade union lodges, and formed the executives in most instances in the most industrial areas. Even in rural areas, he found that the leaders were 'very often men with the ILP outlook and what we might call the ILP mentality'.[39]

Arguably the single event that most influenced the ILP's growth from March 1917 onwards was the Russian Revolution. Marwick states that these upheavals sent a tremendous wave of enthusiasm throughout the party, 'momentarily carrying the whole fabric of its policy forward on its crest, then dropping into a whirlpool of new issues'. This enthusiasm led to the creation of the Convention held

[37] Cardiff University Library Special Collections, Independent Labour Party Papers, 'Annual Conference report, April 1918' (Harvester Microfilms), p. 105; Table 3 provides a list of branches, with affiliation fees paid and money raised for the 'Special Effort' fund.

[38] *Pioneer*, 14 April 1917.

[39] British Library of Political and Economic Science, Independent Labour Party Papers, 6/9/5, Morgan Jones to Francis Johnson, LSE.

Branch	Annual affiliation fees	'Special Effort' fund
Briton Ferry	£11 3s. 7d	£54 7s. 3d
Aberdare	£7 16s. 10d	£5
Merthyr Tydfil	£5 11s. 8d	£4 14s
Cwmavon	£5 6s. 2d	£12
Newport	£5 2s. 8d	£6 11s. 6d
Cardiff	£4 11s. 8d	£7 10s.
Taibach	£3 6s. 1d	£5
Dowlais	£3 1s. 2d	£1 17s.
Bargoed	£2 18s. 7d	£2 15s.
Ebbw Vale	£2 15s. 2d	£3 17s.
Cathays (Cardiff)	£ 2 14s. 1d	———
Rhondda	£2 10s.	———
Mountain Ash	£2 5s. 6d	———
Blaina	£1 18s. 11d	8s.
Pontypool	£1 15s. 3d	£3 5s.
Pontypridd	£1 11s. 11d	———
Garw Valley	£1 10s. 5d	£3
Barry	£1 10s.	£3 10s
Gorseinon	£1 9s. 11d	£2
Ystradgynlais	£1 9s. 6d	£2
Swansea	£1 9s. 4d	£2 10s
Splott (Cardiff)	£1 6s. 4d	£1 11s.
Wrexham	£1 5s. 9d	£1 13s.
Neath	£1 3s. 11d	£1 16s. 6d
Maesteg	£1 3s. 10d	8s.

Table 3: Main Independent Labour Party Welsh branches April 1917–April 1918[40]

in Leeds in June 1917, addressed by the ILP leaders, MacDonald, Anderson and Snowden, that resolved to take the apparently revolutionary course of appointing

---

[40] Cardiff University Library Special Collections, Independent Labour Party Papers, 'Annual Conference report, April 1918' (Harvester Microfilms), p. 105.

a Provisional Committee to form local Workmen's and Soldiers' Councils. Since few attempts were subsequently made to implement this remarkable decision in favour of the Soviet pattern, Marwick suggests that it should be taken rather as a symptom of the 'passionate feeling of communion with the revolution which the ILP then felt, rather than as a practical policy decision'.[41]

This surge of optimism and enthusiasm was crucial to an understanding of the increase in income, members and support for the ILP from the summer of 1917 onwards, until the end of the war and beyond. This growth was aided in south Wales by the appointment of Minnie Pallister, a young and brilliant teacher, public speaker and propagandist from Brynmawr, as a full-time organiser for the ILP in Wales in 1918.[42] She exemplified the close link between the ILP and the anti-war movement, in that she was already well known as a propagandist and public speaker for the ILP, but she was best known as the secretary and main organiser of the NCF in Wales:

> her reputation was fully earned by the wholeheartedness of her propa-
> ganda on behalf of Socialism and the ILP and, in particular by her
> display of her organising ability as honorary organiser of the NCF
> during the past two years. It is in the last sphere, rather than in the ILP
> that she has conspicuously won her spurs as an organiser before the
> eyes of the South Wales movement as a whole.[43]

Known as a 'brilliant platform speaker', she later became the first Welsh woman to sit on the Labour Party's National Executive, and was instrumental in Labour's organisation in Wales in the 1920s.[44]

There is little unanimity amongst historians about the effect of the war on the fortunes of the ILP. Marwick suggests that the effect of the war was to martyr and glorify the ILP, and that the increase in membership from February 1917

[41] Marwick, 'The Independent Labour Party 1918–1932', p. 13.

[42] *Pioneer*, 11 September 1918; *The Labour Who's Who 1927: A biographical directory to the national and local leaders in the labour and co-operative movement* (Labour Publishing Company, 1927), p. 162.

[43] *Pioneer*, 8 June 1918.

[44] Chris Howard, '"The Focus of the Mute Hopes of a Whole Class" – Ramsay Macdonald and Aberavon, 1922–1929', *Llafur*, 7/1 (1996), 70.

onwards was caused by new supporters from the Liberal Party, 'disillusioned by the inconsistencies, immoral and undignified postures they felt their party had assumed'.[45] May, on the other hand, suggests that the consequences of the war for the ILP were 'deleterious' and contends that, while it regained its strength and flourished in parts of the 'increasingly militant cauldron of the south Wales coalfield', the ILP never recovered from 'the distance its attitude towards the war placed between it and the wider labour movement', and that its isolation was compounded by Henderson's reforms to provide for individual membership of the Labour Party, which removed much of its previous *raison d'être*. The party was challenged later by the emergence of the Communist Party, which became the natural home for many critics of the Labour Party's moderation. Thus, May argues that the Great War helped to shift the ILP from the centre stage of Welsh Labour politics.[46]

But May neglects the evidence of the increase in the membership of the ILP from 1917 onwards, and Marwick argues that the ILP had won much of its argument over peace policy and retained its influence over Labour through the involvement of its key leaders in the management of the party. It may be argued that it was more in the trade unions that the ILP was 'not now of great account', and the demand was increasingly for skilled organisers rather than effective propagandists.[47] The legacy of its anti-war policy was that the ILP gained renewed confidence through a 'baptism of common travail',[48] but after the war, it had to adjust to a deeply changed relationship with the Labour Party. The nature and strength of the ILP varied greatly throughout Wales, and its local influence during the war is reflected in the waxing and waning of its financial health and membership numbers. As Pearce suggests, it is only by studying the phenomenon of the anti-war movement on a localised level that it is possible to gain an understanding of how the ILP

[45] Marwick, 'The Independent Labour Party 1918–1932', p. 11.
[46] May, 'The Mosaic of Labour Politics', p. 82.
[47] Marwick, 'The Independent Labour Party 1918–1932', p. 12.
[48] Dowse, *Left in the Centre*, p. 34.

related to the different strands of the anti-war movement.[49] In south Wales, the two areas that witnessed most activity against the war were also those where the ILP was strongest, in Merthyr Tydfil and Briton Ferry.

THE INDEPENDENT LABOUR PARTY
IN THE BRITON FERRY AREA

On the eve of war, Briton Ferry, lying at the mouth of the Neath river, was a prosperous small town of 8,472 people, well connected, with its own dock and a railway network that had grown from the need to transport coal and tinplate from Briton Ferry and south-west Wales. The tinplate industry had developed in the area in the second half of the nineteenth century primarily because of local supplies of particular coals, limestone and sulphuric acid, with plentiful water and coastline ports. The largest tinplate town was Llanelli, with its seven works, and then Pontardulais, Morriston and Briton Ferry with five each, Port Talbot with four, and Neath, Pontardawe and Gorseinon with three works each. By 1913, four out of five of the UK's tinplate workers lived within a twenty-mile radius of Swansea.[50] In common with its neighbours, Briton Ferry was a one-industry town, and shopkeepers and service industries, as well as the workers themselves, depended on the tinplate trade for their livelihood.[51]

The main works were the Briton Ferry Steelworks, the Albion Steelworks, the Gwalia Tinplate Works and the Baglan Engineering and Foundry. Production of Welsh tinplate reached its peak of 848,000 tons before the outbreak of the war,[52] and tinplate manufacturers united with steelmakers, such as the Albion Steelworks with Gwalia Tinplate in Briton Ferry, to accommodate, rationalise and create technological

[49] Cyril Pearce, *Comrades and Conscience* (Francis Boutle Publishers, 2001).

[50] Stephen Hughes and Paul Reynolds, *A Guide to the Industrial Archaeology of the Swansea Region* (Aberystwyth: Royal Commission on Ancient and Historical Monuments, 1988).

[51] W. E. Minchinton (ed.), *Industrial South Wales 1750–1914* (Frank Cass and Co., 1969), p. xxiv.

[52] Minchinton, *Industrial South Wales 1750–1914*, p. xxvi.

advances.[53] The town's sense of civic identity was buttressed by the creation of the Briton Ferry Urban District Council in 1892, and a public park and public hall were both opened in 1911. This was accompanied by the growth of independent working-class representation, and Labour was an important presence on the local council in the decade preceding the war. As early as 1905, the ILP had been active in the town when Keir Hardie had spoken in one of its early public meetings.[54]

The culture and impact of the ILP varied according to physical location and relationship to the workplace, and in Briton Ferry, the ILP branch was made up mainly of tinplaters and steelworkers, with only about a dozen miners. The leadership of the party included Albion men, such as George Gethin, 'a famous Labour man ... a kind of Danton of the labour movement in the Ferry', and tinplaters, such as Joe Branch, who worked in the Gwalia Tinplate Works in Baglan.[55] Branch was the chairman of the party locally, a member of the Briton Ferry Urban District Council, of which he had been chairman, an *ex officio* magistrate on the Neath bench, and would become the regional secretary of the Dockers' Union.[56]

At the end of the Great War, the 'great Briton Ferry' was the most 'virile party' of independent labour in south Wales.[57] The membership of the ILP in the town was approximately one in twenty-two of the town's population of 8,472,[58] numbering approximately 367 members, and representing 6.5 per cent of the town's adult population. The branch had its own choir and community facilities and held debates and literary classes, and its leaders were invariably respectable and sober men of distinction who were chapel-goers, leaders of their trades unions locally, and who dominated Briton Ferry

[53] Philip Adams, *Not in Our Name: War Dissent in a Welsh Town* (Briton Ferry Books, 2015), p. 63.

[54] Adams, *Not in Our Name*, p. 13.

[55] Swansea University Archive, South Wales Coalfield Collection, Len Williams, Aud. 282.

[56] Adams, *Not in Our Name*, pp. 197–8.

[57] Adams, *Not in Our Name*, p. 51.

[58] *Census of England and Wales 1911, County Report on Glamorgan* (HMSO, 1914), p. 21.

Urban District Council. The local membership of the ILP was mainly drawn from the trade union movement, rather than from amongst teachers and the middle class.[59] Marwick attributes the 'virility' of the ILP in the town to Ivor Hael Thomas, who was an office boy in a tinplate works at the age of 15, before becoming a tinplate finisher. He represents the umbilical cord that tied the various parts of the anti-war movement together in south Wales. A trade union activist, he became a member of the National Executive of the Dockers' Union in 1914 for two years.[60] He was a crucial figure in the organisation of the Independent Labour Party within Briton Ferry and throughout south Wales, and was Wales's representative on the national administrative council of the ILP for five years from the beginning of the war. In 1916, he also became the organiser in south Wales and Monmouthshire for the NCCL, and there could be little doubt about Thomas's anti-war credentials, for whilst a number of its founding members, such as the railwayman's leader Jimmy Thomas, were pro-war, Thomas addressed and chaired anti-war meetings in Briton Ferry, took part in NCF fundraisers and celebrations, and was the honorary secretary of the 'Defence and Maintenance' fund, set up when the ILP propagandist, R. C. Wallhead was imprisoned for making anti-war statements.[61] He later took a leading part in the creation of the Aberavon District Labour Party and became its first secretary.[62]

However, Marwick, in ascribing great importance to his individual energy, does not give sufficient consideration to the extensive moral and practical support given by the energetic local labour and socialist movement. Whilst that opposition was a minority view, it received support from a substantial part of the population. Emrys Hughes recorded his experience of ILP political meetings in Briton Ferry as being similar to religious services:

> it had a little hall, which had formerly been a nonconformist chapel, where regular Sunday night meetings were held in wintertime and

[59] Swansea University, South Wales Coalfield Collection, Len Williams, Aud. 282.
[60] Marwick, 'The Independent Labour Party 1918–1932', p. 51; *The Labour Who's Who 1927*, p. 217.
[61] *Pioneer*, 16 February 1918.
[62] Adams, *Not in Our Name*, pp. 204–5.

which were always well-attended. They sang hymns from a Socialist hymn book and it was as much a religious service as a political meeting.[63]

Briton Ferry's reputation for its anti-war activism caused it to be known as 'little Germany'[64] by its detractors and caused concern for the authorities, even in the earliest stages of the war. Even in September 1914, at the height of enlistment to the armed forces, recruiting was thought to be slow in the town, and Briton Ferry was considered to be 'an exceptional place' as it possessed a 'force strongly opposed to warfare'.[65] Briton Ferry became a magnet for anti-war speakers from other parts of Britain, and the number of public anti-war meetings held there increased from only two in 1915, to twenty-two in 1916, twenty in 1917, and a further twenty meetings in 1918.[66] Speakers included the leadership of the ILP, such as Ramsay MacDonald, Philip and Ethel Snowden, George Lansbury, Dick Wallhead, W. C. Anderson and Bruce Glasier, and leaders of the UDC and the NCF, including Bertrand Russell, E. D. Morel, Norman Angell, Charles Buxton, Theodora Wilson and Herbert Dunnico. These nationally recognised speakers were joined by effective Welsh propagandists, invariably ministers of religion, such as T. E. Nicholas, Revd J. Puleston Jones, Pwllheli, and Revd John Morgan Jones, Merthyr. Other speakers included the railwaymen's union leader, Robert Williams, and the ILP and NCF activist and propagandist Minnie Pallister.[67] It was an affirmation of Briton Ferry's role in anti-war activity that the meeting to set up the Wales region of the NCF was held in Briton Ferry in June 1915.[68]

After conscription was introduced in January 1916, the ILP supported local conscientious objectors. The local barber shop was the town's centre for political debate, and Bill

[63] Adams, *Not in Our Name*, p. 118.
[64] National Library of Scotland, Keir Hardie and Emrys Hughes Papers, Dep. 176, Box 8/1, 'Pulpits and Prisons', p. 222.
[65] *Cambria Daily Leader*, 8 September 1914.
[66] Adams, *Not in Our Name*, pp. 272–8.
[67] Adams, *Not in Our Name*, pp. 276–7.
[68] Adams, *Not in Our Name*, p. 273.

Gregory recalls how his uncle, the barber, helped the conscientious objectors:

> when they were on the run, they would come there some times and have a haircut before the shop opened. On one occasion for example, when a chap by the name of Tom Thomas, Tommy Tu'penny he was known as in Briton Ferry, was on the run, his brother came to my uncle and asked if he could cut his hair one morning say about quarter to nine before the shop opened. And I remember my uncle pulling the window of the barber's shop, half way down, taking the tools off the table and setting the table close to the window on a chair, so that if Sergeant Williams came in, Tom would make a dash for it through the window. It didn't come to that but that was the atmosphere.[69]

From the beginning of May 1916, the police, who were presumably exasperated by the widespread anti-war campaigning of the ILP in the Briton Ferry area, responded robustly and started a campaign of intimidation. This approach emanated from the Chief Constable of Glamorgan, Captain Lionel Lindsay, whose confrontational and aggressive attitude towards anti-war activists was not curbed until the following year when the decision on prosecutions against anti-war activists in south Wales was taken over by Special Branch and MI5, whose approach was rather more emollient.[70]

From early May, the police initiated a campaign to dissipate what the *Pioneer* termed the 'prevalent distrust and unrest in South Wales'.[71] Between 7 May and 16 June 1916, the police took out proceedings under the Defence of the Realm Act against twenty ILP members in the Briton Ferry, Cwmavon and Port Talbot area, on five separate occasions, in order to cow the anti-war campaigners. The *Pioneer* accused the authorities of 'pursuing their policy of suppression with a violence that savours of vindictiveness'.[72]

On Saturday 13 May, the police raided the ILP centre in Cwmavon and confiscated anti-war written propaganda as

---

[69] Swansea University Archive, South Wales Coalfield Collection, W. H. Gregory, Aud. 289.
[70] Aled Eirug, 'The Security Services in South Wales during the First World War', *Welsh History Review*, 28/4 (2017), 753–84.
[71] *Pioneer*, 17 June 1916.
[72] *Pioneer*, 17 June 1916.

well as the branch correspondence and minute book.[73] The following day, four prominent ILP leaders were arrested following an anti-war open-air meeting organised by the No-Conscription Fellowship in Bethany Square, Port Talbot; Henry Davies, the leader of the ILP and NCF organiser in Cwmavon, who was to be put forward as the ILP's candidate for the Labour nomination in Aberavon; Councillor Harry Davies, Taibach, and Councillor Mainwaring, both ILP members of the Margam district council; and Councillor James Price, a miner, a member of Aberavon Town Council and, ironically, a member of the local military service tribunal. The first three had been speakers at the 'anti-conscription meeting' and Price had chaired the meeting. These initially appeared in court on a charge of causing obstruction.[74]

A further prosecution was then brought against four prominent local ILP members who had spoken at an outdoor meeting of 400 people, and organised by the NCF in Bethany Square, Port Talbot. They were 'charged with making statements and distributing circulars likely to prejudice recruiting and cause disaffection to the training and discipline of His Majesty's Forces'. In the subsequent hearing, Councillor Taliesyn Mainwaring, from Taibach, who was the NCF organiser in the Port Talbot area, was charged with 'making prejudicial statements' and fined £25 with £5 costs, while Daniel Morris, secretary of the Cwmavon ILP, and Jenkin and William Williams, both members of the Cwmavon ILP, were fined £10 each with £1 costs.[75] Two local NCF and ILP activists, Garnet Watters, the chairman of the Briton Ferry branch of the NCF, and William Davies, were arrested under the DORA legislation for distributing pamphlets, and were each sentenced to one month's imprisonment with hard labour.[76]

A further ten ILP members were charged at Neath Magistrates Court on 16 June, under regulation 27 of the Defence of the Realm Act, with 'distributing articles likely to cause disaffection and prejudice to His Majesty's subjects',

---

[73] *Pioneer*, May 20 1916.
[74] *Pioneer*, 20 May 1916.
[75] *Pioneer*, 17 June 1916.
[76] *Pioneer*, 20 May 1916.

namely the distribution at Easter-time of the anti-war 'Everett' and 'Maximilian' pamphlets, both produced by the NCF.[77] The Everett leaflet protested against the arrest and conviction of a conscientious objector, Ernest Everett, a teacher from St Helens in Lancashire, who had been given the harsh sentence of two years' hard labour in his army court martial,[78] and the Maximilian leaflet was a historical allegory that suggested that Christ would have become a conscientious objector.[79] The ten defendants included Councillor Joe Branch, a number of prospective conscientious objectors including James Adams and William Davies, and Arthur Armstrong, secretary of the Briton Ferry branch of the NCF.

Branch, seen as the ringleader, was bound over in the sum of £50 to be of good behaviour and the remaining nine defendants pleaded guilty on the advice of their barrister, the Liberal Member of Parliament Llewellyn Williams, and were bound over in the sum of £25 each.[80] On the following Sunday another protest meeting to demand the repeal of the Military Service Act was held under the auspices of the NCCL at Taibach, and chaired by the ILP councillor Harry Davies.[81] An indication of the extent of local support given for these activists was the send-off given a week later to Councillor Tal Mainwaring, Port Talbot, and Dan Morris, secretary of the Cwmavon ILP, who had refused to pay their fines and were sent to prison. The columnist Afaneer described the dramatic scene:

> Great waves of enthusiasm witnessed the departure of Coun. Tal Mainwaring and Dan Morris en route to Swansea Gaol from Aberavon station last Saturday evening ... they were followed to the railway station by hundreds of enthusiastic people to see them off. Some of the crowds climbed the platform palings; women weeped [sic]; and the men sang themselves hoarse and waved their headgear ... the 'Red Flag' was sung – this time with renewed vigour and joined in by the Aberavon Male Voice Party, who were leaving by the same train. It was an impressive scene. The singing having ceased a voice shouted out

[77] *Pioneer*, 17 June 1916.

[78] T. C. Kennedy, *The Hound of Conscience: A History of the No-Conscription Fellowship, 1914–1919* (Fayetteville: University of Arkansas, 1981), pp. 128–9.

[79] Adams, *Not in Our Name*, p. 210.

[80] *Pioneer*, 17 June 1916.

[81] *Pioneer*, 24 June 1916.

'Are we downhearted?' 'No' responded a thousand voices. Again and again this cry went up. And now silence reigned. Coun. Harry Davies had suddenly risen to speak and the few remarks he was able to make were generously punctuated with applause and 'hear, hear' ... and thus departed the Comrades – but the spirit remained.[82]

It was to this vibrant centre of dissent that Bertrand Russell, the chairman of the NCF, visited as part of a three-week speaking tour of south Wales in June and July 1916. Russell was the author of the 'Everett' leaflet, which had led to the numerous arrests of ILP and NCF members in May 1916, including those of the Briton Ferry group.[83] This tour was comprised of private meetings of members of the sponsoring organisations, public indoor meetings and outdoor meetings, frequently held on village commons. Its organisation exemplified the close relationship between the various anti-war bodies, since the programme was constructed by the National Council against Conscription and the NCF, with local arrangements made by branches of the NCF or ILP. Russell's account of his visit provides an outsider's eye of conditions in Briton Ferry and the state of the anti-war movement in the area.

His first meeting was a private meeting of about 100 members of the NCF in Briton Ferry, in which he suggested, surprisingly, given the number of court cases against local NCF members, that they had not been subject to much persecution because they were all in starred industries, and that there was a 'higher than average' proportion of reserved, industrial occupations in the town.[84] He contrasted the atmosphere in Briton Ferry with other areas: 'the streets here are as full of young men as in normal times – it is very refreshing'.[100] But he reserved his greatest surprise for the extent of anti-war sentiment that he witnessed in the area, and in Port Talbot he felt that:

> The state of feeling here is quite astonishing. This town subsists on one enormous steelworks, the largest in S. Wales; the men are starred,

[82] *Pioneer*, 1 July 1916.
[83] Jo Vellacott, *Bertrand Russell and the Pacifists in the First World War* (Harvester Press, 1980), p. 78.
[84] Philip Adams, *A Most Industrious Town* (Ludlow: Briton Ferry Books, 2014), p. 125.

and earning very good wages; they are not suffering from the war in any way. But they seem all to be against it. On Sunday afternoon I had an open-air meeting on a green; there were two Chapels on the green, and their congregations came out just before I began. They stayed to listen. A crowd of about 400 came – not like open-air meetings in the South when people stay a few minutes out of curiosity, and then go away – they all stayed the whole time, listened with the closest attention, and seemed unanimously sympathetic. The man who has been organising for me here works twelve hours every day except Sunday in the steel works. Their energy is wonderful.[85]

That evening at Briton Ferry, as news of the Somme offensive filtered through, he had a 'really wonderful' and enthusiastic meeting:

> the hall was packed … they inspired me, and I spoke as I have never spoken before … One needs no prudent reticences – no humbug of any sort – one can just speak out one's whole mind. I thought the great offensive would have excited them, but it hasn't.[86]

The arrests of ILP activists and Russell's visit led to an increase in the number of anti-war meetings and demonstrations. From July 1916 onwards, regular meetings were held in Briton Ferry, Cwmavon and Port Talbot against the war. In the second week of July, for instance, four anti-war meetings were held and addressed by Russell and R. C. Wallhead, calling for peace negotiations.[87] A public meeting of over 900 people on 19 November 1916, listening to the peace activist and founder of the UDC, Charles Roden Buxton, speaking of peace by negotiation, was typical.[88] During the latter half of the war, other prominent national figures came to speak at anti-war rallies in Briton Ferry, including Sylvia Pankhurst, Philip Snowden, Herbert Dunnico, Director of the Peace Society, and Charles Trevelyan, a former Liberal Member of Parliament, who, with Norman Angell, was a founder of the Union of Democratic Control. The ILP in the area also gave recognition to the conscientious objectors when they

---

[85] Vellacott, *Bertrand Russell and the Pacifists in the First World War*, p. 87.
[86] Nicholas Griffin, *The Selected Letters of Bertrand Russell – The Public Years 1914–1970* (Routledge, 2001), p. 70.
[87] *Pioneer*, 15 July 1916; *Pioneer*, 22 July 1916.
[88] *Pioneer*, 23 November 1916.

returned from prison or work camp. On 30 September 1916, three local objectors were welcomed home from prison by a tea and 'entertainment' for between 200 and 300 people. In the same manner that returning soldiers were feted on their return from the front, the brothers John and Sidney Bamford, conscientious objectors from the Cwmavon area who had taken alternative employment in a local tinplate works, were each presented with a gold pendant, a silver cigarette case and a purse of money, which was paid for through subscription.[89]

Of the thirty-three conscientious objectors identified as men from Briton Ferry, most were identified with a chapel, but religious affiliation was often not the sole motivation for their objection.[90] Rather, it was a combination of moral and political objection to the war and based in a belief in the efficacy of the principles of Christianity, as reflected in the Sermon on the Mount. The *Pioneer*'s report of the arrest of nine local men as conscientious objectors is significant because of the close relationship it describes between the ILP, the NCF and the chapels of the area:

> some of these young men will be missed as members of the ILP; others will be missed as workers in the churches to which they belonged, while all will be missed at the meetings of the Fellowship. Of their sincerity, we are convinced, and they will inspire us in this fight for the principles for which we all stand.[91]

Most local chapels supported the war and opposed the anti-war movement. This inevitably caused friction within congregations, and when Councillor Joe Branch and others were arrested for distributing anti-war pamphlets outside Briton Ferry's Bethel Calvinist Methodist chapel on 30 April 1916, the minister of the church and a number of its deacons gave evidence against him, even though he and some of his colleagues were members, and their actions caused Branch and others to leave the chapel.[92]

[89] *Pioneer*, 7 October 1916.
[90] Cyril Pearce, *Pearce Register of Anti-War Activists in Wales* (Wales for Peace, 2016). Available at *http://www.wcia.org.uk/wfp/pearceregister.html*. Accessed November 2016.
[91] *Pioneer*, 2 December 1916.
[92] Adams, *Not in Our Name*, pp. 198, 209.

Jerusalem Baptist Church in Briton Ferry supported the anti-war movement most enthusiastically and provided a platform for numerous ILP and Peace Society gatherings. It was led by its charismatic minister, Revd Rees Powell, and his equally influential wife, Elisabeth Powell, a member of the women's ILP. The introduction of conscription gave an inevitable urgency to anti-war activity in Briton Ferry. Revd Rees Powell was an active member of the town's anti-conscription council and the branch of the NCF, and his church held an increasing number of peace meetings throughout 1916. Nicknamed the 'Kaiser's Church',[93] it became the centre for anti-war meetings in the town after January 1917, when the local council made the Briton Ferry Public Hall unavailable for use by the ILP and other anti-war organisations.[94] The church's official history records that it chose to take what was then the very uneasy course of supporting peace, and describes a period of conflict within the congregation:

> Much bitter opposition and hostile abuse was aroused by a series of peace meetings held in the chapel ... Quite a number of the young men of the chapel and Sunday School joined the army, but others obeyed the dictates of conscience and were imprisoned. In a public meeting at the close of the war, Mr. Powell said; 'I thank God that no young man can ever say that I sent him to the war.'[95]

The influence of the church on conscientious objectors from Briton Ferry was palpable. A remarkable forty-two per cent of them from Briton Ferry defined themselves as Baptist and attended Jerusalem chapel. At least thirteen of them, representing forty per cent, were also members of the ILP. Len Williams recalled:

> There was a very high percentage of conscientious objectors in Briton Ferry, most of them came from the Baptist chapel, most of them moved by religious reasons, but quite a number by socialist ... the minister himself, Rees Powell, well he was a man that was ostracised in his own ... profession ... he was a most Godly type of fellow to look at. But most of them came from his chapel.[96]

---

[93] *Pioneer*, 17 March 1917.
[94] Adams, *Not in Our Name*, p. 214.
[95] *Centenary of the Baptist Cause in Briton Ferry 1837–1937, Souvenir Programme* (Neath, 1938), p. 41.
[96] Swansea University Archive, South Wales Coalfield Collection, Len Williams, Aud. 282.

Powell's radicalism was reflected in his ministry and instances such as his controversial sermon, when he refused to read the king's proclamation demanding that people should make economies:

> He felt that in a church where many worked only two and three shifts a week he could not ask men to economise. At the same church, the Christian Endeavour Society on Thursday last had a paper read, which was written by a conscientious objector who is a guest of His Majesty at Wormwood Scrubs.[97]

In August 1917, the church held the first of a series of seven peace meetings and featured Revd Herbert Morgan, later the Labour candidate in the 1918 election in Neath, who spoke before a 'large audience' on the subject of the futility of war to answer international questions.[98] These meetings brought together peace and anti-war speakers from Wales and Britain, and in January 1918, two leaders of the pacifist movement in north Wales, Revd E. K. Jones, Cefnmawr, Wrexham, and Revd D. Wyre Lewis, Rhos, gave an account of their visit to an anti-war conference of eighty delegates representing sixteen churches in the Swansea Valley, and of their work as visitors to conscientious objectors in camps in north Wales.[99]

Other local chapels, such as Zion Baptist chapel, Cwmavon, also gave opportunities to hold peace meetings. In March 1917, a peace meeting was held in the chapel vestry, with the Revd John Morgan Jones, Merthyr, as main speaker, to call for Peace by Negotiation, and attempts were made to break up the meeting by 'local jingoes and conservatives'. At first they demanded it should be held in English, rather than Welsh, but the crowd quietened them and the meeting continued. The meeting went on to pass a motion to urge the government to 'promote negotiations with the object of securing a just and lasting peace', but as soon as the people began to depart, in 'rushed a dozen sordid, drunken, brutes, singing the National Anthem, who had probably just emanated from the adjacent public house'.[100]

[97] *Pioneer*, 9 June 1917.
[98] *Pioneer*, 18 August 1917.
[99] *Pioneer*, 2 February 1918.
[100] *Pioneer*, 17 March 1917.

This incident had an effect on other chapels and churches and their readiness to provide meeting places for the anti-war movement. Revd T. E. Nicholas had been booked to speak at the Bethania vestry in Cwmavon the following week, but 'with considerable religious prejudice and police pressure', the minister and the deacons cancelled the loan of the vestry, and the meeting was consequently held at the ILP centre.[101]

Other tensions were also developing between local chapels and the ILP. 'Democritus', an ILP member writing from Cwmavon, stated that the Sunday meetings organised by the ILP had become very popular, and although they were timed so as not to clash with religious services, the churches were doing their best to prevent the attendance of the youths by prolonging the religious services to an unusual extent:

> The result of this policy has been that the young people have kicked over the traces and most of them now leave for the meetings in good time, despite the insidious opposition of the church leaders. This narrow-mindedness, vindictiveness and intolerance of the elders of the church is alienating the thoughtful young men from the chapel, especially since it is obvious that opposition to the ILP is mainly due to the disrespect shown by this organisation to the fetishes of Liberalism.[102]

The anti-war movement in Briton Ferry was probably the most significant and effective of any area in Wales. It combined the political and cultural strength of the ILP with the dynamism of the opposition to conscription and the self-sacrifice of those conscientious objectors who came from the town. In spite of the town's involvement in manufacturing arms and serving the war effort, attitudes towards the war remained divided, and those who went to war, and those who refused to do so, were given succour by their different communities. Influential local figures such as Ivor Thomas embodied the network of anti-war activists in the town, and the role of Jerusalem chapel and its minister, Rees Powell, was critically important in giving courage to conscientious objectors and others who opposed the war, whilst the ILP was

[101] *Pioneer*, 24 March 1917.
[102] *Pioneer*, 8 September 1917.

the main political organisation providing practical support and a sense of community to those who might otherwise have felt ostracised and marginalised.[103]

Merthyr Tydfil was the cradle of the industrial revolution and the birthplace of democratic politics in Wales. On the eve of the war, Merthyr was a prosperous town of 83,808 inhabitants, and its growing civic pride was reflected in its elevation to the status of a county borough in 1908. Its economic and civic confidence was built on the pre-war boom in coal and steel production, with Welsh coal production peaking at 56.8 million tons of coal in 1913, of which 3 million tons were mined in the Merthyr area.[104] The largest single employer was the Guest Keen and Nettlefold Dowlais Iron and Steel Works, which also owned numerous coalmines in the area. Forty-three per cent of the electorate of Merthyr Boroughs worked in the small and scattered mines of the borough, and the unemployment rate was a paltry 1.4 per cent.[105] Merthyr miners' militancy was exemplified by their lonely opposition to a resumption of work in the south Wales coalfield after the minimum wage strike of 1912.[106]

The Merthyr Tydfil and Aberdare area, which together constituted the Merthyr Boroughs parliamentary borough, was the heart of the socialist movement and labour representation in south Wales. The ILP's network of branches combined with active trades and labour councils and an energetic co-operative movement, which was an significant addition to the quality of life for many. On the eve of the war,

[103] *Pioneer*, 12 April 1919. A significant postscript to the war was the municipal election to Briton Ferry Borough Council in March 1919, and the electorate's verdict on the ILP in Briton Ferry after the profoundly difficult and divisive period of war. In spite of a strong campaign against them by Discharged Soldiers and Sailors candidates, two of the three ILP candidates, George Gethin and D. L. Mort, were re-elected on top of the list.

[104] Merthyr Tydfil Teachers' Centre, *Merthyr Tydfil: A Valley Community* (Merthyr, 1981), p. 330.

[105] K. O. Morgan, 'The Merthyr of Keir Hardie', in Williams (ed.), *Merthyr Politics: The Making of a Working-Class Tradition*, p. 61.

[106] Joe England, 'The Merthyr of the Twentieth Century', in Williams (ed.), *Merthyr Politics: The Making of a Working-Class Tradition*, p. 83.

there were four co-operative societies in the area, in Dowlais, Treharris, Troedyrhiw and Merthyr, with a total of over 2,000 members and a remarkable sales volume of £116,063 in 1911. Labour's growth in the town before the war occurred in the context of greater industrial militancy, and the locally produced brochure of the ILP national conference, held in Merthyr in 1912, looked forward confidently to their efforts bearing fruit: 'the unification of the great parallel movements of the labour world, the trades unions, political and socialistic movements and the gradual conversion of the present Co-operative movement into a real collection effort is to be the greatest accomplishment of the near future.'[107]

In 1900 the constituency returned J. Keir Hardie as its first Member of Parliament to be elected as an unequivocal socialist and member of the Labour Representation Committee, and his political philosophy suffused the labour movement locally with his radical commitment to workers' rights, his loyalty to a working-class cooperative tradition, and his anti-militarism, which found expression in his opposition to the South African War and subsequently his objection to the Great War. Much of his local appeal lay in his ability to translate socialist ethics into the imagery of popular Nonconformity,[108] and his anti-war stance reflected the pacifist heritage of his predecessor, the Liberal Henry Richard, whose campaigning for an international system of peace arbitration earned him the sobriquet of 'Apostle of Peace'. Hardie's opposition to war set him firmly in this political lineage of radical Liberalism and anti-militarism and he was considered a 'voice of sanity' and 'pacific tolerance' at the outbreak of the war,[109] but he was shattered and crushed by his experience in a peace meeting in Aberdare, which was disrupted by angry pro-war demonstrators, and he reflected that he now understood the sufferings of Christ at Gethsemane.[110] The Labour organisation in Merthyr was henceforth divided between those who agreed with the official Labour leadership in supporting the war, and the

[107] *Souvenir ILP 20th Annual Conference Easter 1912* (Merthyr: ILP, 1912), pp. 49–50.
[108] Morgan, 'The Merthyr of Keir Hardie', pp. 70, 67.
[109] Morgan, 'The Merthyr of Keir Hardie', pp. 80, 262.
[110] Morgan, 'The Merthyr of Keir Hardie', p. 266.

pacifist supporters of Hardie and the ILP who stood out against the 'passions of the time'.[111]

The strength of Merthyr's ILP branch was gained from Keir Hardie's strong personal following, and, even in the early part of the war, as other branches declined, the Merthyr and Aberdare Valleys could report the 'surprising fact' that branches which had fallen away before the war were now increasing in membership and activity.[112] By 1918, the ILP's Merthyr and Aberdare Federation area had eleven branches in the Merthyr and Aberdare area; at Merthyr, Aberdare, Abercanaid, Abercynon, Bedlinog, Dowlais, Hirwaun, Merthyr Vale, Mountain Ash, Troedyrhiw and Ynysybwl. During the war, Aberdare ILP's affiliation fees and membership were second in south Wales only to those of Briton Ferry. In 1917–18, for instance, Aberdare's paid affiliation fees reflect a membership of approximately 260, with another 160 in Merthyr. These two branches were part of a Merthyr division that included another nine branches, and would probably have included at least 300 other members in the area.[113]

The local ILP newspaper, the *Pioneer*, was one of the 'most interesting of the official provincial ILP papers at this time',[114] and its ownership by over 800 local subscribers was testament to the vigour of the ILP in the Merthyr area. Created in June 1911, it fulfilled a need for a local journal to express an 'unofficial but constitutionally orientated militancy of which Hardie himself was the supreme symbol'. At the time, it lent new momentum to the flagging ILP in the Welsh industrial valleys,[115] and the list of subscribers included a high proportion of teachers, but the overwhelming majority of subscribers were associated with the mining industry.[116] The *Pioneer*'s circulation was calculated at 'usually in excess of ten

---

[111] Morgan, 'The Merthyr of Keir Hardie', p. 77.

[112] *Pioneer*, 22 May 1915.

[113] Cardiff University Library Special Collections, Independent Labour Party Papers, 'Annual Conference report, April 1918' (Harvester Microfilms), p. 105.

[114] Marwick, 'The Independent Labour Party 1918–1932', p. 51.

[115] K. O. Morgan, *Keir Hardie, Radical and Socialist* (Weidenfeld and Nicolson, 1975), p. 237; Deian Hopkin, 'The Membership of the Independent Labour Party, 1904–10: a spatial analysis', *International Review of Social History*, 20 (1975), 185.

[116] Hopkin, 'The Membership of the Independent Labour Party', 185, 193.

thousand',[117] and its policy was to support the rank and file of the SWMF, especially the emergent leaders of the militant left, like Vernon Hartshorn, Charles Stanton and George Barker.

From the beginning of the war, it supported the ILP in taking a strong and uncompromising anti-war stance. At the end of the week when war was declared, the *Pioneer* called on the workers of south Wales to unite with the trade unionists and socialists of Europe to oppose the war:

> Workers, don't fail your comrades at this great moment. Stand by your fellow workers here. Stand by your fellow-workers in Europe. Whoever else deserts the ranks, whatever you have to face, stand firm. The future is dark, but in the solidarity of the workers lies the hope which shall, once again, bring light to the peoples of Europe. Down with the war-mongers. Up with the Banner of peace.[118]

The Union of Democratic Control (UDC), founded by middle-class radicals such as E. D. Morel, the Liberal C. B. Trevelyan, MP, and the propagandist Norman Angell, whose study of militarism and the arms trade influenced a generation of peace activists,[119] attempted to define the means by which international peace could be established and maintained once the war ended. Its strength lay amongst London radicals and intellectuals,[120] and its first meeting in Wales was held in January 1915, at Shiloah chapel, Merthyr, in order to set up a local branch. The speaker was C. B. Trevelyan, who addressed 'an attentive and appreciative audience'.[121] Later in 1915, the Aberdare ILP mandated its delegates to affiliate to the UDC, and in the first meeting of the General Council of the UDC, with Ramsay MacDonald in the chair, there were delegates from Cardiff, Merthyr and Newport, representing a tenth of the UDC's branches.[122] At the beginning of 1916 the Merthyr Tydfil Trades and Labour Council, representing 10,000 unionists, affiliated to the

---

[117] Hopkin, 'The Membership of the Independent Labour Party', 60.
[118] *Pioneer*, 8 August 1914.
[119] Norman Angell, *The Great Illusion* (Putnam and Sons, 1910).
[120] Marvin Swartz, *The Union of Democratic Control in British Politics* (Oxford: Clarendon Press, 1971), p. 89.
[121] *Pioneer*, 30 January 1915.
[122] *Pioneer*, 6 November 1915.

UDC, but in April, an indication of the tension with the local anti-war movement was the Union's Executive Committee's refusal to send a speaker to a meeting in Merthyr because it appeared to be part of an unconditional 'stop the war' campaign. By September 1916 however, the UDC's views on Merthyr's anti-war movement seem to have changed, and one of its founders, E. D. Morel, spoke at a rally of 3,000 people organised by the Merthyr Peace Council, the umbrella group for the anti-war movement in the town.[123]

Regular anti-war meetings were usually held in the largest public meeting hall in Merthyr, which was the Olympia skating rink. These meetings of up to 3,500 people were organised by the ILP, the local Peace Council, the NCCL and other anti-war and anti-conscription bodies, and the frequency of these meetings reflects the increasing momentum of the anti-war movement throughout this period. An indication of the shock with which the outbreak of war was greeted was that the first meeting was not held until 25 October 1914, fully ten weeks after the outbreak of war. Only two big anti-war meetings were held in 1915, and it was only in the second half of 1916, that their frequency increases noticeably. Four meetings were held in the first half of 1916, and a further four in the second half. In 1917, a total of eleven meetings were held in the rink, and a further six meetings in 1918 prior to the Armistice.

George Protheroe, a local ILP member, recalled the anti-war feeling in the town during the war:

> there was a bigger spirit of anti-war in Merthyr, I think it was recognised at the time, than in any other town in the country. And some of the greatest speakers had been over there, which the ILP were organising peace meetings for. I attended practically every one of them, which were held in the Rink ... and there were between three and four thousand people in those peace meetings on a Sunday evening.[124]

The FoR's assistant secretary, George M. Ll. Davies, based in London in 1915, was delighted at the large size of his

---

[123] Swartz, *The Union of Democratic Control*, pp. 149–51; *Pioneer*, 9 September 1916.
[124] Swansea University Archive, South Wales Coalfield Collection, George Protheroe, Aud. 309.

audience and the respectful silence with which he and other anti-war speakers were greeted:

> Yn y dyddiau hynny (1915) arfer heddychwyr oedd cyfarfod mewn ystafelloedd o'r neilltu ... er fy syndod, aeth a mi i neuadd mwyaf y dref. Pan welais gynulliad o ddwy fil yn disgwyl amdanom tybiais eu bod am ein gwaed ... Cawsom wrandawiad astud a chefnogaeth i syniadau a fuasai'n tynnu'r dorf am ein pennau yn Llundain.[125]

> (in those days (1915) pacifists used to meet in private rooms ... to my surprise we went to the largest hall in town. When I saw a crowd of two thousand waiting for us I thought they were for our blood ... We were given an attentive hearing and support for ideas that would have caused a crowd to attack us in London.)

At the end of the war, Alderman Frank James, formerly military representative for the Merthyr Borough, drew the attention of the Merthyr Watch committee to the reputation of the rink as one of the 'most seditious parts of the country' and challenged the chief constable to take action. The town mayor absolved the police of responsibility for the lack of action against ILP activists and blamed the Home Office for its reluctance to allow prosecutions:

> Speakers are brought here from all over the country every Sunday, and it gives the borough a reputation it does not deserve. The audience is drawn from Aberdare, Pontypridd, Bedlinog etc., but it gives Merthyr an opprobrious name, and results in its being stigmatised as the hot-bed of Bolshevism and Socialism of the broadest and most violent type.[126]

The first meeting, at the end of October 1914, was held with a crowd of between 2,000 and 2,500 who congregated to hear two of the leaders of the ILP, Ramsay MacDonald and Bruce Glasier, as well as Keir Hardie himself:

> The meeting held at the Olympia Rink on Sunday afternoon last must have been a grievous disappointment to the Jingoes. Merthyr people have again shown during this crisis, as during the South African War, that whilst other towns may not be prepared to give a fair hearing to the 'other side of the question'. Merthyr is always prepared to do so.[127]

---

[125] M. R. Mainwaring, 'John Morgan Jones 1861–1935', in D. Ben Rees, *Herio'r Byd* (Liverpool: Cyhoeddiadau Modern Cymreig, 1980), p. 64.
[126] *Pioneer*, 13 February 1919.
[127] *Pioneer*, 31 October 1914.

The speeches reflected the uncertainty of the ILP at the time. Macdonald denied he was anti-war, though he stated his refusal to embark on recruiting campaigns with his political enemies, but Glasier was more forthright in his condemnation of the war:

> I hope that you don't believe in a possible alliance between Christ and the sword – that civilisation cannot advance but by the sword. (Applause) I am proud to be here with Keir Hardie to stand for the great principles of peace for which our movement stands.

Hardie closed the meeting in an unscheduled speech in which he railed at diplomatists and warned against militarism:

> It is not enough to denounce war, men. It is not enough to preach peace, we must change the conditions which make war inevitable. (Applause) Richard Cobden and John Bright, and that man who brought honour to Merthyr, Henry Richard. (Cheers) They were hated and lied about, but they stood true to their principles, and when the war of madness was over, the country turned to honour the men who had held to their principle.[128]

The next rallies were not held until almost a year later, in the autumn of 1915, when Hardie's memorial meeting in the Rink on 23 October 1915 provided the opportunity to celebrate his life and his anti-militarism. A further rally of 3,000 people in November 1915, at which Robert Williams of the Transport Workers' Union spoke, declared 'its strongest opposition to compulsory military service', and the 'utmost opposition to any proposal to impose upon the British people a yoke which is one of the chief curses of Prussian militarism'.[129]

The Rink hosted the first public meeting of the 'Merthyr Stop the War and Peace Council', which brought together the Fellowship of Reconciliation, the ILP, the NCF, the UDC and trade union lodges,[130] in April 1916, with 2,000 people present. A further meeting, organised by the Merthyr District Peace and Anti-Conscription Council, with an audience of 1,600 people, highlighted the plight of the conscientious

---

[128] *Pioneer*, 31 October 1914.
[129] *Pioneer*, 1 December 1915.
[130] *Pioneer*, 22 April 1916.

objectors,[131] and a meeting sponsored by the Peace Society on 25 June 1916 attracted a reported crowd of 5,000 people to listen to Philip Snowden.[132] The Rink meetings increased in frequency, with another four large anti-war rallies held between July and December 1916, and in the following year, meetings were held every six weeks from January 1917 onwards and sustained until the end of the war. Most of these meetings were held on Sunday afternoons, and they attracted crowds from a ten-mile radius of 'Aberdare, Bargoed, Bedlinog and elsewhere',[133] but their timing could affect church or chapel attendances. At least half of the Rink audiences were reported to be regular attendants of chapels and churches.[134]

The only chapel to support the anti-war movement consistently in Merthyr Tydfil was Hope Methodist chapel, under the ministry of Revd John Morgan Jones, a distinguished scholar and theologian:

> he was ... about the only one, if I can remember rightly, that preached against war. And he was holding his services there and the place started to fill and over-fill as the war went on ... Then of course after the Peace meetings, well there would be a rush home to tea and then it would be to Hope Chapel for another anti-war sermon ... And that kept on well practically the whole duration of the war.[135]

Another enthusiast compared the spiritual journey from the Rink to most chapels with 'going from the glorious sunshine to a thick fog. There is, I understand, one grand exception to this; at the chapel (Hope) I have in mind, there is a continuation of the Rink meetings spirit there.'[136] In addition to the regular public meetings to oppose the war, the local ILP also played an important part in supporting conscientious

---

[131] *Pioneer*, 24 June 1916.

[132] *Pioneer*, 31 July 1916.

[133] *Pioneer*, 25 January 1918.

[134] *Pioneer*, 11 January 1918: 'if a man from Abercanaid, Cefn or Dowlais, attends a Rink meeting which commences late, and afterwards wants to go to church or chapel, he has hardly any time for his Sunday tea. Among the Rink audiences are people from Pant, Caeracca and Dowlais Top, all of which are very far from Merthyr.'

[135] Swansea University Archive, South Wales Coalfield Collection, George Protheroe, Aud. 309.

[136] *Pioneer*, 25 January 1918.

objectors. The secretaries of the NCF in Aberdare and Merthyr were both members of the ILP, and Revd John Morgan Jones's daughter worked in the Conscientious Objector Information Bureau in the NCF's head office in London. A total of thirty-two objectors appeared before the local tribunal in its first hearing on 13 March 1916,[137] and at least seventy-one conscientious objectors in total were to emerge from the Aberdare and Merthyr area. Of the thirty-six objectors who declared an affiliation, fourteen men declared themselves as members of the ILP, and sixteen declared themselves members of the No-Conscription Fellowship.[138]

By the end of 1916, because of its anti-war meetings in the Rink, and the militancy of the ILP locally, Merthyr had become synonymous with the anti-war movement. The term 'Merthyrism' was fashioned by the special correspondent of the *Times*, who warned of the peril of the confluence of an anti-war movement in south Wales with the possibility of a strike in the coalfield in December 1916, unless the men's claim for an increase in wages was met.[139] This concern was heightened by the ongoing controversy over the disruption of a conference organised by the NCCL in the Cory Hall, Cardiff, in November 1916, which was reconvened for December in Merthyr, and which is considered in further detail in chapter 3.

A report, written in August 1916 by an intelligence officer for the Ministry of Munitions, reviewed attitudes in Merthyr towards the war, and stated that although miners individually showed no wish to 'hamper Imperial efforts', nowhere else in the mining industry had he encountered such distrust between coal owners and their employees. He found that 'tacked on' to the trade unions' organisation were 'combinations' such as 'a Council for Civil Liberties, a Council for Peace and the like'. He warned that although there was no secret about the objective of these organisations, 'they are slowly but surely bringing about an attitude which to a certain extent is bound to become prejudicial to major interests'. He highlighted the failure of local prominent figures, including

---

[137] *Pioneer*, 18 March 1916.
[138] *Pearce Register*.
[139] *The Times*, 23 November 1916.

Labour Members of Parliament, to support the war effort and to 'help the average man to keep in the right frame of mind':

> At the moment, Socialists with whom the ILP is identified, and a section of the Welsh clergy, are out to either mould new ideas or disturb fixed ones, and thus divert essential enthusiasm. I do not think that very much assistance need be expected from Labour members *in* Wales; it seems to me they are the slaves of local dictation.

He identified local 'juveniles' as slackers and most ready to cause trouble. But amongst the causes of 'considerable irritation' locally were the increasing high cost of living, and the tendency for shopkeepers and merchants to raise prices, so that whilst miners were not so affected because of their rates of pay, others, like railwaymen, municipal employees and shop assistants, could not keep pace. He warned that 'the agitators are out to engineer difficulties' and referred to the representation of 116 representatives of trade unions, together with political and religious organisations, at a recent meeting of the NCCL in the area.[140]

One of the leaders of the local anti-war movement, the miners' agent for Merthyr and Dowlais, John Williams, led the opposition to conscription within the industry:

> South Wales was quite clear that there was to be no more cooperation with the Government, in order to secure their young men, and he knew that the men of Merthyr would be prepared to take any measure, however drastic, to protest against this damnable thing.[141]

Whilst the 'comb-out' of men for the armed forces was supported by a margin of 77 per cent to 23 per cent across the coalfield, the margin of the vote in Merthyr and Dowlais was the closest for any Federation division in south Wales, at 44 per cent opposed to the 'comb-out', to 56 per cent in favour.[142] This tradition of militancy was affirmed by the

---

[140] Bodleian Library, Addison Papers, Dep. c 88, fos 44–6, 'Report by 'A.B.', an intelligence agent'. Whilst the note is anonymous, his further report, Security Services Papers KV/2/663/20444, 13 November 1916, suggests that an 'A. Barker' was the likely author.

[141] Bodleian Library, Addison Papers, 21 April 1917.

[142] *Western Mail*, 16 November 1917.

appointment of Noah Ablett, a stormy firebrand, to succeed John Williams as miners' agent for Merthyr in 1918. He was one of the leading 'advanced men' of the URC and associated with the syndicalist philosophy of *The Miners' Next Step*.[143] He had been the only member of the SWMF Executive in August 1914 who had held out for an international miners' strike to end the developing war,[144] and although he had broken with the ILP in 1910, the readiness of Merthyr miners to employ him suggests an appetite amongst them for a radical transformation of the Miners' Federation into a means for striving for miners' ownership of the mines.[145] Another new agent elected for Dowlais, S. O. Davies, had been a check-weighman in the Great Mountain colliery in Tumble, was a prominent ILP member and anti-war activist, and shared Ablett's radicalism.[146]

Merthyr Tydfil was one of the main centres for the opposition to the war in south Wales due to its radical anti-war tradition, the development of an influential labour movement through the labour and trades council, a strong ILP and co-operative movement, and a clear voice through the pages of the *Pioneer*. The Olympia Rink was the location for the greatest anti-war demonstrations in south Wales from the autumn of 1916, and whilst many of its audiences were drawn from outlying districts, the size of these congregations of many thousands suggests strongly that attitudes in the town were more opposed to the war than in other parts of south Wales.

Merthyr and Briton Ferry were the most significant centres of opposition to the war in south Wales, and the organisation of these local anti-war movements was intrinsically linked with the ILP's activities, that orchestrated anti-war and anti-conscription protests, leafleted and gave practical support to the families of imprisoned conscientious objectors. Whilst these were unquestionably the two strongest ILP branches in

[143] Morgan, 'The Merthyr of Keir Hardie', p. 78.
[144] Swansea University, South Wales Coalfield Collection, Minutes of Executive Council of the SWMF, August 1914 *passim*.
[145] Egan, 'Noah Ablett', 25.
[146] Robert Griffiths, *S. O. Davies – A Socialist Faith* (Llandysul: Gomer Press, 1983), pp. 34–40.

south Wales, other areas also had both strong ILP branches and anti-war activity. These included Aberdare, the Swansea Valley and Swansea town itself, and the Rhymney Valley. In the 'new communities' of the coalfield, such as the Rhondda and Monmouthshire's eastern Valleys, the vanguard of the anti-war movement was the grouping of 'advanced men' associated with the Unofficial Reform Committee, who propagated industrial unionism and workers' control, and were instrumental in resisting the introduction of conscription within the mining industry for a full eleven months in 1917.

THE 'ADVANCED MEN' AND THEIR OPPOSITION TO WAR

The south Wales coalfield was the area of Britain most influenced by the 'advanced men', who supported the amalgamation of all labour within one union, believed in industrial unionism at the point of production, and demanded workers' control.[147] In no part of the country was this belief so widely held, and the South Wales Miners' Federation's decision in 1917 to call for the abolition of capitalism as one of its aims reflected their rapidly growing influence within the Federation.[148]

The mining industry dominated the economy of south Wales. Its output peaked in 1913 and it employed an annual average of 212,000 men throughout the Great War, approximately two-thirds of whom were members of the SWMF.[149] Before the war, the militant element within its rank and file had grown substantially and had expressed its frustration in the Cambrian Combine dispute in 1910–11 and through the pages of *The Miners' Next Step*, published by the Unofficial Reform Committee (URC), which spurned conventional electoral politics, and emphasised the 'syndicalist virtues of direct industrial action'.[150] This element was reflected in the

[147] Commission of Enquiry into Industrial Unrest, No. 7 Division, *Report of the Commissioners for Wales, including Monmouthshire*, Command 8668 (1917), p. 17.

[148] Hywel Francis and Dai Smith, *The Fed: A History of the South Wales Miners in the Twentieth Century* (Lawrence and Wishart, 1980), p. 24.

[149] Francis and Smith, *The Fed*, p. 508.

[150] Francis and Smith, *The Fed*, p. 10.

increasing power of the SWMF's delegate conferences, although only gradually by the composition of its Executive Council. Chris Williams describes this strand of thinking as a 'fierce burst of intellectual endeavour'[151] and traces industrial unionism and syndicalism to the 'common, socialist culture of mining communities'.[152] Electoral political action was seen as an ineffectual means for gaining working-class emancipation, and Ablett became one of its most vocal and effective spokesmen:

> In politics things were done for the workers; in industrial matters they were, from the bottom up, beginning to do things for themselves. The weapon of political action was a speech, its end hot-air in a gas-house on the way to become a dung-heap ... The industrial union did not need the backing of a political organisation, therefore it was foolish to swim the river to fill the bucket on the other side[.][153]

W. F. Hay's pamphlet, *WAR! And the Welsh Miner*[154] is the most coherent and explicit expression of the thinking of the 'advanced men' on the question of the war. A miner at the Standard Colliery, Wattstown, Rhondda, he became a member of the industrial Syndicalist League and wrote before the war for the *Rhondda Socialist*.[155] His pamphlet described the war as a 'cyclone of death' created by militarism and high finance, and urged his readers to understand that the coalminer's duty in the first place was to himself to obtain the best possible conditions under the 'slave system', and that the only patriotism he had any use for was class patriotism.

He advocated that the state should take over food supplies with a scale of maximum prices and that workers should insist on better rates of pay, and this strategy, he believed, would also hasten the end of the war by 'squeezing the pockets of the Capitalist'.[156] Ness Edwards, a working miner and a later historian of the SWMF, considered that 'the tone

---

[151] Chris Williams, *Democratic Rhondda: Politics and Society, 1855–1951* (Cardiff: University of Wales Press, 1996), p. 6.
[152] Williams, *Democratic Rhondda*, p. 7.
[153] *Pioneer*, 10 November 1917.
[154] W. F. Hay, *War! And the Welsh Miner* (Tonypandy, 1914).
[155] Egan, 'The Swansea Conference', 18.
[156] Hay, *War! And the Welsh Miner*, p. 7.

laid down in Hay's pamphlet was quietly permeating the rank and file of the organisation'.[157]

Egan contends that the extent of the anti-war movement in south Wales during the Great War has been underestimated by historians, and that by the end of 1915, there had occurred 'a regroupment and strengthening of anti-war tendencies within the movement'.[158] Paul Davies states that the growing anti-war feeling among the south Wales miners should not be minimised in 1915 and 1916, and argues that after February 1917 this sentiment took off and became a mass movement.[159] Advocates of this 'advanced' tendency did not oppose the war on pacifist grounds, but wished to take advantage of the circumstances afforded by the war to further a social and industrial revolution. J. L. Williams, a miner and anti-war activist, considered that Noah Ablett typified this approach:

> he was against it but not in the way that the ILPers were ... there was a tendency I would say amongst the more revolutionary to regard the war as more or less inevitable and the war has to be accepted as a stage in the development of capitalism. So we shouldn't be concerning ourselves unduly with opposing the war but rather take advantage of the war situation.[160]

The security services' view of Ablett was as a 'well-known Socialist agitator and avowed Bolshevik',[161] and he considered that the war 'was of no concern or interest to South Wales miners other than they should use the strong bargaining power it presented them with to wrest as much as they could from their employer and the State'.[162] Egan describes this burgeoning critique of the war as one that affected the rank and file of the trade union movement, the ILP 'and other

---

[157] R. Page Arnot, *South Wales Miners: A History of the South Wales Miners' Federation (1914–1926)* (Cardiff: Cymric Federation Press, 1975), p. 94.

[158] Egan, 'The Swansea Conference', 28.

[159] Paul Davies, 'The Making of A. J. Cook: His Development within the South Wales Labour Movement 1900–1924', *Llafur*, 3 (1978), 47.

[160] Swansea University Archive, South Wales Coalfield Collection, J. L. Williams interview, Aud. 396.

[161] National Archives, Security Services Papers, KV3/327, 'Revolutionary Tendencies behind the Labour Unrest', 6 April 1919.

[162] Egan, 'Noah Ablett', 25.

minuscule socialist organisations in South Wales, such as the Rhondda Socialist Society, along with the No Conscription Fellowship and the Union of Democratic Control'.[163]

The first eighteen months of the war saw patriotic support given to the war effort, and prominent 'advanced men' and supporters of *The Miners' Next Step*, such as Noah Rees and Ted Gill, spoke on recruiting platforms. Forty thousand south Wales miners had joined up by the summer of 1915, but the combustible nature of industrial relations in the coalfield led to the coal strike in July 1915, which was declared by the SWMF Executive against the terms of a Treasury agreement, for a new and higher standard wage rate. It was only due to the intervention of Lloyd George, the Minister of Munitions, with two other government ministers, Walter Runciman, Minister of the Board of Trade, and Labour's Arthur Henderson, that further industrial action was averted, and the miners won their main demands.[164]

Francis and Smith assert that this strike was the expression of a 'growing antiwar feeling, largely at this stage unconscious',[165] whilst Mor-O'Brien argues to the contrary, that the 1915 Strike was due to 'the intense patriotism of the south Wales miners'.[166] For most contemporary newspapers, this strike was viewed as a display of anti-war feeling, but more considered observers viewed it as a display of miners' frustration, and this bitterness continued and intensified up to the government's takeover of the mining industry in December 1916, and beyond.[167] The influential syndicalist *Plebs Magazine* argued that the strike was not an anti-war protest, but rather an attempt to stop 'the profiteers who, organised politically as "the State", have done their utmost, under cover of a real national crisis, to rob labour of practically every safeguard it

---

[163] Egan, 'The Swansea Conference', 28.

[164] Egan, 'The Swansea Conference', 28.

[165] Francis and Smith, *The Fed*, p. 22.

[166] Edward May, 'Charles Stanton and the Limits to "Patriotic" Labour', *Welsh History Review*, 18/3 (1997), 498: Anthony Mor-O'Brien, 'A Community in Wartime: Aberdare and the First World War' (unpublished PhD thesis, University of Wales, 1986).

[167] D. K. Davies, 'The Influence of Syndicalism and Industrial Unionism on the South Wales Coalfield, 1898–1921: a study in ideology and practice' (unpublished PhD, University of Wales, 1991), p. 74.

had won for itself during the long struggle against exploitation'.[168] The strike comprehensively flouted the government's attempted imposition of the Munitions Act, and one of the most prominent of the 'advanced men', W. H. Mainwaring, one of the authors of *The Miners' Next Step*, argued that whilst the miners had not won everything demanded, yet the strike could be described as 'a great defeat of Capitalism' and 'one of the greatest victories in the history of Trade Unionism'.[169]

The URC had been moribund in the first year of the war until the July 1915 Miners' Strike, and lacked the confidence to take action explicitly opposed to the war until the campaign against conscription developed from January 1916 onwards. In August 1915, they regrouped in the 'Aberystwyth' restaurant in Tonypandy,[170] and the radicalising effect of the war quickened a shift in emphasis to a proletarian internationalism, in which patriotism was challenged by a belief in international brotherhood and a conviction that the war was caused by the expansionary needs of imperialist capitalist powers. This analysis developed into an active anti-war position as military conscription was introduced and civilian conscription was feared, and was further inspired by the Russian Revolution in 1917. The 'advanced men' worked to resist the introduction of conscription into the mining industry, and although this campaign was to lead to failure in the 'comb-out' ballot in November 1917, the extent of the vote against conscription, at thirty per cent of the total of votes cast, alarmed contemporary commentators,[171] and gave added momentum to the revived URC.

The Commission of Enquiry into Industrial Unrest identified the influence of the 'advanced men' as one of the underlying reasons for industrial unrest in the coal industry in the summer of 1917:

> they see in the strengthening of the union a means of forging a firmly-welded weapon which will ultimately be sufficiently powerful

---

[168] *Plebs Magazine*, August 1915, 146.
[169] *Plebs Magazine*, August 1915, 150.
[170] Francis and Smith, *The Fed*, p. 24.
[171] *Welsh Outlook*, December 1917. The result of the 'comb-out' ballot was 98,948 in favour, to 28,903 opposed.

to overcome and reorganise the capitalist forces ranged against them. To these men political action is of temporary and deluding value; to them legal enactment is but a means either of oppression or of stupefaction ... In no part of the country is this creed so widely held and constantly preached as amongst the miners of Glamorganshire and Monmouthshire.[172]

As Egan suggests, some of the 'big battalions' of labour were won over to the anti-war movement by the summer of 1917, especially so within the SWMF, where growing pressure for a peace settlement from key districts, such as the Western District and the Merthyr and Aberdare districts, and numerous lodges were forcing the SWMF's Executive to reluctantly adopt a peace programme.[173]

The broader significance of the 'comb-out' ballot lay in its implications for the image of south Wales as part of the Empire at war. This study suggests that the controversy over the ballot was a proxy for attitudes towards the war, and while not all those miners who voted against the 'comb-out' were necessarily opposed to the war, the campaign certainly portrayed them as such. The most garish and apocalyptic language was employed by many contemporary newspapers and commentators, to reflect a sense of crisis and the critical importance of a favourable decision in the 'comb-out' ballot for the future supply of coal to the Empire's armed forces.

The *Welsh Outlook*'s editor argued that the URC was not only anti-capitalist, but also 'to a large extent anti-war', and that it was primarily due to their influence that the 'comb-out' ballot was held in November 1917:

> The opposition (to combing out) comes from the pacifist organisations, whose influence is increasing very rapidly in the mining towns and villages. The men who dominate the pacifist movement are the same men who dominate the political and industrial movement. Their propaganda is perfectly legitimate but they wield power beyond their numerical strength.[174]

He argued that these activists had influence beyond their numbers, and were permitted by the majority of the

---

[172] *Report of the Commissioners for Wales, including Monmouthshire*, p. 17.
[173] *Report of the Commissioners for Wales, including Monmouthshire*, p. 28.
[174] *Welsh Outlook*, November 1917.

Federation's members to dominate its business so that it was 'transacted by the few'.[175]

The URC had been revived in Pontypridd at a meeting on 13 April 1917, with Noah Tromans in the chair and W. H. Mainwaring as secretary.[176] This body of men had formed a coherent network of activists across the south Wales coalfield before the war, and a number of those who had taken part in the drafting of *The Miners' Next Step*, such as Noah Rees, George Barker and Ted Gill, had become members of the SWMF's Executive Council, and now passionately supported recruiting and the war effort.[177] It was the introduction of conscription and support for the Russian Revolution in February 1917 that revived the anti-war movement. The Rhondda miner W. H. Mainwaring exemplified the network of relationships between the anti-war organisations, for in addition to his role as secretary of the URC, he was also secretary of the local NCF, the chairman of the Rhondda anti-conscription committee, a member of the ILP, a late student of Ruskin College and Central Labour College, a leading light of the Plebs League and supporter of the Russian Revolution.[178]

In addition to their involvement in the Federation, a number of the anti-war URC activists, including George Dolling, Nun Nicholas and George Phippen were also members of the ILP,[179] and others, such as Noah Ablett, S. O. Davies and A. J. Cook, were influential miners' agents. A small number of its supporters, such as Ness Edwards in Abertillery and A. E. Cook from Cardiff were members of the British Socialist Party (although also associated with the ILP) and the Socialist Labour Party, respectively. A young member of the URC, Will Cockrill, from Pontnewynydd in Monmouthshire, encapsulated these men's beliefs:

---

[175] *Welsh Outlook*, November 1917.

[176] Nina Fishman, *Arthur Horner: A Political Biography 1894–1944* (Lawrence and Wishart, 2010), p. 506.

[177] David Egan, 'The Unofficial Reform Committee and the Miners' Next Step: Documents from the W. H. Mainwaring Papers', *Llafur*, 2/3 (1978), 79.

[178] National Archives, Security Services Papers, KV3/327, 'Revolutionary Tendencies behind the Labour Unrest'.

[179] Paul Davies, 'The Making of A. J. Cook: His Development within the South Wales Labour Movement 1900–1924', *Llafur*, 2/3 (1978), 44.

we weren't pacifists or anything of that nature. But on the other hand we believed that it was being waged by the imperialists, either by the German imperialist and our imperialists, because our history was just as bad as theirs. So the attitude was that we would fight to defend but we believed that they ought to negotiate and come to a settlement.[180]

In the charged atmosphere of the war, many failed to understand this nuanced approach, but in Cockrill's view, the Russian Revolution inspired anti-war activists. Only a handful of conscientious objectors from Wales appealed on the grounds of their political beliefs as Marxists and revolutionary socialists, and the miners amongst them only became objectors after the 'comb-out' was introduced into the mining industry in November 1917. David John Davies from Aberdare, in his statement to the court martial, explained that his refusal to conform to the Military Service Act was because of his belief that the war was fought 'in the interests of Capital and not the workers':

the workers are being used as pawns in the game of the ruling classes and it is only when the workers of all Countries realise that their interests are alike that they have in common the same enemy i.e. Capitalism to fight and overthrow, then only will war become a thing of the past. Believing so I therefore refuse to participate in war and obey military commands.[181]

Mark Starr's explanation for his conscientious objection was rooted in an analysis of the war as the inevitable product of imperialism and militarism:

I disobey military orders: – because one section of militarism can never by threatening and menacing another section remove the thing itself. The helpless pawn can never destroy the game. Because I put class before country, and thus refuse to kill my fellow class-member at the bidding of fellow countrymen ... Because I thus oppose that section of militarism which is nearest to me despite the high sounding phrases with which, aided by the mighty press, it cloaks its real aims in every country. Because I desire to advance another cure for all war – the education of the workers.[182]

---

[180] Swansea University Archive, South Wales Coalfield Collection, Will Cockrill, Aud. 339.
[181] Sheila Parry private papers, David John Davies, court martial speech, 28 August 1918.
[182] *Pioneer*, 19 August 1918.

Since war mainly benefited the 'capitalist class', the leading activist, Arthur Horner, could not consent to 'take the life of my fellow workers, or sacrifice my own'.[183] In retrospect, he explained his uncompromising attitude against the war as being because 'I saw in the coal owners and the Government that supported them a nearer enemy than the Kaiser'.[184]

An important factor that developed the confidence and influence of the 'advanced men' was their link with the Central Labour College, founded by students disillusioned by Ruskin College, Oxford, which 'they considered to be propping up the existing capitalist social and economic system, instead of challenging and overthrowing it on Marxist lines'.[185] The Commission of Inquiry into Industrial Unrest identified this link as the dynamic spirit in the lodges of the SWMF and the trades councils, in which they had become 'centres of educational work and potent social and political activity'. This independent working-class movement, primarily delivered through Central Labour College (CLC) and Plebs League classes, reached its height in 1917–18 and was 'without doubt the most formative influence in the coal-field and did much to instil a deep antipathy towards capitalism'.[186] By November 1917, some 1,200 students were members of forty classes in south Wales,[187] which had the highest concentration of classes for any part of Britain.[188] The largest number of classes was in the Rhondda, with eighteen branches, and most were sponsored by either the SWMF or the ILP.[189]

Its main tutors included many who were anti-war activists, such as A. J. Cook, a miner in the Lewis Merthyr colliery in Trehafod in the Rhondda, a member of the ILP before the war who spent a year at the Central Labour College. He became a leading member of the URC and a lecturer on economics and industrial history for the Plebs League, and

[183] *Pioneer*, 19 August 1918.
[184] Arthur Horner, *Incorrigible Rebel* (MacGibbon and Kee, 1960), p. 9.
[185] Morgan, *Rebirth of a Nation*, p. 149.
[186] Richard Lewis, *Leaders and Teachers: Adult Education and the Challenge of Labour in South Wales, 1906–1940* (Cardiff: University of Wales Press, 1993), p. 122.
[187] *Welsh Outlook*, November 1917.
[188] *Plebs Magazine*, December 1917, January 1918.
[189] *Plebs Magazine*, January 1918.

was arrested on a charge of sedition in the spring of 1918 and given a three-month prison sentence. He was elected agent for Rhondda No. 1 district in June 1919.[190] Nun Nicholas, a checkweigher at a colliery in the Swansea Valley, became a conscientious objector, was 'one of the most charismatic of the Marxist lecturers'[191] and revived 'Plebs' classes by the end of 1917 in the Swansea Valley. Other classes, held in Garnant and Gwaun-cae-Gurwen, were run by David Rees Owen, a local checkweigher and the first person from the area to enter the Central Labour College.[192] He and another tutor, Jack Griffiths, Cwmtwrch, held classes on economics and Marxism under the aegis of the college, in the 'White House' in Ammanford. This centre, styled a 'Communist Hall' by the local newspaper,[193] had been bought by George Davison, a colourful and prosperous businessman who had made his fortune in the Kodak company. A socialist supporter of the ILP, he took a close interest in anarchist thought and funded the 'White House' as a library and meeting place. Of the fifty or so attenders of the Ammanford group, nine became conscientious objectors, and the White House became the local 'home of those who were opposed to the war'.[194]

A network of independent working-class education classes was also established in the west Monmouthshire valleys, in Risca, Tredegar and Abertillery, which were described as a 'hotbed of political activity and dissent'.[195] These 'advanced men' included Sam Fisher of Wattsville, the young Aneurin Bevan of Tredegar, Bryn Roberts, Ness Edwards and Will Hewlett of Abertillery, and were led by Ted Gill of Abertillery and Sidney Jones of Blackwood.[196] As the war drew on, although Gill joined in the recruiting campaign, most of this group became anti-war activists and involved in the campaign

[190] John Saville and Ralph Desmarais, 'A. J. Cook', *Dictionary of Labour Biography*, vol. 3 (Palgrave Macmillan, 1976), pp. 38–45.

[191] Lewis, *Leaders and Teachers*, p. 97.

[192] *Amman Valley Chronicle*, 9 February 1956.

[193] *Amman Valley Chronicle*, 13 October 1913.

[194] Griffiths, *Pages from Memory*, pp. 20–1.

[195] Alun Burge, 'Labour, Class and Conflict', in Chris Williams, Andy Croll and Ralph A. Griffiths (eds), *Gwent County History. Volume 5: The Twentieth Century* (Cardiff: University of Wales Press, 2013), p. 320.

[196] Burge, 'Labour, Class and Conflict', p. 323.

against the 'comb-out' in the mining industry.[197] These classes were seen as centres of Bolshevism and pacifism, and the Glamorgan Constabulary accused A. J. Cook's classes of constituting an 'insidious campaign against law and order'.[198] The CLC classes played an 'important role in the militant and revolutionary groundswell which made South Wales, ideologically, the most advanced area of Great Britain',[199] and a reflection of their influence was the amendment of the objects of the South Wales Miners' Federation in June 1917 to include the revolutionary aim of the 'complete abolition of capitalism'.[200]

The success of the URC in 1917 lay in the agitation against conscription within the mining industry, and its achievement in postponing the combing-out of men in the mining industry for eleven months after the War Cabinet had initially proposed that 20,000 mine workers who had hitherto been exempt should be conscripted. This marked the high point of its political and industrial influence during the war, but its influence, as reflected by the result of the 'comb-out' ballot in November 1917, whilst significant, also reflected its limitations.

THE IMPACT OF THE RUSSIAN REVOLUTION

Smith and Francis view the influence of the Russian revolutions of 1917 as the catalyst to more widespread 'conscious and open hostility to the war', which hitherto had been confined to small local socialist societies and individual conscientious objectors.[201] Whilst this interpretation ignores the evidence of widespread anti-war activity led by the ILP throughout 1916, the first Russian Revolution in February 1917 undoubtedly excited a new fervour and gave added vigour to the anti-war movement. The first report of the Ammanford and Llandybie Trades Council, presented by

---

[197] Harold Finch, *Memoirs of a Bedwellty MP* (Risca: Starling Press, 1972), p. 33.

[198] National Archives, Home Office Papers, HO45/10743, 'A. J. Cook' folio, J. Williams to Chief Constable Lindsay, 9 February 1918.

[199] Davies, 'The Making of A. J. Cook', 49.

[200] Swansea University Archive, South Wales Coalfield Collection, Minutes of SWMF Special Conference, 12 June 1917.

[201] Francis and Smith, *The Fed*, p. 22.

its young secretary, the future Labour Cabinet Minister Jim Griffiths, captures the excitement and enthusiasm with which the Revolution was greeted:

> the Russian Revolution burst upon the vision of an oppressed Democracy like the streaks of a dawning day ... The Russian Revolution, despite its recent apparent failure, gave new life and hope to the Democratic movement in Europe ... Its influence was felt in all parts of the world, reviving the spirit of Revolt ... a silent revolution has taken place in our midst. The mental outlook of the people has changed; an atmosphere has been created that is responsive to the kind of progress we of the Labour movement desire.[202]

The first display of support for the Revolution in Wales was a mass public meeting organised by the Merthyr ILP in April 1917.[203] Further, mass 'Russia Free' meetings were held in Merthyr and Bargoed in May, and a meeting in Gwaun-cae-Gurwen, addressed by Noah Ablett and J. L. Rees, a local miners' leader, passed a motion that congratulated the Russian Revolution and demanded international action to end the war.[204] The call for a convention of labour, socialist and 'democratic' organisations to 'Follow Russia', to be held in Leeds, appeared in May 1917 and called on its supporters to 'work for a complete and real international peace based upon working-class solidarity and therefore calculated to be honourable and enduring'.[205] It was intended to be a pacifist rather than a revolutionary event, and 'reflected an opposition to the continuation of the war for a "knock-out blow"'.[206] In June 1917, the Western District of the SWMF, representing 7,000 miners, approved of Russia's demand for an Internationalist Socialist and Labour conference in order to end the war.[207]

This conference, held in Leeds, convened over 1,000 delegates, of whom half came from the trade unions, trades

---

[202] Swansea University Archives, South Wales Coalfield Collection, SC 118/1, Annual Report of the Ammanford Trades and Labour Council, 1917–18.

[203] *Pioneer*, 7 April 1917.

[204] *Pioneer*, 26 May 1917.

[205] *Labour Leader*, 17 May 1917.

[206] Stephen White, 'Soviets in Britain: The Leeds Convention of 1917', *International Review of Social History*, 19 (1974), 166.

[207] *Pioneer*, 16 June 1917.

councils and constituency Labour parties. A total of 294 delegates represented ILP branches, and eighty-eight came from the less influential British Socialist Party.[208] There were only twelve delegates from Wales, including representatives of the Western, Merthyr and Dowlais districts of the SWMF, one SWMF lodge, four ILP branches and the South Wales Socialist Society, and although the conference also received a message from James Winstone, president of the SWMF, its content was not reported.[209]

Although the Convention was called jointly by the ILP and the British Socialist Party (BSP) their aims were divergent. Whereas the ILP sought to propagate peace by negotiation, the BSP interpreted the conference as a revolutionary act.[210] Hinton suggests that the shop stewards' movements in Scotland and England saw a parallel with the Russian soviets, but in contrast, the URC showed no interest in making comparisons between conditions in south Wales and Soviet Russia.[211] Four substantive motions were passed, first congratulating the Russian Revolution on their revolution, and expressing the hope that it might quicken peace, secondly calling for international negotiations to end the war on the basis of no annexations or indemnities, thirdly calling on the British government to present a charter of liberties, and lastly, setting up Councils of Workmen's and Soldiers' delegates.[212] This last motion would be interpreted as the most revolutionary, but the dissonance between its mover and seconder betrayed a fundamental difference of emphasis between the revolutionary and gradualist interpretation of the purpose of the motion.

The proposer, the ILP MP W. C. Anderson, emphasised this was not a subversive organisation and that its main purpose was to unite working-class soldiers and civilians, but the seconder, the transport union leader, Robert Williams

[208] John Slatter, 'Learning from Russia: A History of Soviets in Britain', *Labour History Review*, 61/1 (1996), 5–29.
[209] Egan, 'The Swansea Conference', 15.
[210] *The Call*, 14 June 1917.
[211] James Hinton, *The First Shop Stewards' Movements* (Allen and Unwin, 1973), p. 307.
[212] *What Happened at Leeds* (Council of Workers and Soldiers Delegates, Pelican Press, 1917).

called for the 'dictatorship of the proletariat'. Noah Ablett, there as a representative of the Maerdy lodge of the SWMF, had been mandated to vote for all four motions but complained at the Convention's failure to offer practical advice of how to set up these local Councils of Workmen and Soldiers.[213] Indeed, the motivation of most of those in the conference was not revolution but the 'banner of pacifism'.[214] The Convention agreed to set up a committee to establish thirteen 'district councils' of workers' and soldiers' deputies, including one in Wales, and, significantly, the address given for this provisional Committee was that of the NCF's offices in London.[215]

The first district meetings were held on 28 July 1917 in six locations, including Swansea for the Welsh district. On the two weekends following the Convention, mass meetings to hear reports back and to celebrate the Russian Revolution were held in Merthyr Tydfil, Taibach, Clydach, Cimla, Porth and Ynyshir. Meetings of 2,000 people in Merthyr, Ynyshir and Porth voted to support the decisions made in Leeds, and in Porth supported a resolution, proposed by Ablett and seconded by A. J. Cook, that demanded an immediate peace conference 'to negotiate an immediate cessation of hostilities on the lines of the Russian manifesto, of no annexations, no indemnities'.[216]

The conference in Swansea to establish a district council for Wales was organised for 29 July 1917, whilst north Wales was allocated to the Lancashire district and the Newport Labour Party sent its delegates to the West Country conference in Bristol.[217] The delegate list for the conference gives an indication of the breadth of support within the labour and trade union movement in Wales, and included twenty-six trades and labour councils, which constituted the majority of trades and labour councils Wales, sixty-six lodges of the SWMF, which included a large proportion from the Rhondda, thirteen branches of the National Union of Railwaymen and

[213] White, 'Soviets in Britain', 176.
[214] The Times, 5 June 1917.
[215] Cumbria Archives, Catherine Marshall Papers, f. 24, 21 June 1917.
[216] Pioneer, 7 July 1917.
[217] Egan, 'The Swansea Conference', 17.

another forty-six assorted trade union branches, the Maesteg ILP branch, the SWMF's Anthracite District and the South Wales Socialist Society.[218]

Whilst those meetings in Leicester, Bristol and Norwich passed peacefully, the meetings in London and Newcastle were disrupted and abandoned, as were later meetings in Glasgow and Manchester. The Swansea meeting was targeted by members of the Naval and Military Pensions and Welfare League, a government-sponsored organisation of discharged soldiers and sailors (known as 'bit-badge' men), and a crowd of 500, including munitions workers, attacked the delegates and invaded the Elysium Hall, where the meeting was to be held. With no police presence, Arthur Horner, for example, 'had his teeth punched out of his head and his eye and upper face badly bruised', and the *Cambria Daily Leader* reported that the delegates who remained were 'bleeding profusely and half-stunned. Fire extinguishers were turned on them, and with their faces half covered with blood, and the water streaming down their clothes, they appeared deplorable specimens'.[219]

The organisation quickly lost momentum, as only four districts succeeded in meeting and its National Council met only once. The October Russian Revolution undermined the 'somewhat shaky coalition of Socialists of varying hues which February's blurring of political differences had made possible'.[220] A postal ballot was subsequently held for a Wales representative to sit on the central Provisional committee. The list of candidates reflect an impressive range of talented advocates across the range of trade union and party political activity, most of whom were anti-war activists, and the vote was won by the president of the SWMF, James Winstone, who although not considered as an anti-war candidate, yet spoke forcefully in favour of a peace settlement from the summer of 1917 onwards.[221] The first – and only – meeting of the full

[218] Egan, 'The Swansea Conference', 24, 25.
[219] Egan, 'The Swansea Conference', 22, 23.
[220] Slatter, 'Learning from Russia', 24.
[221] *Cambria Daily Leader*, 30 July 1917; the candidates were George Barker (miners' agent, SWMF), Harry Davies (Cwmavon ILP and NCF), D. R. Grenfell (miners' agent, SWMF), George Gethin (Briton Ferry ILP), H. Hiles (Cardiff Trades and Labour Council), Revd John Morgan Jones (Merthyr ILP), T. C. Morris (Rhondda

National Soldiers' and Workers' Council was held in the third week of October 1917 and adopted a seven-point statement of the Council's aims, which stated that it should be a propaganda body with no intention to supplant existing organisations. It would campaign for a people's peace, the defence of civil liberties, the protection of soldiers' and sailors' rights and the elimination of profiteering,[222] but when the government banned the holding of further district conferences, the enthusiasm for the councils dissipated. By mid-October 1917, Basil Thomson, the head of the Special Branch, could report that the 'Workers and Soldiers Councils were moribund'.[223]

Activists within the SWMF however, attempted to maintain the momentum of the Leeds conference. The adoption of motions by the Merthyr and Dowlais Districts and a 'host of lodges'[224] forced the Executive to put forward a resolution to a coalfield conference in August 1917 that required the SWMF to:

> take such action with the view of ascertaining the opinion of the organised labour movements of this country on the question of Peace, so as to offer to the labour movement of the belligerent powers the British working-class view of a peace settlement ... and to take such action as will compel their respective Governments to adopt it.[225]

This resolution was adopted by a south Wales coalfield conference on 2 August 1917, by 212 votes to 43,[226] but in the late summer and early autumn of 1917, as the dream of workers' soviets faded, anti-war activity was directed increasingly towards frustrating the conscription of miners in the 'comb-out' ballot.

---

organiser, NUR), Noah Tromans (Mountain Ash ILP), James Winstone, David Williams (Swansea ILP) and John Williams (miners' agent, SWMF).

[222] *The Call*, 25 October 1917; *Pioneer*, 27 October 1917.

[223] National Archives, Cabinet Office Papers, CAB 24/22, Basil Thomson, 'Bolshevism in England', 1917.

[224] *Pioneer*, 21 July 1917.

[225] Swansea University Archive, South Wales Coalfield Collection, Minutes of SWMF Special Conference, 2, 3 August, 1917.

[226] Swansea University Archive, South Wales Coalfield Collection, Minutes of SWMF Special Conference, 2, 3 August 1917.

THE 1917 'COMB-OUT' BALLOT

In the wake of the Leeds Convention and the disrupted District Committee in Swansea, the anti-war element deployed the special conference of the SWMF on 2 and 3 August 1917 to reject the attempt made by its Executive Council, on behalf of government, to introduce a scheme for 'combing-out' men for military service. Prior to the conference, the URC had campaigned for its motion, on the basis that the scheme should be opposed as an 'act of rejection of the war itself'.[227] The resolution rejecting the advice of the Executive had been drafted by the URC and circulated beforehand to lodges,[228] and although the 'comb-out' scheme had been accepted by the Miners' Federation of Great Britain (MFGB) and recommended for acceptance, the special conference overwhelmingly rejected the proposal, by 236 votes to 25. The conference then decided to hold a coalfield ballot to establish whether the membership would support strike action if the government attempted to impose the scheme.[229] The SWMF's Executive Council subsequently resolved to hold a ballot for strike action if the government took steps to compel the 4,000 unmarried men between the ages of 18 and 25 required for military service from the south Wales collieries under the 'comb-out' order, agreed between the government and the MFGB.

The 'comb-out' ballot was undoubtedly a proxy for anti-war and pro-war sentiment, and a significant litmus test of attitudes towards the war within the SWMF and beyond. The Marxist historian Page Arnot interpreted the holding of the ballot as a manifestation of the spreading of 'the widespread longing for peace' in the coalfields following the Russian Revolution,[230] and Matthews's study of miners in the anthracite district of west Wales also suggests that the vote

[227] Egan, 'The Swansea Conference', 29.
[228] Swansea University Archive, South Wales Coalfield Collection, Lady Windsor Lodge, SWMF, Minutes of General Meeting, 30 July 1917; Swansea University Archive, South Wales Coalfield Collection, Blaenavon Lodge, Minutes of Committee Meeting, 1 August 1917.
[229] Egan, 'The Swansea Conference', 28.
[230] R. Page Arnot, *South Wales Miners: A History of the South Wales Miners' Federation (1914–1926)* (Cardiff: Cymric Federation Press, 1975), p. 133.

demonstrated the existence of a strong lobby for a termination of hostilities.[231]

In 1917, south Wales was the area of greatest opposition to
conscription in the mining industry in Britain. May argues
that the 'comb-out' controversy, combined with an increasing
sense of war weariness and the radicalising effect of the
Russian Revolution, produced a more militant anti-war attitude within the south Wales coalfield, and this provided the
springboard for the re-emergence of a revolutionary unofficial rank and file movement. This movement was able to
channel this anti-war mood and launch a serious challenge
to the state's war effort.[232] He points out that there were also
other aspects to miners' conditions which came to the fore in
the controversy over the 'comb-out':

> it raised momentous questions with regard to industrial conscription,
> civil liberties, equality of sacrifice, and the relative importance of the
> working class to the war effort – the impact of this had been delayed by
> the initial exemption of the mining workforce from military conscrip-
> tion – but the comb-out brought this to a fore.[233]

Most contemporary newspapers and commentators interpreted the 'comb-out' controversy as an indication of
anti-war or 'pacifist' feeling, and the very fact that the ballot
was held was interpreted as evidence of the existence of a
strong anti-war current amongst the south Wales miners.
The government felt so apprehensive about the result of the
ballot that a succession of pro-war propagandist 'War Aims'
public meetings were held throughout the coalfield.[234] John
Thomas, active in the ILP and the adult education movement, believed that the anti-war movement within the SWMF
was strengthened by the impact of the government's control
of the mining industry from December 1916 onwards, the
growing strength of the ILP and the revival of the URC from
1917 onwards, the spread of the Central Labour College

---

[231] Ioan Matthews, 'The World of the Anthracite Coal Miner' (unpublished PhD
thesis, Cardiff University, 1995), p. 290.
[232] Eddie May, 'A Question of Control: social and industrial relations in the South
Wales coalfield and the crisis of post-war reconstruction, 1914–1921' (unpublished
PhD thesis, Cardiff University, 1995), p. 94.
[233] May, 'A Question of Control', p. 99.
[234] Egan, 'The Swansea Conference', 28–9.

classes, the impact of the Russian Revolution, and a more general sense of war weariness. He believed that the report of the Commission of Enquiry into Industrial Unrest had underestimated the strength of anti-war feeling in south Wales in the summer of 1917:

> in many official Conferences of the SWMF, speeches of an Anti-War character were often made and applauded by the delegates. Often at these Conferences speeches were made directing fierce criticism, and expressing resentment against prominent Miners officials appearing on recruiting platforms, when they as officials were specially exempt from Military Service.[235]

Mor-O'Brien dismisses the 1917 'comb-out' ballot as showing that pacifist and anti-war sentiment remained a minority response, yet he also accepts that the vote against the 'comb-out' was sufficiently large to be worrying for the authorities.[236] Whilst Keith Davies has emphasised the limits of syndicalist influence, he argues that the 1915 Strike, far from representing miners' desire for recognition of their patriotism, represented the beginnings of a rejection of the social consensus which was subsequently corroborated by the growing 'anti-conscription, indeed anti-war, movement' in the south Wales coalfield.[237] May's examination of changing working-class attitudes to the war in south Wales concludes that whilst anti-war feeling may have been exaggerated, it was clear that the interpretation of the 'comb-out' controversy as an expression of an increasingly militant mood of rejection of the war effort in the coalfield is valid. In his view, 'conscription was one contributory factor to the emergence of a class-based view of the war', which meant that outside observers such as politicians and government officials found it difficult to comprehend the prevailing mood within the coalfield.[238]

---

[235] John Thomas, 'The South Wales Coalfield under Government Control 1914–1921' (unpublished MA thesis, Swansea University, 1925), pp. 81–3.

[236] Anthony Mor-O'Brien, 'Patriotism on Trial: the strike of the South Wales miners', *Welsh History Review*, 12/1 (1984–5), 100; Anthony Mor-O'Brien, 'A Community in War-time: Aberdare and the First World War' (unpublished PhD thesis, Swansea University, 1986).

[237] Davies, 'The Influence of Syndicalism and Industrial Unionism', p. 177.

[238] May, 'A Question of Control', p. 96.

As evidence for the link, May cites the two motions passed by 800 men of the Blaenavon lodge in July 1917, which melded opposition to the war with opposition to the 'comb-out':

> i) that this meeting of eight hundred men request an immediate conference for considering the best ways and means of bringing an end to the terrible slaughter which is going on in various parts of Europe today, and ii) we protest against any further comb out on the ground that is a scandalous waste of human life and because we firmly believe that the time has come when negotiations should begin.[239]

But some local lodges could give confused signals, and resistance to the 'comb-out' was not always synonymous with opposition to the war. The Coegnant lodge opposed the 'comb-out', but in July 1917 supported the action of Havelock Wilson's seamen's union in refusing to take British Labour delegates to the Stockholm peace conference. Yet two weeks later, the Coegnant lodge voted in favour of moves to secure an early end to the war.[240]

Ness Edwards, a supporter of the URC, and a conscientious objector, emphasised that opposition to conscription did not necessarily mean opposition to the war:

> It was an easy attitude to adopt among the miners, and found many adherents in the organisation, especially among those who believed in the War but preferred that others should do the fighting. The cowards and the courageous, the pacifist and the class conscious, all coalesced in this anti-conscription agitation.[241]

In an MFGB conference held on 7 September 1917, the proposition that the MFGB take no part in assisting in the recruitment of miners for the army was put forward from the south Wales, Somerset and the Forest of Dean areas. Both representatives from the Forest of Dean and Somerset complained that their mandate to oppose the 'comb-out' and

---

[239] Swansea University Archive, South Wales Coalfield Collection, UCS Blaenavon lodge minutes, 25 July 1917.
[240] Swansea University Archive, South Wales Coalfield Collection, UCS Coegnant lodge minutes, 7, 26 July 1917.
[241] Ness Edwards, *History of the South Wales Miners' Federation* (Lawrence and Wishart, 1938), p. 93.

to ballot for strike action had been influenced by 'an influx into my district of other men from some other county, who got among our young men and started the flame'.[242] Whilst they did not refer to south Wales by name, it resembled the modus operandi of the URC. The conference agreed to the 'comb-out' but subject to the unanimous agreement of all areas. In a stormy special conference of the SWMF on 8 October, the Executive Council's attempt to prevent the ballot was defeated by 1,712 to 897; the business committee subsequently prepared a motion that the 'comb-out' ballot be taken, and that the question asked should be:

> the South Wales Miners' Federation take no part in assisting in the Recruitment of Colliery Workers for the Army and Navy.

> Are you in favour of a down tools policy in South Wales in the event of the Government proceeding with their comb-out scheme in the mines?

> Yes/No.[243]

Tom Richards, SWMF's general secretary, whilst regretting the necessity for the ballot, hoped that the loyalty and patriotism of the Welsh miner would not fail:

> I shall be very astonished and grieved if it is not found to be above reproach. I am glad that the leaders, at least, have been convinced that it is their duty in this great crisis to act their part and perform the functions which they have been elected by their fellow-workmen to discharge; and they have given … their recommendation regarding downtools policy.

He warned that a rejection of the 'comb-out' would not lead to peace negotiations but would only 'deprive our kith and kin in the various battlefields of the necessary means of fighting against the devastating German hordes'.[244]

At the beginning of the campaign, the *Pioneer*'s editor had no doubt about the link between the ballot and peace. He saluted the south Wales miner for having 'so often and unmistakably expressed himself as the enemy of Militarism':

[242] Swansea University Archive, South Wales Coalfield Collection, Miners' Federation of Great Britain Special Conference minutes, September 1917.
[243] Page Arnot, *South Wales Miners*, p. 133.
[244] *Western Mail*, 24 October 1917.

'In South Wales he [the miner] is actively attached to the advanced Socialist wing of that [Labour] party. In that position, he is a vigorous exponent in peace time, as in war time, of the economic doctrine of a class war'.[245] The campaign itself was ill-tempered and immoderate, and portrayed by the belligerent press as a battle between pacifists, 'shirkers', and pro-Germans on the one hand, and patriots and supporters of the war effort on the other. The *Western Mail* encouraged the belief there were malign influences at work behind those opposed to the 'comb-out' and welcomed the authorities' investigation of the 'origin of pacifistic propaganda ... for the purpose of discovering the authors and the source of the financial assistance with which they appear to be lavishly endowed'. It criticised the government for being too lenient to 'these peculiar people', and accused 'pacificist agents', who appeared to be more numerous in south Wales than elsewhere, of having captured the trade union machinery on an extensive scale. It attributed the refusal of miners to support the 'comb-out' to a 'physical or moral cowardice, and in part to a selfishness of a most odious kind, especially in view of the fact that many of the SWMF's delegates were of military age'.[246]

The SWMF Executive Council issued a manifesto to the workmen urging them to vote and support the 'comb-out',[247] and in meetings in the coalfield, the virulently pro-war Miss E. Bowerman of the Women's Social and Political Union warned of German influence:

> pacifists were assisting international financiers of German origin who desired a compromised peace, and she advised Trades Unionists to attend their lodge meetings so that the views of the pacifist minority should not go out as the convictions of the patriotic majority of the workers.[248]

The Liberal *South Wales Daily News* blamed the ballot as having been engineered by a small minority bent on wrecking the Federation: 'They have rarely missed the opportunity of

---

[245] *Pioneer*, 13 October 1917.
[246] *Western Mail*, 9 October 1917.
[247] *Western Mail*, 20 October 1917.
[248] *South Wales Daily News*, 24 October 1917.

flouting their leaders in recent controversies, and their attitude has been determined largely by this perverse disposition and by the intrigues of a small pacifist group.'[249] Vernon Hartshorn, a leading member of the SWMF Executive and a scourge of the URC, described the ballot as one that had been 'forced upon us through the pro-Kaiser policy of peace-at-any price extremists'[250] and became increasingly vitriolic towards the URC, denouncing it as a secret caucus scheming to usurp the authority of the SWMF, with the aim of 'inducing a chaotic coalfield strike for the purpose of forcing a German-inspired surrender peace on the allies'.

Thomas Richards had also lost his customary forbearance by the end of the ballot campaign. After being heckled at the end of a miners' meeting by a 'prominent pacifist section of the audience ... many described as being young men holding extreme views', he replied that every man who voted 'Yes' for strike action would be voting in favour of Germany.[251] As the campaign wore on, more lodges supported the 'comb-out'. The *Pioneer* reported resolutions passed by seven lodges against down-tools, with only the Merthyr District and Cilfynydd passing a resolution in favour of a down-tools policy. Even those miners' leaders such as the president of the SWMF, James Winstone, who had spoken out previously in favour of a negotiated peace and against conscription, campaigned in favour of the 'comb-out'. Although Winstone deplored the hysteria and prejudice in the coalfield over the ballot, he warned that a vote for strike action would 'lead to nothing but disruption and anarchy', and he believed that its effect on the war would be disastrous, although paradoxically he disagreed with those who said it would benefit the enemy.[252]

The *Western Mail* trumpeted that pacifists were getting so alarmed at the probable result of the miners' ballot that on the last Saturday before the ballot, members of the URC held 'unofficial conferences' in Cardiff, Swansea and Newport to gather their supporters. The ferocity with which newspapers

[249] *South Wales Daily News*, 20 October 1917.
[250] *South Wales Daily News*, 24 October 1917.
[251] *South Wales Daily News*, 27 October 1917.
[252] *Western Mail*, 23 October 1917.

and executive members of the Federation targeted the activists of the URC caused Noah Tromans to criticise the 'vigorous press campaigns' and the attacks by miners' leaders that had been carried on during the past fortnight against active men in the organisation.[253] During the month leading up to the ballot, the 'War Aims' Committee organised a series of eight meetings to drum up support for the war, and the last meetings in the series, in Cardiff and Tonypandy, were addressed by the South African War leader, General Jan Smuts. The chairman of these meetings, William Brace, the Under-Secretary of State at the Home Office and miners' leader, was appalled by those who opposed the 'comb-out', and believed that 'the name of the South Wales miner was stinking all over the country ... and the ballot should not come off because if we were in Germany, we would not even be allowed to talk of a ballot'.[254] On the day of the vote, the *Western Mail* issued a rousing clarion call:

> the eyes of the Empire are turned on the Welsh coalfield to-day, and anxious hearts in the trenches are waiting to know the results of the voting. Let it be an emphatic and overwhelming repudiation of the wreckers of the Empire ... Fill up every ballot paper. Mark your cross against the word NO, and send that reply crashing into the eyes of those who would shelter the pacifists, the disloyalists and the cowards.[255]

The result of the ballot, by a margin of three to one, was a substantial victory for those who supported the 'comb-out'[256] and was heartily welcomed by the king.[257] One explanation for the result amongst those newspapers who supported the 'comb-out' was that the number who voted for strike action approximated to the 27,000 who had entered the industry since 1914. It was these 'refugees from the recruiting officer'[258] who would be selected as the most likely to serve, as a result of the 'comb-out' process, from amongst the

[253] *Western Mail,* 29 October 1917.
[254] *Pioneer,* 3 November 1917.
[255] *Western Mail,* 2 November 1917.
[256] *The Times,* 16 November 1917.
[257] *The Times,* 19 November 1917.
[258] *Western Mail,* 16 November 1917.

unmarried men fit to serve between the ages of 18 and 41. Clement Edwards, the Member of Parliament for South Glamorgan and persecutor of the URC, estimated that three out of every five who voted were of military age and thus liable to the 'comb-out', and therefore had a personal interest in its rejection.[259]

Following the vote, Clement Edwards MP made scurrilous and extravagant accusations of venality, corruption and bribery by 'German gold' against 'various syndicalists and pacifists' in their campaign to defeat the proposals for the 'comb-out':

> Secret conclaves have been held in different districts of the coalfield with the utmost regularity, and there has been wholesale canvass by professors of pacifism and advocated of syndicalism in favour of voting for down-tools. There has been money spent in great streams in South Wales, the likes of which we have not had with the ordinary syndicalist propaganda of the four or five years preceding the war ...
>
> Treating has not always been in the form of intoxicants – that is not suggested – but expensive cigars and expensive meals at well-known Cardiff restaurants have been a form of entertainment by 'Comrades' from colliery villages up the valleys. Railway fares have been paid, motor-cars have been hired, and all apparently out of the modest earnings of young day wagemen and very subordinate agents of syndicalism and pacifism from afar ... there has been carried on within the last 18 months or two years more active syndicalist propaganda than ever before.[260]

In Parliament, he questioned why more prosecutions had not been made in Glamorgan against those who had made 'seditious utterances'.[261]

The propaganda engendered by both local and British newspapers turned on the 'sinister' motives of those who agitated for the ballot. The editor of the conservative *Western Mail*, for instance, accused those opposed to the 'comb-out' of being disloyal 'pacifistics' and unpatriotic:

> certain men are attempting to use the Federation for the purpose of achieving objects of a grossly unpatriotic and seditious character,

---

[259] *The Times*, 12 November 1917.
[260] *Western Mail*, 15 November 1917.
[261] *Western Mail*, 15 November 1917.

which if carried out, would plunge the country and its Allies into difficulties, would endanger the fleets and armies and would cause the Welsh miner to be excoriated all over the world ... Let everyone, therefore, who values his country and his good name, and who is loyal to his relatives and comrades in the trenches, give a vote against this infamous and dastardly proposal to make the Welsh collier the ally of the Hun.[262]

SWMF Districts	For 'down-tools'	Against
Anthracite	4,588	6,000
Aberdare	2,079	3,633
Afan Valley	1,189	4,864
Blaina	1,183	2,148
Dowlais	1,033	1,848
Eastern Valley	894	4,823
East Glamorgan	477	4,136
Ebbw Vale	362	3,428
Garw	707	4,048
Maesteg	1,031	4,563
Merthyr	1,116	1,382
Monmouth Western Valley	1,753	5,752
Ogmore and Gilfach	332	3,262
Pontypridd and Rhondda	1,166	5,591
Rhondda No. 1	5,563	23,392
Rhymney Valley	909	7,141
Saundersfoot/Reynoldston	54	236
Taff and Cynon	466	4,129
Tredegar Valley	946	5,462
Western	3,056	3,308
Total	**28,903**	**98,946**

Table 4: The vote of the SWMF districts in the ballot to down tools in the event of the government proceeding with their 'comb-out' scheme in the mines[263]

The overall result of the ballot (see Table 4) was that 77 per cent had voted against the down-tools policy and less than 23 per cent in favour. Each one of the twenty districts of the

---

[262] *Western Mail*, 1 November 1917.
[263] *Western Mail*, 16 November 1917.

SWMF had voted in favour of the 'comb-out', but the size of the majority varied widely.

The greatest percentages of those who opposed the 'comb-out' came from the two western-most areas, the Anthracite District (43 per cent) and the Western District (48 per cent), and from the Merthyr, Dowlais and Aberdare districts (44 per cent) of the coalfield. Whilst the 5,563 who opposed the 'comb-out' in the URC's heartland in the Rhondda was a substantial number, it represented only 18.5 per cent of the total vote of 29,955 in the district.[264] The total turnout of 127,849 was 87 per cent of the possible turnout of 147,089.[265] The *Western Mail* alleged that this majority might have been even greater if miners in districts such as Risca had not refused to participate in the ballot in protest, because they believed that the war effort should be supported unconditionally.

The explanation given for the comparatively high minority vote in the Western and Anthracite Districts was that these districts had suffered more than any other area from the impact of the war, with local coal production being diverted from commercial to war work, and 'the better judgement of the men had been overborne by a settled cause of grievance'.[266] Two weeks after the ballot, a *South Wales Daily News* reporter travelled the coalfield in order to assess whether the opposition to the 'comb-out' was indeed caused by German bribery. He found that in the Western coalfield many collieries had been working on short time and that the want of employment had made the men 'restless and dissatisfied', so that while there was 'obvious pacifist feeling', he believed it could be countered by 'fairly regular work'. He thought the URC was responsible for spreading industrial discontent:

> I found that the leaflet of the URC, which works with somewhat secret methods within the ranks of the Federation had been sent to various lodges and distributed among the men. The members of the URC

[264] *Western Mail*, 16 November 1917.
[265] Swansea University, South Wales Coalfield Collection, Miners' Federation of Great Britain, Special Conference Credential Committee report, 8, 9 August 1917.
[266] Swansea University, South Wales Coalfield Collection, Special Conference report, 8, 9 August 1917.

however, contend that this leaflet was not in any sense a peace manifesto, but one which had purely an industrial object in view. The leaflet
itself was vaguely worded. It asked the workmen to 'read between the
lines' but it certainly does not contain any definite reference to peace
… It is not the cause of pacifist feeling, such as it is, but it may have
given a form of expression to some unrest previously existing.[267]

Frank Hodges, miners' agent for the Garw valley, had
supported the 'comb-out' but felt that the pressure for the
ballot emanated from an 'embittered political outlook'
and 'industrial resentment', which 'finds its expression in
a pacifist movement'. The reporter interviewed two of the
local leaders of the campaign to oppose the 'comb-out' in
the Rhondda, George Dolling and A. J. Cook. Both were
members of the URC, which, Cook explained to the reporter,
was a 'ginger group' within the Federation. They emphatically denied receiving any money for peace propaganda,
denied that the policy of the URC was pacifist and emphasised that the URC would accept the ballot result and take no
further action in the matter if the vote was lost.[268]

J. L. Rees, a prominent SWMF official of the Trebanos
Lodge in the Swansea Valley, a member of the URC and
involved in the local Plebs League classes, suggested that
anti-war feeling and the impact of the Russian Revolution
were the most significant factors in the comparatively high
vote against the 'comb-out' locally:

Down in the West great meetings have been held during the last two
years at which the impossibility or at least the costliness of the 'knock
out blow' has been advocated. The mass of miners in this district have
had that lesson driven into their minds and they realise that some
other way than conquest must be found from the impasse of war. The
way a large number of us think has been found in the Russian formula
of peace, and it cannot be doubted that this formula has seized the
imagination of thousands of miners down in the West.[269]

He denied that the reason why six of the seven lodges in
his area returned a majority for 'down-tools' was the influence of 'German gold', and welcomed any inquiry into the

[267] *South Wales Daily News*, 21 November 1917.
[268] *South Wales Daily News*, 21 November 1917.
[269] *South Wales Daily News*, 23 November 1917.

campaign's expenses that had been contributed by various trade unions in the locality.[270] Matthews considers that the ballot result in the anthracite district demonstrated 'the existence of a strong lobby for a termination of hostilities'.[271] The reasons for the opposition of other lodges to the 'comb-out' could also be traced to the influence of prominent URC members and active ILP branches. For instance, the only lodge in the Tredegar Valley district that voted against the 'comb-out' was chaired by Sidney Jones, a prominent URC member, and the 'foremost exponent of independent working class education in the Sirhowy Valley'.[272]

The *Western Mail* pressed the SWMF's Executive Council to take advantage of its victory to show greater moral fibre: 'the recent episode should stiffen the backbone of the council; it provides it with every justification to withstand the efforts of the extremists and to appeal to the general body of the miners should the delegate conference once be guilty of treacherous conduct'.[273] But criticism of the activists who campaigned for strike action was not confined to the opponents of the URC and the 'advanced men' within the Federation. The *Pioneer* blamed the press and the 'official coterie' of the SWMF for a 'campaign unsurpassed in the virulence of its abuse of opponents, in its hysteria and in its misrepresentation; a campaign so entirely one-sided as to give the lie to all idea of British fair-play and justice'.

But surprisingly, the *Pioneer*'s editorial declared for the first time its disagreement over the holding of the ballot, and revealed a fundamental split between the 'advanced men' and those who placed their trust in constitutional politics. The editor had failed to share his concern before the ballot was conducted:

> Personally we have all along felt that the ballot was a huge mistake from every point of view, and we have exhibited only regret that the industrial organisation of the miners should have been subjected to such a very risky experiment as its use for purposes quite outside of its

[270] *South Wales Daily News*, 23 November 1917.
[271] Matthews, 'The World of the Anthracite Coal Miner', p. 263.
[272] Susan E. Demont, 'Tredegar and Aneurin Bevan: A Society and its Political Articulation' (unpublished PhD thesis, Cardiff University, 1990), p. 158.
[273] *Western Mail*, 16 November 1917.

legitimate activities; an experiment calculated to introduce the seeds
of anarchy quite irrespective of the final result of the ballot.

The *Pioneer* believed the ballot had shown that whilst only
a minority favoured the 'out-and-out policy' of opposition
to the war, this number would add 'tremendously' to the
number of conscientious objectors, and the Federation
would take a more direct and active interest in the treatment
of conscientious objectors. The editor believed that the
ballot had displayed the limitations of industrial unionism
and 'even the most advanced unions are, outside of a few well
defined lines of action, floating aimlessly on an unchartered
sea'. However, he also warned that anyone who portrayed the
result as:

> a 'patriotic' answer to the German-gold-bought Pacifists of the
> S.W.M.F. is too superficially informed … His very belief that the ballot
> gives the quietus to pacifist effort on the part of the Federation, and
> commits it to a Jingoist policy shows his inability to grasp the issue. An
> inability that will have a rude awakening in the very near future.[274]

Another critic from the left, the revolutionary socialist J.
Walton Newbold, a supporter of the British Socialist Party,
an ILP candidate in the 1918 General Election and a close
friend of W. H. Mainwaring,[275] concluded that the result
of the ballot should not have been a surprise, given public
feeling about the war, and warned that the 'advanced men'
should not waste their efforts in an ineffectual peace movement, comparing it to 'trying to stop the Flying Scotchman
[*sic*] in full career by throwing one arm's round the smoke-
stack'. The opponents of the 'rank and file' movement, in his
view, constantly confused the public in south Wales as to the
identity and aims of this school, representing them as pacifists and at one in spirit and thought with the NCF, the UDC
and other similar 'individualist' organisations:

> let us hope that it will teach our pacifist friends that their tactics and
> their ideas have no attraction for the working class, and that they are

---

[274] *Pioneer*, 10 November 1917.
[275] Robert Duncan, 'John Turner Walton Newbold', *Dictionary of Labour Biography*,
vol. 10 (Palgrave Macmillan, 2000), pp. 150–6.

alien to the minds of the proletariat, however proper they were to those of the small traders and their kind.

Newbold's opinion of the strength of the anti-war movement in south Wales was influenced by his knowledge of the large ILP branch in the Merthyr and Aberdare areas, which he compared with other areas of the coalfield such as the Rhondda, where the tradition of independent working-class organisation was less rooted:

> It would be strange if all the work of the ILP and the Hardie tradition, the great Rink meetings, and the years of literature and lectures had had no effect. In other areas, where customary ILP methods of propaganda have been in vogue as long as those of the CLC classes system in the Rhondda, the results have not justified any such confidence in the efficiency of the former. Merthyr, Aberdare and Dowlais have historic traditions and a Radical tendency which go far to explain matters. The size of the minority vote is by no means disconcerting to those who know the ground and who recognise that great and enthusiastic audiences are often a mixed lot and comprise a very small proportion of the whole population.[276]

The delay of eleven months in the introduction of the 'comb-out' in the mining industry across Britain at the height of the war in 1917 was due totally to the intransigence of the south Wales miners. The factors that contributed to the ballot being won in favour of a 'comb-out' include the patriotism of the majority of south Wales miners, and their conviction that the miners should be seen to be supporting their comrades in the trenches. The immediate impact of the ballot result was that approximately 11,000 additional miners were conscripted into the army. In January 1918, the government again asked for a further 50,000 men from the mining industry, and the MFGB supported a resolution moved by south Wales that a ballot should be taken to ascertain whether the Federation should assist the government in 'combing out' more men. The government went on regardless, and whilst the ballot on 22 March 1918 produced a small majority against the 'comb-out', it did not reach the two-thirds majority threshold

---

[276] *Plebs Magazine*, December 1917.

for the MFGB to reject the scheme.[277] This suggests that the support for the 'comb-out', as shown in the November ballot, had waned by the following spring, whilst May considers that although the vote for industrial action was lost, it 'nonetheless popularised the concept throughout the coalfield'.[278]

The 'comb-out' ballot campaign gave added momentum to the URC, and in April 1918 it held a special conference to consider the further 'comb-out' and the implications of the recent ballot. The delegates represented nearly 100,000 of the south Wales miners, and they demanded that the Executive should call an official conference to explain to the rank and file why their decision on the 'comb-out' question should 'be diverted to a channel which the men never intended'. Several delegates alleged that the policy of the Executive was 'directed by outside influence'.[279] This demand was treated with contempt by Vernon Hartshorn, who described the URC as a 'set of nincompoops without the intelligence of a tom-tit', who had attempted unsuccessfully to dragoon the Executive into action. The result of the November 1917 ballot had 'put them in their proper place', and they did not possess any 'intellectual honesty'.

> They had their cronies on the E.C. [Executive Council] and had come to know that a conference was to be called in the proper constitutional manner. So they met and decided to hold an unofficial conference and passed resolutions and appointed a deputation to meet the Executive Council that day (Friday) to bring the necessary pressure to bear upon the E.C. to force a conference, and then they would turn round and say, 'We made them (the E.C.) call the conference.' But they were told by the E.C. to go home, and were not allowed an interview. (Cheers.)[280]

The immediate effect of the 'comb-out' in south Wales was a reduction in the number of working miners and in total output, leading to the rationing of coal. The 'comb-out' of men was effectively reversed by the summer of 1918, when the demand was for as many miners as the military could

[277] *Pioneer*, 30 March 1918.
[278] May, 'A Question of Control', p. 106.
[279] *South Wales Daily News*, 2 April 1918.
[280] *Pioneer*, 13 April 1918.

spare to be brought back into the mines.[281] The early post-war years would see the URC 'gain disproportionately large influence as circumstances changed in their favour',[282] but the effect of the 'comb-out' ballot was to energise the URC and the anti-war movement within the SWMF, and to radicalise the ordinary membership of the SWMF. The prominence of URC members and anti-war activists such as Noah Ablett, S. O. Davies, Arthur Horner, A. J. Cook and W. H. Mainwaring, who all gained key posts as miners' agents in 1918–19, reflected the Federation's growing industrial militancy and the influence of the rank and file.

In common with other industrial parts of Britain, the ILP provided an organisational framework for the anti-war movement in south Wales and ensured that opposition to the war was not merely confined to individual conscientious objectors. The moral case for peace was an important element of the ILP's collective political outlook, and it bridged the religious and political justification for opposing war. As the case studies of Merthyr Tydfil and Briton Ferry suggest, the ILP was an integral part of the community and its members played a significant part in its political and social life. They undoubtedly took a largely unpopular stance, yet in such areas they received succour and support from the wider community. Attitudes towards the war fluctuated dramatically, and ranged from the initial enthusiasm in August 1914 to a greater understanding of the 'grim reality of modern warfare' and a 'war weariness' as the casualty list grew.[283] By 1917 the introduction of military conscription, growing industrial militancy, and the excitement engendered by the Russian Revolution gave impetus to the left and its allies within the SWMF. An alliance between various strands, such as the ILP and the 'advanced men', coalesced within the URC and drove the political agenda within the SWMF from 1916 onwards, and whilst the vote against the 'comb-out' was defeated, it also marked the consolidation of the growing influence of the 'advanced men'.

[281] Page Arnot, *South Wales Miners*, p. 148.
[282] Burge, 'Labour, Class and Conflict', p. 320.
[283] Mari Williams, 'In the Wars: Wales 1914–1945', in Gareth Elwyn Jones and Dai Smith (eds), *The People of Wales* (Llandysul: Gomer Press, 1999), pp. 182–4.

As Smith and Francis suggest, the Great War quickened the pre-war processes in which the anti-capitalist views of many of the 'advanced men' developed into support for the Bolshevik Revolution and an international perspective 'rooted in the direct and indirect experience of the South Wales miners'.[284] Mounting concern about the growing influence of the left in the labour movement and its symbiotic relationship with the anti-war movement explains to a large extent why the security services became increasingly active against the left from 1917 onwards, and the perceived threat of Bolshevism ensured that the security services monitored their activity beyond the end of the war, in order to combat peacetime economic and political subversion.[285]

[284] Smith and Francis, *The Fed*, p. 28.
[285] Aled Eirug, 'Spies and Troublemakers in South Wales: How British intelligence targeted peace and labour activists in south Wales at the height of the Great War', *Llafur*, 12/1 (2016), 103–15.

3

THE ORGANISATION OF OPPOSITION – THE NATIONAL COUNCIL FOR CIVIL LIBERTIES AND THE NO-CONSCRIPTION FELLOWSHIP

A distinctive aspect of anti-war activity in Wales was the extent to which those trade unions and trades councils who were concerned by the extension of military conscription to industry combined with avowedly anti-war organisations, such as the Independent Labour Party (ILP) and the No-Conscription Fellowship (NCF). The National Council against Conscription, later re-named the National Council for Civil Liberties (NCCL), included these two elements, and its initial founders were the NCF and the Quakers' Friends' Service Committee, formed in November 1915 to lobby Members of Parliament to oppose conscription. In doing so, they also privately campaigned for a conscience exemption clause to be inserted in the Bill, whilst publicly opposing conscription.[1] London and Wales were the two areas of Britain where the NCCL was most successful in gaining trade union support for its aims and for mobilising trades councils and trade unions to oppose the extension of conscription.

The NCF was the only organisation specifically created to give a voice to those war resisters in Britain who became conscientious objectors. It gave practical and moral support to these young men, whose beliefs included a moral objection to carrying arms, but was not exclusively religious in believing that war was morally wrong. These conscientious objectors included Christians who rejected state violence and those who opposed an imperialist war, or that conscription should be opposed because it was a 'fatal infringement of human liberty'. All of these views were represented, and

---

[1] T. C. Kennedy, *The Hound of Conscience* (Fayetteville: University of Arkansas Press, 1981), pp. 78–81.

views shifted and changed in response to their experiences as conscientious objectors.[2] In Wales, the organisers of both bodies were interchangeable and mutually supportive in spite of their ostensibly different aims.

THE NATIONAL COUNCIL FOR CIVIL LIBERTIES

The failure of the 1915 Derby scheme's canvass of eligible men for voluntary enlistment led to the Military Service Act of January 1916, which conscripted all unexempted single men and childless widowers between the ages of 18 and 41. The ILP's *Labour Leader* threatened that if the government continued 'its foolish attempts to impose military servitude upon the people of this country, it will meet with a resistance which may easily develop into revolution'.[3]

The NCCL's objectives were to work for the repeal of the Military Service Act, to prevent conscription from becoming a permanent part of British life, and to safeguard all civil liberties. It attempted to broaden its support beyond the ILP, the NCF and the Union of Democratic Control (UDC), and one of the UDC's paid organisers, Bernard Langdon-Davies, became its first secretary, whilst Robert Smillie, the anti-war President of the Miners' Federation of Great Britain, became President of the NCCL. Its executive included the NCF chairman, Clifford Allen, Dr Henry Hodgkin of the Fellowship of Reconciliation, the ILP leader George Lansbury, and the trade unionist leader Robert Williams. It included both pro- and anti-war campaigners, and was initially created as a body of some fifty people, most of whom were prominent in labour or civil libertarian politics.[4]

The government regarded the NCCL as dangerously subversive and consisting of active opponents of the war, 'who have not raised a finger to help their country in her hour of need'.[5] The NCCL's first meeting in Wales, in

---

[2] *No-Conscription Fellowship Souvenir 1914–1919* (NCF, 1919), pp. 8–10.

[3] *Labour Leader*, 6 January 1916.

[4] Keith Robbins, *The Abolition of War: The 'Peace Movement' in Britain, 1914–1919* (Cardiff: University of Wales, 1976), p. 75.

[5] Kennedy, *The Hound of Conscience*, citing MI5 report, HO45/10801/307402, 78–81, NA.

February 1916, in Briton Ferry, illustrated the precarious balance the new organisation attempted to achieve between those who opposed the war, and those whose sole aim was to oppose conscription. Its organiser in south Wales and Monmouthshire, Ivor Thomas, was at pains to state that the NCCL was not an anti-war movement as such, and insisted that its object was to 'protect the democracy, and if possible to prevent the Conscription Act being placed on the Statute Book or to secure its repeal'. He refuted the accusation that the campaign was aimed at discouraging men to join the army, but the chairman of the meeting disallowed a question as to whether Thomas and the organisers had done anything to encourage voluntary recruiting. The vote to create a branch was passed, but the division between those who supported the war effort and those who opposed it was clear in the debate.[6]

Although Thomas may have wished to convey the impression that the NCCL welcomed pro-war elements, he was personally firmly anti-war. His role as Wales's representative on the ILP's National Advisory Council and his activity in the Briton Ferry NCF placed him in the engine-room of the anti-war movement in south Wales. His links with the labour movement were crucial to his effectiveness, and before the war he had been a member of the national executive of the Dockers' Union, whilst after the war he became the Labour Party agent for the sitting MP, Ramsay MacDonald, in Aberavon. Another key figure in the anti-conscription campaign was Morgan Jones, who was elected President of the South Wales Council against Conscription, as well as chairing the ILP in Wales, and also served as Wales's representative on the National Committee of the NCF.[7] The national organiser of the NCCL was Catherine Marshall, who had headed the NCF's political lobbying operation in its first two years and been its secretary.[8] She recognised the NCCL's success in Wales in attracting the trade unions and labour and trades councils to its anti-conscription message, described Ivor Thomas as an 'extremely effective organiser',

---

[6] *South Wales Daily Post*, 24 February 1916.
[7] *The Labour Who's Who, 1927* (Labour Publishing Company, 1927), p. 217.
[8] Kennedy, *The Hound of Conscience*, pp. 95, 107–11.

and related how, in the autumn and winter of 1917, he organised a 'raging, tearing campaign' in south Wales in order to persuade miners' lodges and divisions to affiliate to the NCCL, in the face of the growing threat of conscription and the 'comb-out' ballot within the coal industry. His work mainly consisted of circularising trades and labour councils, visiting and addressing trade union branches, arranging for the sale and distribution of literature, liaising chiefly with the ILP, and organising large conferences on such matters as the threat of industrial conscription, and militarism and education.

Marshall considered that the NCCL's success in Wales in attracting 195 organisational affiliations by July 1918 was due 'from 80 to 90% to Thomas's efforts'. She stressed that each affiliation meant not merely that 'our propaganda has spread to that organisation but that something of what we stand for has gone to a number of other organisations at the same time'. She emphasised Thomas's value as a local organiser:

> the fact of these affiliations being due to a local organiser is perhaps shown by the comparison of the affiliations of Wales and London on the one hand, in both of which we have a local organiser, and of Scotland and Lancashire, where we have not on the other. They are Wales 195; London and Home Counties 468; Lancashire 92; Scotland 142.[9]

Significantly, Marshall also noted that whilst the affiliations for Lancashire and Scotland were mainly branches of overtly anti-war organisations, the affiliations in Wales and London were predominantly from trade unions and less dependent on the membership of the ILP, NCF and UDC, whilst Wales's fundraising record for the NCCL was markedly better than other districts. The NCCL accounts for 1917 showed 1,105 affiliated organisations in Britain, exclusive of Wales, contributing £322 each, an average of 5s. 9d per organisation. In Wales 195 organisations contributed an average total of £128 each, an average of 13s. 2d per organisation, contributing over double on average for each affiliate. Ivor

---

[9] Cumbria Archives, Catherine Marshall Papers, D/MAR/4/95, 'Report on the organisation of the NCCL in Wales, 1 July 1918'.

Thomas received £200 per year salary and approximately £80 of expenses, and whilst this represented about one-sixth of the total spent on salaries, he had collected considerably more than one-third of the total affiliation fees.[10] Thomas's work resulted in the rapid growth of local anti-conscription councils throughout the region in the first half of 1916, and Anti-Conscription Leagues were set up in the Rhondda, Swansea Valley, Aberbargoed, Merthyr Tydfil, Aberdare, the Rhondda and Briton Ferry.[11]

The anti-conscription campaign in Wales was led in key industrial areas, such as the Rhondda and the eastern Monmouthshire valleys, by members of the Unofficial Reform Committee.[12] The creation of the Rhondda Anti-Conscription Committee, for instance, was heralded by the *Pioneer* not as another 'cranky pacifist organisation', but as a 'determined corporate body of Trade Unionists, Industrialists and Socialists who carry with them the huge masses of the workers'. If conscription was implemented, this organisation, it was said, would take around 'a fiery cross' to 'awaken the proletariat in the coalfield to a determination such as it has never seen even in its historic resistance in industrial warfare'.[13] The Committee's manifesto concentrated on the danger of conscription being introduced into the mining industry, in particular, and warned against the resultant undermining of the trade unions:

> The menace of conscription is upon us. It is creeping on in such an insidious form that most of the trade unionists of the country seem to be unaware of its proximity … We are therefore justified in assuming that there are ulterior motives in the minds of those who promote the scheme. It is being pushed and advertised by a powerful section of capitalists, who, by means of their great influence with the press, use every opportunity to further the agitation.[14]

The *Pioneer* reflected that the alliance of miners and railway, engineering and transport workers, who were mostly

---

[10] Cumbria Archives, Catherine Marshall Papers, 'Report on the organisation of the NCCL in Wales', D/MAR/4/95, 'Report on the organisation of the NCCL in Wales', 1 July 1918.

[11] *Pioneer*, January–May 1916.

[12] Burge, 'Labour, Class and Conflict', p. 323.

[13] *Pioneer*, 1 January 1916.

[14] *Pioneer*, 1 January 1916

exempt at the time, could soon come under the 'tyranny' of conscription.[15] The conference called by the Rhondda Anti-Conscription League in January 1916 was held in Cardiff and brought together over a hundred delegates of trade union lodges, branches of the ILP, the NCF, socialist societies and 'all the revolutionary and fiery spirits in South Wales', such as Noah Ablett and A. J. Cook.[16] It called for a propaganda war against conscription and unanimously adopted a radical resolution that went much further than any action being considered by the anti-conscription movement elsewhere, in calling for a 'down-tools' policy to be initiated on the day that conscription became law. The meeting also concluded that if England refused to take part in industrial action, south Wales should go it alone. The meeting included many of the younger Marxist miners' leaders who had been at Ruskin College, Oxford and opposed the war on revolutionary grounds. But whilst Emrys Hughes recalled a good attendance there, with many delegates from the miners' lodges in particular, and whilst he felt it represented an undoubted growing anti-war feeling, he questioned whether there was popular support for a strike against conscription at the time:

> two or three delegates (were) quite insistent that it would be successful, and when I doubted it, I met with some criticism. But it was quite evident that apart from a few districts, there was absolutely no prospect of the rank and file of the miners being prepared to strike on that issue:

> The conference agreed to send a deputation to visit Clydeside to assess rumours that there was a strike there against conscription. But when the deputation reported back, it was evident that no such event had occurred, and the leaders in Clydeside held out no hopes of any effective action against the Government's policy. In fact, things were very much the same in Glasgow as they were in south Wales ... There would be no popular revolt against conscription, the Derby scheme had paved the way well enough to safeguard against that. Individuals who intended to fight conscription would have to go out alone.[17]

[15] *Pioneer*, 1 January 1916.

[16] National Library of Scotland, Keir Hardie and Emrys Hughes Papers, Dep. 176, Box 8/1, 'Welsh Rebel', p. 78; 'Pulpits and Prisons', p. 85.

[17] National Library of Scotland, Keir Hardie and Emrys Hughes Papers, Dep. 176, 'The Journal of a Coward', p. 25.

An undated list of the 179 NCCL's branches throughout Britain, obtained by the security services, included a total of twenty branches in Wales, mostly located in those areas where the ILP was at its strongest. They were concentrated in Swansea, Swansea Valley, the Afan Valley, the western Monmouthshire valleys, Cardiff and Merthyr, and the only branch outside the proximity of the south Wales coalfield was in Caernarfon, where the ILP remained influential.[18]

From the summer of 1916, the NCCL attempted to organise large conferences in south Wales to oppose the extension of conscription into civilian life. The first, held in Swansea in August 1916, went off without incident, and the delegate list exemplifies the coalition of groups that came together to oppose conscription. There were delegates representing a total of fifty-eight trade unions, eleven trades councils and three co-operative societies, in addition to eight NCF branches, twenty-one branches of the ILP and three of the Women's Labour League, one women's co-operative guild and eleven 'religious societies' (mostly individual chapels). The chairman, Swansea-based John Twomey, General Secretary of the National Amalgamated Labourers' Union, described the campaign's 'uphill fight', as its active supporters had been gaoled, their homes raided, and they had been forced to become conscientious objectors. The formal resolution passed in the meeting warned of what it considered to be the inevitable step from military to industrial conscription:

> this conference, holding that Military Compulsion cannot be separated from Industrial Compulsion, and that this form of compulsion in the workshops endangers the whole standard of industrial conditions and places the men in the mines, the factories, railways, docks, etc., practically under military or semi-military law, and that this puts a weapon of great power in the hands of private employers working for their own profits and dividends, pledges itself to offer unrelenting opposition to any such proposals.

---

[18] National Archives, Security Services Papers, KV 2/665. The NCCL branches were Ystradgynlais, Aberavon, Gorseinon, Glais, Port Talbot, Swansea, Maesteg, Cardiff, Splott, Barry, Bargoed, Troedyrhiw, Merthyr, Rhondda, Tredegar, Nantyglo, Brynmawr, Blaina, Brithdir, Pontypool and Caernarfon.

The speakers were all recognised anti-war activists. Twomey was joined on the platform by W. C. Anderson, MP, Councillor Stan Awbery of the Swansea ILP, Harry Thomas, representing the National Amalgamated Labourers' Union, and Councillor David Williams, a respected trade unionist and local magistrate who would become the Labour MP for Swansea East in 1922.[19]

The second large-scale meeting to be organised by the NCCL in Wales in 1916 was due to take place in Cardiff at the Cory Hall, on 11 November. It was to be chaired by James Winstone, miners' agent and President of the South Wales Miners' Federation, and J. H. Thomas, the railwaymen's leader, and Ramsay MacDonald, MP, were scheduled to speak. The speakers reflected the breadth of opposition to conscription and was not limited to anti-war speakers. Thomas, whilst actively supporting recruiting for the army, viewed compulsory military service as the inevitable precursor to industrial compulsion. Whilst Winstone would gradually develop a view in favour of peace by negotiation in 1917, he was certainly not opposed to the conduct of the war at this time. There were 900 in the audience, including 445 registered delegates, representing 290 trade union branches; thirty-seven trades and labour council delegates, representing a total of 81,000 affiliated members; 100 representatives of Socialist and Peace Societies, and two adult school delegates, representing 7,375 members; thirteen religious organisations, representing a total of 1,500; sixteen Co-operative delegates, representing a membership of 23,000; and women's societies sent twenty-nine delegates, representing 687 members.[20]

However, the meeting was disrupted by a mob, organised by Captain Atherley Jones, a 'one-time National Service League organiser, a failed recruiting officer and semi-professional rabble rouser',[21] and led by two jingoists, the mercurial C. B. Stanton, Hardie's successor as MP for Merthyr Boroughs, and Captain Tupper of the Seamen's Union.

---

[19] *Pioneer*, 26 August 1916.
[20] *Pioneer*, 18 November 1916.
[21] Brock Millman, *Managing Domestic Dissent in First World War Britain* (London: Frank Cass, 2000), p. 150.

Millman exaggerates the impact of this disruption, termed 'The Battle of Cory Hall', which illustrated the conflict between pro-war and anti-war elements in south Wales. He states that 'ultimately it put paid to the effort to consolidate dissent into a combination capable, in 1916, of shifting the national agenda',[22] but his judgement is coloured by his failure to examine its aftermath, and to consider that the meeting was subsequently reconvened to the Rink in Merthyr Tydfil the following month, where a 'an impressive unity of purpose' was displayed.[23]

The more sober assessment by the intelligence services of the events surrounding the disruption of the anti-conscription meeting in the Cory Hall highlighted the strength and potential of the anti-war movement rather than the success of the 'patriots' in disrupting the conference. The rescheduled meeting was held on Saturday 9 December 1916, and the crowd of over 2,500 people were drawn from all parts of south Wales, with individuals from as far as London and the Midlands. In comparison with the Cory Hall conference, there was an increase of twenty-five per cent in registered delegates, from 445 to 593. These delegates represented an aggregate membership of 324,767, as against the 445 delegates representing 220,000 people in Cardiff. These included 307 trades union delegates, representing 89,000 members; sixty-two Labour parties and trades councils, with an affiliated membership of 197,684; twenty Co-operative societies, representing 27,410; twenty-nine women's organisations, representing 785 members; thirty-one church organisations, representing 2,100 members; 139 socialist Peace Societies, representing 7,120 members; and fifteen 'unclassified' delegates.[24]

The meeting drew together a wide cross-section of opinion that went beyond the anti-war movement, and included those opposed to the further encroachment of the state in extending conscription. The delegates' torrid experience of the Cardiff mob seems to have steeled the Merthyr delegates, and the *Pioneer*'s editor argued that the destructive tactics of

[22] Millman, *Managing Domestic Dissent in First World War Britain*, p. 138.
[23] Millman, *Managing Domestic Dissent in First World War Britain*, pp. 138–66.
[24] *Pioneer*, 16 December 1916.

the disruptive 'patriots' had encouraged more delegates to attend:

> I spoke with several delegates before the meeting who did not see eye to eye with me on the pacifist position, but their determination to preserve the right of free speech, of open discussion, was something to remember ... I believe that it was the opposition of the rank and file of democracy to these that had determined many of the lodges and unions who were not represented at Cardiff to send delegates to Merthyr, and thus was explained the great increase in the delegates.[25]

Whilst not a pacifist, Winstone set out his opposition to industrial conscription and the present conduct of the war, and supported 'peace by negotiation'. He condemned the government for its insistence on fighting the war 'to the finish', and its lack of clarity on its war aims. He was glad to see, he said that there was 'growing up in every country involved in this terrible war a peace party which is growing in strength from day to day'. Ramsay MacDonald then moved a motion expressing alarm at the reduction in civil liberties, and the pacifist Mrs Swanwick's motion demanded peace by negotiation. The conference then called on the government to review and correct what was termed the disastrous administration of the Military Service Act, in relation to conscientious objection, domestic hardship and to any further extension of the Act.

J. H. Thomas, who had recruited actively for the army, avowed that whilst he was not anti-war, he was certainly anti-conscription. To large cheers, he lent support to MacDonald, and, although they disagreed on their attitudes to the war, yet defended his right to state his views: 'I am not going to stand by and allow a man like MacDonald, because he is temporarily unpopular, to be hounded out of public life by men who are today enjoying what he is responsible for.' The motion that military compulsion should cease was moved by Thomas and seconded by the local miners' activist Noah Tromans, Mountain Ash, who warned prophetically that industrial action was inevitable, and that 'in all probability, in the event of a struggle for industrial freedom coming, the

[25] *Pioneer*, 16 December 1916 .

brunt would fall on the south Wales miners'.[26] This show of unity against the extension of conscription into civilian life and against the operation of military conscription reflected the NCCL's strategy of bringing together the anti-war movement with the wider labour movement, and the impressive array of sixty-two local Labour parties and labour and trades councils represented a significant achievement for the NCCL's organisers, and for Ivor Thomas in particular. From December 1916 onwards, the NCCL concentrated on developing the opposition to the extension of conscription in the essential industries, and within the mining industry in particular.

The influence of the NCCL can be traced to Ivor Thomas's activities in this period, and his energetic attempts to secure the support of Federation lodges and districts. He reported on 1 November 1917, on the eve of the momentous ballot on the 'comb-out' of men in the mining industry, that he had received only one refusal among fourteen districts of the Federation he had requested to affiliate, and on 4 November, he reported that out of the nineteen districts, comprising 417 lodges of the SWMF, a total of ten districts, comprising 201 lodges, had affiliated.[27] This spate of activity coincided with the virulent and highly charged campaign conducted in south Wales over the 'comb-out' ballot.

Marshall highlighted the advantage of having a local organiser for such a large area as Wales 'as the geographical and other conditions are exceedingly difficult', and she cited Thomas's organisation of conferences on the theme of militarism in schools in north Wales in support.[28] This north Wales conference in Llandudno was described by the *Pioneer's* editor, perhaps with some exaggeration, as one in which 'the whole weight of north Wales Nonconformity will join in with the Labour elements in the area in setting about the establishment of a first line of resistance to the most sinister and

---

[26] *Pioneer*, 16 December 1916.

[27] National Archives, Security Service Papers, KV/665, seized NCCL papers following a police raid by Scotland Yard on its offices.

[28] Cumbria Archives, Catherine Marshall Papers, D/Mar 4/95, 'Report on the organisation of the National Council of Civil Liberties in Wales to the Executive committee of the National Council for Civil Liberties, 1 July, 1918'.

[29] *Pioneer*, 22 June 1918.

dangerous movement that Militarism has yet made in this nation'.[29] Its ostensible aim was to oppose the introduction of military education into schools, but in addition to the involvement of the NCCL, the conference included a number of prominent anti-war activists in north Wales, including Principal Thomas Rees, Revd H. Harris Hughes, Bangor, and Principal John Graham, Manchester, and it was addressed by a number of local religious and trade union leaders, including Revd H. Barrow Williams, Llandudno, and S. Rowlands from the National Union of Railwaymen. The conference secretary, J. E. Thomas, Penygroes, a prominent member of the ILP, informed delegates of the aims of the NCCL and asserted that the conference represented most Nonconformist chapels in Meirion, Arfon and Anglesey. Present were 173 church and chapel representatives, twelve representatives of local Free Church councils, and ten from trade union and labour councils, and letters had also been received from a further fifty-nine churches supporting the aims of the conference.[29]

This conference reflected the NCCL's attempt in north Wales to unite the anti-war movement with those elements who were concerned with the militarisation of schools, and the unanimous vote for the motion that opposed military exercises for children under 18 reflected a consensus that went beyond the anti-war movement. Speakers such as Revd H. Barrow Williams were anxious to assure listeners that they did not wish to inhibit the government's efforts to win the war:

> ond yr oeddynt am i'r Llywodraeth brysuro i'w chael i ben gyda sefydliad heddwch cyfiawn, anrhydeddus a sefydlog.[30]

> (but they wanted the Government to bring it [the war] to an end with the creation of a just, honourable and stable peace)

An indication of the broadening influence of the NCCL in Wales after the end of the war were the anti-conscription protests held on the fourth anniversary of the Military Service Act, on Sunday 2 March 1919. Meetings to call for the

---

[29] *Y Dinesydd Cymreig*, 24 July 1918.
[30] *Y Dinesydd Cymreig*, 24 July 1918.

repeal of the Act were held in sixteen towns across Wales and included speakers, such as the pro-war Vernon Hartshorn, newly elected Member of Parliament for Ogmore, who months earlier might have baulked at sharing a platform with the NCCL. In Maesteg, before 1,200 people, he joined with the NCCL and the local labour and trades council to call for the end of conscription. Similar meetings were meet throughout south Wales, and in Merthyr, for instance, 2,000 people at the Rink heard John Bromley, secretary of the Amalgamated Society of Locomotive, Enginemen and Firemen, and the local miners' agent, Noah Ablett, call for the repeal of the Military Service Act.[31]

The significance of the NCCL during the war lay in its ability to provide a bridge between the anti-war movement, the trade union movement, and the trades and labour councils. It stoked the fear of the further extension of military conscription and the creation of civilian conscription within vital industries, such as coal, steel, tinplate and transport. Whereas the NCCL gained most support in other parts of Britain from predictable sources of opposition to the war, such as the ILP, NCF and the UDC, the particular strength of the NCCL in Wales, as in London, lay in its ability to gain support from trade unions and trades councils to campaign against the extension of conscription. In doing so, it also broadened the extent of anti-war activity in Wales from the end of 1916 onwards to include support for the Russian Revolution, demands for a negotiated peace, and opposition to conscription within the mining industry. The personal connections and influence of its organiser, Ivor Thomas, within the labour movement and the ILP in Wales were crucial, and he embodied the symbiotic relationship between the NCCL, the trade union movement, trades and labour councils (often dominated by the ILP) and the anti-war movement.

[31] *Pioneer*, 8 March 1919.

THE NO-CONSCRIPTION FELLOWSHIP IN WALES

From the outset, a 'conscience clause' was included in the Military Service Act in January 1916, which provided that those with a conscientious objection to military service could be granted various forms of exemption from conscription by applying to a tribunal system. The new Act created a category of men described as conscientious objectors and defined as men whose bona fides were established by a tribunal, or who, having failed to satisfy or appear before a tribunal, still refused combatant service on conscientious grounds.[32]

The military was ill-equipped and increasingly unprepared to deal with this novel phenomenon. Those conscientious objectors who were prepared to work under the authority of the army joined the Friends' Ambulance Unit (FAU), the Non-Combatant Corps (NCC), or, in certain circumstances, the Royal Army Medical Corps (RAMC), and from the summer of 1916, opportunities to engage in 'work of national importance' were also provided, primarily through the Home Office Scheme, whilst a comparatively small number were directed to the Pelham Committee's schemes for employment. But of the 16,500 conscientious objectors, there were almost 6,000 conscientious objectors who either refused to accept the tribunals' decision or failed to apply to a tribunal on the ground of conscientious objection, and after initial periods in prison for these men, from July 1916 inwards they were subsequently offered alternatives to military service.[33] Most accepted the government's alternative schemes, although approximately one-twelfth of the total of conscientious objectors, including approximately eighty men from Wales, brooked no compromise and became 'absolutists'.

To the extent that such a varied group of independently minded and wilful men could be organised, it was the NCF who supported conscientious objectors, through its branches, its visitors, its information bureau, and its political

---

[32] John Rae, *Conscience and Politics: The British Government and the Conscientious Objector to Military Service 1916–1919* (Oxford: Oxford University Press, 1970), pp. 14–21, 70.
[33] National Archives, Ministry of Health Papers 47/3, 'Report of the Brace Committee's Central Tribunal', February 1919, p. 24.

campaigning and lobbying of politicians to improve conditions for conscientious objectors. This section considers the organisation and activity of the NCF and its significance to the wider anti-war movement in Wales.

The NCF was created in the spring of 1915, following an appeal by the editor of the *Labour Leader*, Fenner Brockway, and described itself as an organisation of 'men created to refuse from conscientious motives to undertake military service and bear arms and that it would oppose every effort to introduce compulsory military service into Great Britain'. This call to action attracted over 16,000 young men, whose religious and political beliefs were 'as various as the nation's religions and political theories'.[34] Its first Convention, in April 1916, attracted 1,500 delegates, representing 10,000 members,[35] and the majority of members resisted the war on religious grounds, and drew inspiration from the Christian tradition of pacifism. Only about a tenth of conscientious objectors described themselves as socialists, but it was they, and specifically the young members of the ILP, who invariably led the work of the NCF and composed its officers and activists. Brockway became its secretary, and Clifford Allen, born in Newport, a member of the ILP's City of London branch, was appointed chairman. The political background of most of its leaders was overwhelmingly that of the Independent Labour Party, and on its executive committee the ILP members included C. H. Norman, James H. Hudson, a Lancashire schoolmaster, William J. Chamberlain, a journalist on the *Daily Citizen*, and south Wales's representative, Councillor Morgan Jones, from Bargoed in the Rhymney Valley.

In May 1916 most of the NCF's national executive committee, including Morgan Jones, were arrested under the Defence of the Realm Act for publishing the leaflet *Repeal the Act*, that the authorities thought contained material prejudicial to the recruitment to and discipline in His Majesty's forces. They were fined a hundred pounds, and Jones was imprisoned, before then being re-arrested and imprisoned

---

[34] *The No-Conscription Fellowship*, p. 8.
[35] Kennedy, *The Hound of Conscience*, p. 280.

for his conscientious objection to military service in June 1916. His organisational roles illustrate the close links between the various anti-war and anti-conscription organisations in south Wales in this period, for in addition to his membership of the NCF national committee, he was chairman of the ILP in Wales and President of the South Wales Council against Conscription.[36] After the war, he became the first conscientious objector to be elected as a Member of Parliament, in the 1921 Caerphilly by-election.[37]

The symbiotic relationship between the ILP and NCF is illustrated by the correspondence between the secretary of the NCF Aberdare branch and Percy Wall, an imprisoned conscientious objector from the area:

> Your stand as an Absolutist is much appreciated by the Branch Percy ... the Branch members are anxious to welcome you back to the District ... today you are a Comrade and friend of the Aberdare NCF and ILP who will never be forgotten. Keep the flag flying Percy.[38]

The active membership of both organisations, as in Aberdare, were often one and the same. At the end of the war, the *Welsh Outlook* described Aberdare as an area where 'speakers who were bitterly assailed in other parts of the country, received attentive audiences'.[39]

In the British context, the NCF allied closely with two organisations of Christian pacifists, the Young Men's Service Committee of the Society of Friends, and the Fellowship of Reconciliation. The former represented those Quakers of military age who adhered to the Society's traditional rejection of military service, whilst the latter united Christian pacifists from most denominations. This alliance helped to coordinate resistance to conscription, though for some members of the NCF 'the sanctity of human life was a flag of convenience rather than a banner of faith',[40] but in Wales, the Quakers were numerically insignificant. Whilst the FoR

---

[36] *Llais Llafur*, 3 June 1916.
[37] Dylan Rees, 'Morgan Jones, educationalist and Labour politician', *Morgannwg*, 31 (1987), 66–83.
[38] Imperial War Museum, Percy Wall Papers, 86/53/1, 14 April 1918.
[39] *Welsh Outlook*, 'Aberdare 1910–1920 – a Social Study' (January 1922).
[40] Rae, *Conscience and Politics*, p. 12.

was weak or non-existent in south Wales, it was an important presence in north Wales, in particular, where it was centred on the Bala-Bangor Theological College.[41] Much of the NCF's energy was directed towards blending its diverse elements into a united anti-conscription and anti-war movement, but much of its weakness lay in the political and religious diversity of its membership. The well-known journalist Percy Ogwen Jones, from Anglesey, compared his fellow conscientious objectors to dissimilar threads of a rope:

> Rhaff ac iddi amryw geinciau oedd mudiad heddychwyr 1914–1918. Ar un ystyr nid oedd yn fudiad o gwbl: yn hytrach damwain a chyd-ddigwydd a ddug y ceinciau hyn at ei gilydd yn un rhaff, a Deddf Gorfodaeth 1916 a wnaeth y rhaff.[42]

> (The pacifist movement in 1914–1918 was like a rope with many strands. In one respect it was not a movement at all; rather, it was accident and coincidence that brought these strands together into a rope, and it was the Conscription Act 1916 that made the rope.)

The first south Wales branch was set up in June 1915 in Briton Ferry, and in the following weeks, local groups were set up in Monmouthshire, Cardiff, Mid Glamorgan and the Swansea area.[43] The Fellowship's manifesto appeared on 11 September 1915 on the *Pioneer*'s front page, and Emrys Hughes, Abercynon, one of the most prominent members of the ILP in south Wales, and one of the earliest members of the NCF, set the resistance to conscription in the context of pre-war industrial unrest and struggle in south Wales:

> if the Bill becomes law, there will be resistance and determined resistance throughout the country, and south Wales will again do its share. In the Valleys we have seen the cavalry clattering up the hills to intimidate the strikers of Tonypandy and Aberdare. These facts are not easily forgotten.[44]

If the government was to introduce conscription, he warned the NCF would fill the prisons:

[41] T. Eirug Davies, *Prifathro Thomas Rees* (Llandysul: Gwasg Gomer, 1939), p. 70.
[42] Percy Ogwen Jones, *Ceinciau Cymysg*, 6 November 1964 (BBC Radio Talk), p. 3.
[43] *Llais Llafur*, 19 June 1915.
[44] *Pioneer*, 15 December 1915.

we will not be Conscripts. The South Wales Valleys have seen many
struggles for liberty and freedom; Keir Hardie is dead but the idea
is alive, and when the time comes we will be true to the memory of
Hardie and fight conscription whatever the consequences may be.[45]

The authorities kept a close eye on the NCF from March
1915 onwards, and the Attorney General was warned by intelligence services that the 5 August 1915 edition of the *Labour
Leader* had contained a direct incitement by the NCF not to
obey the Munitions of War Act 1915, and that this 'mischief'
had been 'gravely enhanced by the success' of Mr Clifford
Allen's proselytising efforts in South Wales.[46]
    By October 1915, over fifty branches had been formed
throughout Britain, with a membership of over 5,000. At
NCF's first national convention in November 1915, each
branch was advised to set up a committee of 'six energetic
and able' associate members, who would henceforth meet
with the regular branch committee to become familiar with
the activity of the branch.
    NCF membership was initially only open to young men
who were liable to be conscripted, but it then agreed to
accept women and older men as associate members. During
the first six months of 1915, due to its belief that the government was keen on crushing the NCF, a 'complex and
clandestine infrastructure' of autonomous local groups was
created, with safe methods of communication and a system
in which every official would have a shadow or replacement,
who would automatically assume his position if they were
arrested or otherwise neutralised.[47] The decision to admit
associate members seemed to be incidental at the time, but
eventually it proved to be momentous for the viability of the
organisation.
    By May 1916, Wales had twenty-three branches of the NCF,
primarily in West Glamorgan, Cardiff, Swansea, the Aberdare
and Merthyr areas, and the western valleys of Monmouthshire
(see Table 5). The administrative office for south Wales was

[45] *Pioneer*, 1 January 1916.
[46] National Archives, Home Office Papers, HO45/10786/297549/10, cited in
Kennedy, *Hound of Conscience*, p. 64.
[47] Kennedy, *Hound of Conscience*, pp. 65, 66; Rae, *Conscience and Politics*, p. 12.

Briton Ferry	H. Armstrong
Cwmavon	J. Morris
West Glamorgan	W. J. Roberts, Gorseinon
Port Talbot	Councillor T. Mainwaring
Swansea	Miss M. Harris, c/o Swansea Socialist Centre, the 'Bomb Shop'
Swansea Valley	Tom Evans, Ynismudw
Aberdare	J. Thomas BA, Aberdare
Abercynon	J. R. Taylor
Bargoed	Moses Price
Cardiff	E. F. Williams
Mid Glamorgan	T. Mainwaring
Maesteg	A. Jones
Merthyr	A. Brobin
Pontypridd	D. J. Williams
Tonyrefail	T. J. Williams
Abertillery	Henry Gale
Bedlinog	J. M. Williams
Blaenavon	F. Marchant
Newport	R. H. Ley
Nantyglo	J. E. Jones
Risca	G. Dardis
Pembrokeshire	B. T. L. Jones, Boncath
Cardiganshire	Revd T. E. Nicholas

Table 5: No-Conscription Fellowship branches and secretaries in Wales, May 1916[48]

located in Cardiff, and its secretary, Ieuan Peter Hughes, coordinated activity between local branches and the NCF centrally, before he was imprisoned in May 1916. Most of the branch secretaries were also prominent local ILP activists and at the end of May, the secretaries for West Glamorgan, Merthyr and Risca branches had to be replaced, after each was imprisoned as conscientious objectors.[49] At least a quarter of these secretaries became conscientious objectors or were

[48] Cumbria Archives, Catherine Marshall Papers, D/MAR/4/4, 'List of NCF branches, May 1916'.
[49] Cumbria Archives, Catherine Marshall Papers, D/MAR/4/4, 'List of NCF branches, May 1916'.

arrested for offences under the Defence of the Realm Act, related to sedition and circulating materials thought to be prejudicial to recruitment.[50]

The NCF's Welsh Divisional Conference, held in June 1916 in Cardiff, reflected its concerns for the increasing numbers entering the prisons, and as if to amplify this challenge, Henry Davies, Cwmavon, was required to take the chair, since the officeholder, Morgan Jones, had been taken into military custody. The NCF's secretary, Fenner Brockway, addressed the meeting where seventeen NCF branches, and a number of ILP branches were represented.[51] The following day, the NCF national committee met in Cardiff and agreed to ask the Welsh Liberal MP, the barrister W. Llewellyn Williams, to act on its behalf in appealing against the Glamorganshire police's recent prosecutions against NCF for circulating anti-war leaflets. The committee also considered the growing issue of supporting the families of those men who had been prosecuted in south Wales, and it was agreed that the main office should forward to the Welsh Divisional secretary a sum of money which could be drawn upon by the dependants of imprisoned men, if local effort did not realise the necessary funds.[52]

The introduction of conscription divided communities in south Wales, as reflected in debates, often initiated by the NCF, in council chambers, trades councils and miners' lodges. In January 1916, a meeting of Mountain Ash council considered a request from the Aberdare branch of the NCF for the council to oppose conscription and the Military Service Bill before Parliament. A motion to effectively ignore this demand, by 'laying it on the table', was narrowly carried, by seven votes to five, in spite of protests by the ILPer councillor and pacifist Revd George Neighbour.[53] The Bargoed and District Trades Council resolved to oppose conscription, and the NCF's Merthyr branch lobbied the local district of miners successfully to oppose the Military Service Act. The first quarter of 1916 for the NCF was taken up by a series of

[50] *Pearce Register.*
[51] *Pioneer,* 17 June 1916.
[52] Cumbria Archives, Catherine Marshall Papers, D/MAR/4/6.
[53] *Pioneer,* 29 January 1916.

public protest meetings against conscription in collaboration with trades councils and miners' lodges. These meetings were held mainly in ILP strongholds, such as the Swansea and Amman Valleys, Aberdare, the Merthyr area and Pontypridd, and the speakers included the Marxist educationalist and miner Nun Nicholas and prominent local officials of the SWMF, such as J. L. Rees, Pontardawe.[54]

The NCF organised sessions to advise young men how to fill their exemption forms and to explain procedures for their appearances before the military tribunals. and such an event was held in Glais in February 1916. Revd T. E. Nicholas, recently a local minister before moving to Llangybi in Cardiganshire, where he was secretary of the local NCF branch, gave introductory words of encouragement, and the secretary of the NCF in Pontardawe, the ILPer Tom Evans, gave a brief history of the NCF.[55] In March 1916, new branches were created in the Swansea Valley and mass anti-conscription meetings were held in Cwmtwrch, Gwaun-cae-Gurwen and Pontardawe, with 2,000 present, and Clydach, with 1,500 present.[56] The anti-conscription campaign, organised by the NCF and ILP, gathered momentum across the south Wales coalfield, with large-scale meetings in Swansea,[57] Blackwood, Aberbargoed, Aberaman and Merthyr, where the first public meeting of the local 'Stop the War and Peace Council', jointly organised by the anti-war organisations and trade union lodges, was held with 2,000 present, followed by another mass meeting in May.[58]

From the end of February onwards, conscientious objectors started appearing before the tribunals. In two sessions of the Bangor tribunal, a total of thirty-five students appealed as conscientious objectors,[59] and another thirty-two conscientious objectors appeared before the Merthyr tribunal on 13 March. Individual COs appeared before Ystradgynlais and Tregaron tribunals,[60] and on 21 March, sixty-two

[54] *Pioneer*, 26 February 1916; *Pioneer*, 4 March 1916.
[55] *Pioneer*, 4 March 1916.
[56] *Pioneer*, 4, 11, 25 March, 1 April 1916.
[57] *Pioneer*, 22 April 1916.
[58] *Pioneer*, 15, 22 April, 13 May 1916.
[59] *North Wales Chronicle*, 3 March 1916.
[60] *Pioneer*, 18 March 1916.

conscientious objectors, the largest number of COs to appear
before a tribunal at a single sitting in Britain throughout the
war, appeared before the Pontardawe tribunal.[61] In the
Glamorgan appeal tribunal, most appellants who were COs
were members of the NCF and ILP, and their solicitor,
Edward Roberts, Dowlais, came into immediate conflict with
a number of tribunal members who were easily provoked
and inflamed by the NCF. In his appeal to the West
Glamorgan Appeal Tribunal, for instance, Albert J. Lewis,
chairman of the Neath Trades Council and the Neath
Socialist Society appealed against non-combatant service,
and stated that he was a member of the NCF. One of the
tribunal members, Alderman Davies responded violently:
'then you belong to one of the most pernicious bodies in the
country. Its members are going all over the place distilling
poison, and are greater enemies to Britain than the
Germans.'[62]

The creation of the 'shadow' system for replacing those
officials who had been arrested and imprisoned, in the
second half of 1916 and by 1917, sustained the NCF's activity,
albeit under difficult circumstances. In Wales, the leadership
of the NCF was increasingly entrusted to women supporters,
and Emrys Hughes's sister Agnes became its divisional organiser in south Wales.[63] As soon as conscientious objectors
began to be arrested, the NCF was re-organised and divided
into ten departments, including the Conscientious Objector
Information Bureau (COIB) which tracked the records of
each conscientious objector, including the grounds of objection, the details of his appearances before courts, and of the
prison or Home Office settlement in which he was placed.
The press and literature departments produced propaganda,
and the political and campaigning departments focused on
lobbying Parliament on behalf of conscientious objectors,
and on agitating for the release of conscientious objectors.
The Visitation department had representatives in each
region who informed the NCF's Conscientious Objector
Information Bureau of the whereabouts of conscientious

---

[61] *Pioneer*, 25 March 1916.
[62] *Tribunal*, 6 April 1916.
[63] *Pioneer*, 1 December 1917.

objectors in military camps and prisons, and reported on their progress through the court martial and prison system.[64]

Thirteen of the 232 visitors who reported to the COIB covered Wales. They included Minnie Pallister, Agnes Hughes and Revd John Morgan Jones, Merthyr, who mainly visited south Wales prisoners,[65] whilst Revd Gilbert Jones, Llangloffan in Pembrokeshire, visited objectors in Pembroke Dock military barracks and Carmarthen prison. In north Wales, the sprawling military camps outside Rhyl and Park Hall outside Oswestry were mainly visited by Revd E. K. Jones, Cefnmawr, who was aided by Principal Thomas Rees, Revd Wyre Lewis, Oswestry, and two Quakers from the Deganwy area, Watson Webb and Frederick Pane.[66] Jones visited and kept meticulous records of 467 conscientious objectors in five army camps in Kinmel Park, near Rhyl, and the Park Hall camp, near Oswestry.[67] His prodigious activities on their behalf were unpaid, and included letter writing to relatives and their families, attending tribunal hearings of COs, in which he acted as a friend and witness, appearing as character witnesses at military court martials, and interviews with conscientious objectors, which he then reported back to the NCF's Conscientious Objector Information Bureau.[68]

Other supporters who liaised with conscientious objectors' families in Wales included the Jewish novelist Lilian Tobias, living in Rhiwbina, who supported the mother of two Cardiff objectors, Thomas and Robert Bassett, in complaining about the conditions which Robert had endured at Llanddeusant camp, where he had been working under the Home Office scheme.[69] Tobias, originally from Ystalyfera in the Swansea Valley, was part of a small group of socialist Jewish intellectuals in south Wales, a novelist who was a member of the

[64] *The No-Conscription Fellowship*, pp. 24–6.

[65] Cumbria Archives, Catherine Marshall Papers, D MAR 4/95.

[66] National Library of Wales, E. K. Jones Papers, Box 29, 'Goss to E. K. Jones, 27 October, 1916'.

[67] National Library of Wales, E. K. Jones Papers, Box 2, 'Conscientious Objector case files'.

[68] E. K. Jones, *Atgofion am Dri Rhyfel*, Wales Peace Pamphlets, No. 9.2 (Denbigh: Gwasg Gee, 1944), p. 22.

[69] Cumbria Archives, Catherine Marshall Papers, D/MAR/4/55 , 'Letter from Tobias to Miss Rinder'.

Zionist movement and co-founded the Cardiff and Swansea branches of the Daughters of Zion. Her brothers were COs, and she had been secretary of the Swansea branch of the ILP before the war, before becoming active in the NCF. Fenner Brockway described her as a 'young, battling, aggressive socialist pacifist' and praised her 'daring challenges to authorities'.[70] She helped the families of Jewish COs in particular, of whom about half a dozen were COs in south Wales.

Other local ILP activists, such as Councillor Tal Mainwaring of Port Talbot, raised the case of individual conscientious objectors, such as Richard Mainwaring, who was ill at home, and was forcibly given a medical examination there by a military doctor.[71] The NCF supported conscientious objectors and their families and raised money to help those dependants who had been punished by court appearances, police prosecutions and debt, such as the ten Briton Ferry members fined for distributing 'seditious material'. Minnie Pallister appealed for money to support conscientious objectors and their families and recalled the support given to Councillor Tal Mainwaring and his family during his imprisonment and subsequent illness.[72] An appeal by Agnes Hughes for funds for the dependants of conscientious objectors, at a meeting of the ILP in Maesteg in November 1917, for instance, raised 11s. 1d.[73] Support for conscientious objectors was displayed by a number of labour and trade union organisations, and the south Wales division of the Cooperative Wholesale Society, for instance, passed a resolution by a 'large majority', demanding that the same allowances be made to dependants of members who were conscientious objectors as were made to the dependants of members of the armed forces.[74] The NCF branch in Gorseinon supported the dependants of conscientious objectors by making weekly collections and raising money through picking coal from tips and selling it,

---

[70] Lily Tobias, *Eunice Fleet*, foreword by Jasmine Donahaye (Dinas Powys: Honno Classics, 2004), pp. xi–xiii.
[71] Cumbria Archives, Catherine Marshall Papers, D/MAR/4/66, letter to Miss Rinder, 26 March 1917.
[72] *Pioneer*, 15 December 1917.
[73] *Pioneer*, 1 December 1917.
[74] *Pioneer*, 15 December 1917.

gathering and selling cast-off lumps of wood, trudging five miles to a wood to cut pea and bean sticks to sell, and raffling a 'white duck'. The branch circulated an appeal leaflet to every church in the neighbourhood, and in six months it was reported that Gorseinon had raised £150, 'in spite of the fact that many of their members are in prison and camp'.[75]

The NCF was an intense social grouping of like-minded and principled young men, but its effectiveness as a campaigning organisation was curtailed by the rapid increase in the arrest and incarceration of its members from the summer of 1916. As in the case of other branches scattered throughout south Wales, its Gorseinon branch included a 'small but committed' group of COs and their supporters, and the branch was not ostracised by the community, although the majority of the local population was pro-war. The Western District Miners' Federation responded positively to its appeal for money to assist the dependants of imprisoned conscientious objectors:

> it was decided to vote a sum of £10 'without prejudice' to the fund, the District meeting making it quite clear that they would not express any opinion upon the conduct of the conscientious objectors, but from a humanitarian point of view wished to relieve such dependents as may be suffering want of the necessities of life through the internment or imprisonment of their men.[76]

This jaunty description of an excursion to mid Wales by members of the Gorseinon branch imparts the sense of joy and comradeship in the group:

> Bip, Bap; Bip, Bap!
>
> Last Saturday the No-Conscription Fellowship took their outing by open-motor bus to Llanwrtyd Wells. The drive was magnificent. During the day sport of many kinds was indulged in, best of all being the sculling competition for the men … Tea was provided at the Carlton, after which excellent speeches were made by Fellows Stanley Rees, Mansel Grenfell, and MacGinnes; and a most encouraging speech by the vicar (Rev. Richard Jones). He said that success must inevitably follow the Fellowship; possibly they could not agree on some

[75] *Pioneer*, 22 December 1917.
[76] *Cambria Daily Leader*, 2 July 1917, cited in David Cleaver, 'Conscientious Objection in the Swansea area', *Morgannwg*, 28 (1984), 53.

things, but that we were as one banded together to save humanity. Many thanks are due for such an enjoyable day to Herbert Rees and Mansel Grenfell.[77]

Later that summer, the NCF members of the four branches covering the Dare, Merthyr and Lower Rhondda Valleys converged in Abercynon for a joint ramble:

over the hill to Llanfabon where a 'spread' had been arranged. The mountain walk served to have given them a good appetite, for as soon as they arrived at the appointed place they fell to. After tea they all entered the Parish Room, where Mr Brobyn (Merthyr) was appointed chairman for the evening. He made a nice little speech on the present position and our duty to our comrades in prison. Guardian Noah Tromans and Miss Agnes Hughes followed with short addresses. Then Mr Warren sang one of his favourite songs. After singing the 'Red Flag,' and giving cheers to the International and the boys in prison, they started to journey home. Everybody seemed to enjoy the ramble, and it has been decided to hold another within a month's time. It is worthy of note that the four branches represented were at one time all combined in one branch called the Aberdare and Merthyr Branch, of which our Comrade Emrys Hughes was secretary.[78]

A central activity of NCF branches was to support imprisoned COs and their families in prison and after release. In October 1916, Briton Ferry's NCF branch held a large social gathering to welcome back three of their members who had been imprisoned in Swansea prison for distributing anti-war leaflets, and the celebration included the ubiquitous NCCL organiser, Ivor Thomas:

We welcome back into our midst three of our gallant comrades, who, after having the pleasure of being the guests of his Majesty the King, have returned to civilian life for a time which his Majesty's Ministers think fit ... After tea, a short entertainment was held [and] Florrie Lambert opened with ... 'There's a long, long train'... Mr. Arthur Armstrong, chairman of the local branch, followed with a short speech ... Item No. 3 was a song by Miss Thomas, who rendered 'A Canadian Boat Song' in splendid style. Councillor Henry Davies (Cwmavon), the South Wales and Monmouthshire Divisional representative on the National Executive, followed with a short but lucid speech ... referring to the suffering [of COs]. The entertainment was concluded

[77] *Pioneer*, 15 July 1916.
[78] *Pioneer*, 26 August 1916.

by singing the 'Red Flag'. Dancing followed, in which I perceived Comrade Ivor Thomas skipping about well to the front, as he always is in great progressive movements ... The Briton Ferry Co-operative Society catered for the Social.[79]

The same evening, the *Pioneer*'s Cwmavon and Port Talbot correspondent reported a separate event where two conscientious objectors, the brothers John and Sidney Bamford, were each presented with a gold pendant, a silver cigarette case and a purse of money, subscribed by a number of friends. Both had accepted alternative service and were now employed by the Copper Miners' Tinplate Company. Another social event, to welcome Tal Mainwaring following his release from Swansea prison, was held in Taibach with 200 people present, and it was reported that 'thanks to the ILP element in the local branch' of the British Steel Smelters Union, the branch had decided that conscientious objectors belonging to it should be 'accorded the same welcome as soldiers returning from the front'.[80] The NCF's Pontypridd branch held a tea and social evening:

> A recitation was given by Miss Rowlands, the Rev. Geo. Neighbour, Mountain Ash, following with a short speech, humorous yet redolent with propaganda. A song was sung by Miss Thomas, and a few remarks on the influence of the N.C.F. were made by Mr. Ted Williams. Mr. Tom Rowland recited 'The Red Dawn,' and the meeting closed to the strains of the 'Red Flag' and cheers for the International.[81]

The NCF also organised events to raise the spirits of CO prisoners by organising singing outside prisons, including Cardiff.[82]

From the summer of 1916 to the summer of 1918, the 'honorary' organiser, albeit part-time, of the NCF in South Wales was Minnie Pallister. She was based in the main office in London for a short time in the summer of 1916, and Catherine Marshall had found her contribution useful. It seems they discussed the creation of a full-time organiser's post for the NCF in south Wales, for Marshall thanked her

---

[79] *Pioneer*, 7 October 1916.
[80] *Pioneer*, 7 October 1916.
[81] *Pioneer*, 22 June 1918.
[82] *Tribunal*, 17 May 1917.

for her work, but thought that the position in south Wales did not merit such an appointment:

> after carefully considering the S. Wales position, in relation to the work in the Divisions, we have come to the conclusion that we should not be justified at present in putting a wholetime organiser then. We would however very much like you to undertake to carry on the maintenance work so far as you are able to do so.

However, the relationship seems to have been of value to Marshall: 'I am so glad you enjoyed your brief sojourn in London and felt it worthwhile. I am always keen on keeping the work in the provinces and the work of headquarters in close touch. *Both sides need it.*'[83]

Pallister was appointed the ILP's organiser for south Wales in June 1918. *The Pioneer* condescended to compliment her organisational ability with the NCF, 'it is in the last sphere rather than in the I.L.P. that she has conspicuously won her spurs as an organiser before the eyes of the South Wales movement as a whole',[84] but warned that she should concern herself more with organisation than propaganda:

> Miss Pallister always has been a successful platform propagandist, probably the best of her sex that we have in Wales, and we must not overlook the fact that the intoxicating effects of the great meeting possesses a charm that might seduce even one of her level-headedness and cool sanity to occasionally forget that organisation is a genius for taking pains in the little things of the movement.[85]

Another important link with the NCF's head office in Wales was the daughter of Revd John Morgan Jones, Merthyr, Margaret Morgan Jones, who worked in the NCF's office in London in the Conscientious Objectors' Information Bureau, and helped to compile the case files of conscientious objectors.[86] By May 1917, the NCF had twenty-six branches of the NCF and one Sunday school in south Wales, but because

[83] Cumbria Archives, Catherine Marshall Papers, D/MAR/4/9, correspondence between Pallister and Marshall, 29 August 1916.
[84] *Pioneer*, 8 June 1918.
[85] *Pioneer*, 8 June 1918.
[86] Cumbria Archives, Catherine Marshall Papers, D/MAR/4/53, letter from Marshall to Pallister.

of what Pallister referred to euphemistically as the 'migratory character' of the population of conscientious objectors, 'it has been found beneficial in some cases to change the Branch centres in this Division', and by the end of the year the number had declined to twenty (see Table 6).

Division 1	Scotland	15
Division 2	North West of England	20
Division 3	North East of England	10
Division 4	Yorkshire	13
Division 5	Midlands	15
Division 6	South of England	24
Division 7	London area	31
Division 8	Wales	20

Table 6: NCF branches in December 1917[87]

This was in the context of a total of 150 branches across Britain, split into seven divisions, of which the strongest division was the London area, with thirty-one branches. There was no formal branch presence in north Wales, and the NCF primarily covered the south Wales industrial districts, whilst only two branches, Cardiganshire and Pembrokeshire, were located beyond those areas. There was a close correlation between the location of the NCF's branches and the ILP's strongest membership in Wales. Most of the twenty NCF branches in Wales in 1917 were in those areas where the ILP had its strongest branches, based on their financial contribution to the party in 1917–18.[88] A number of the NCF's branches had been amalgamated to create regional branches by 1917, but the low turnover of branch secretaries between May 1916 and the end of 1917 reflects a surprising stability to the NCF's organisation, in spite of its inherent weakness as its young members were increasingly arrested and sent to prison or to undertake alternative work as conscientious objectors.

[87] *Tribunal*, 24 May 1917.
[88] *Pioneer*, 26 August 1916.

THE POLICING AND THE PERSECUTION OF THE NCF

An inevitable concern for the NCF was the extent to which its activity was monitored by the security services and the police. From March 1916 onwards, the Glamorganshire Police increased their activity markedly against the NCF. Two members of the NCF, who later became conscientious objectors, D. J. Evans and T. Thomas, were arrested and fined ten shillings with one month's imprisonment with hard labour, under the Defence Of the Realm (DORA) legislation, for distributing NCF literature at Cefn, near Merthyr, on Good Friday,[89] and four of the Briton Ferry and Port Talbot NCF branch were fined and imprisoned following an anti-conscription public meeting in Port Talbot on 7 May. By the end of the month, twenty-five of the NCF's members in Wales had either been imprisoned or were in military barracks awaiting court martial. Two more NCF and ILP activists, William Davies and the chairman of the Briton Ferry NCF, Garnet Watters, were arrested under the DORA legislation for distributing pamphlets and sentenced to one month's imprisonment with hard labour.[90]

In May 1916, the police raided the offices of the NCF in the ILP centre in Cwmavon and confiscated all the branch propaganda literature and the branch's correspondence and minute book. The secretary of the Briton Ferry branch of the NCF, A. H. Armstrong, wrote that day to NCF headquarters, warning that police action locally imperilled the organisation's effectiveness:

> I suggest that the distribution of future leaflets should be seriously considered or we shall *all* be imprisoned, not that we fear imprisonment, but our services, and the services of many many men we cannot afford to lose will be lost to us. Our ILP premises here was raided by the Police, a Superintendent, Inspector, two sergeants, and a constable, we were holding a branch meeting in the small room over our shop, discussing matters concerning our two comrades who were summoned. When the police arrived, they said they did not want to disturb everything in our little shop (stationery, sweets, literature, tobacco) if we would show them and produce for them, all our

---

[89] *Pioneer*, 29 April 1916.
[90] *Pioneer*, 20 May 1916.

publications on the War, we willingly complied of course, they then took the names and addresses of the chairman, secretary and treasurer. So we are awaiting events. The fact is that any matter published in the war can be held to be 'prejudicial to training and discipline in His Majesty's Forces' we are under the Iron Heel.

The following week, a branch meeting at the ILP office in Briton Ferry was raided by five policemen, again led by Superintendent Ben Evans, and they took away leaflets and pamphlets. The NCF's paper, the *Tribunal*, reflected on the intense police activity in the Briton Ferry area and warned against the bullying of the NCF's solicitor in south Wales, Edward Roberts, a 'small pale-faced solicitor from Merthyr', who was a well-known socialist, a regular attender at Merthyr's Sunday anti-war meetings, and who represented Emrys Hughes in his first court martial in Cardiff Barracks: [91]

> The police are very busy in South Wales just now, especially in the Neath Division. Raids have been made on ILP and NCF centres in search of literature 'prejudicial to recruiting' and one expects an outburst of political intelligence from the man in blue in this Division. Over a dozen summonses under the Defence of the Realm Act have been taken out in Briton Ferry, Port Talbot and Cwmavon, secured by the police, and the military representative for the Aberavon Borough Tribunal (Mr F. B. Smith) paid a personal visit to the solicitor engaged for the defence of the Port Talbot and Cwmavon cases and warned him that if he appeared in any of the Defence of the Realm cases he would immediately apply for a variation of his certificate of exemption and get him arrested as an absentee! One wonders what the Incorporated Society of Law Servants has to say in reference to this grave interference with the privileges of its profession.[92]

In Wales, the raids continued and the ILP rooms in Bargoed were raided by police on 29 May: 'fresh faces were seen in these premises. They left with a good deal of convincing Socialist literature. The raid was carried out in the best of spirits.'[93] More prosecutions were brought against a second group of Briton Ferry ILP members, who were accused of 'distributing articles likely to cause disaffection and

[91] National Library of Scotland, Keir Hardie and Emrys Hughes Papers, Dep. 176, Box 9, *Welsh Overture*, *Pioneer*, 6 May 1916.

[92] *Tribunal*, 8 June 1916.

[93] *Pioneer*, 3 June 1916.

prejudicial to His Majesty's subjects'. The *Pioneer*'s editor described this police activity as the pursuit of a 'policy of suppression with a violence that savours of vindictiveness' which caused distrust and unrest in community, and contrasted it with the series of 'moving Democratic conferences' against conscription and for peace by negotiation.[94]

Large anti-conscription meetings continued to be held in Merthyr, Swansea Valley, Bargoed and Cwmavon throughout the summer, and invariably included a motion that opposed the government's treatment of conscientious objectors. The Merthyr Anti-Conscription meeting, reportedly attended by representatives of 20,000 people, supported a motion to protest against the 'persecution of men who had conscientious objection to military service', and Bargoed, Aberbargoed and Brithdir Councils against Conscription called for an inquiry into the methods of dealing with conscientious objectors. Anti-conscription meetings in the Swansea Valley attracted crowds of 1,000 in Ystradgynlais, 1,500 in Pontardawe, and a 'large crowd' in an open-air meeting in Glais. All three meetings passed a motion that urged the government to open for 'a just and lasting peace' and to protest against the 'harsh treatment meted out to conscientious objectors',[95] and these meetings increased in size throughout the summer and autumn of 1916. A peace meeting addressed by Philip Snowden in Abertillery reportedly drew an audience of 3,000 people, and a meeting of the Merthyr Peace Society with his wife, Ethel Snowden, speaking drew an audience of 5,000, demanding that persecution of conscientious objectors by the government should come to an end.[96]

Bertrand Russell, the acting chairman of the NCF, entered the febrile atmosphere of south Wales in July 1916 and conducted a three-week speaking tour of the south Wales valleys, where he contrasted the difficulty of conducting anti-war activity in London with the enthusiastic support he received in Wales:

---

[94] *Pioneer*, 17 June 1916.
[95] *Pioneer*, 24 June 1916.
[96] *Pioneer*, 1 July 1916.

I spent three weeks in the mining areas of Wales, speaking sometimes in halls, sometimes out-of-doors. I never had an interrupted meeting, and always found the majority of the audience sympathetic so long as I confined myself to industrial areas. In London however, the matter was different.[97]

In addition to the crowded meetings described in the profile in chapter 2 of the ILP in Briton Ferry, he addressed further meetings in the Swansea Valley and the Merthyr area, at the Rink in Merthyr, in Abercanaid, Troedyrhiw and Dowlais, and in Pontypridd, Abertillery and Cwmavon.[98] At the last meeting of his three-week tour, at the Friends Meeting House in Cardiff, for the first time he was greeted by hecklers. Following this meeting, at which its audience was denounced as a 'lot of miserable, pro-German, sentimental traitors' by Captain Atherley Jones, the Home Office took legal action against him and he was barred by military decree on 31 August 1916 from entering any 'prohibited area' and stopped from making public speeches. The Minister for Munitions, Lloyd George, accused Russell of preparing lectures that would lead to 'weakness, inefficiency, and if tolerated, would hamper us in the prosecution of the War'.[99] Significantly, his reception in Cardiff was in stark contrast to the supportive and thoughtful response he had received in the south Wales coalfield.[100] Russell subsequently voiced his concern that perhaps he should have gone to more hostile districts because south Wales was 'merely a picnic', but his observations suggest that the presence of such a level of support for the anti-war movement in south Wales, in contrast to his unhappy experiences elsewhere, impressed him deeply.[101]

Throughout the summer of 1916, the NCF worked with other anti-war organisations to create 'Peace Councils' in industrial areas such as Aberdare and Gorseinon:

---

[97] Bertrand Russell, *The Autobiography of Bertrand Russell 1914–1944* (George Allen and Unwin, 1968), pp. 24–5.

[98] *Pioneer*, 15 July 1916.

[99] House of Commons Papers, Hansard, Oral answers, cols 533, 534, 18 October 1916 (HMSO).

[100] Jo Vellacott, *Bertrand Russell and the Pacifists* (Brighton: Harvester Press, 1980), pp. 88–9.

[101] Nicholas Griffin, *The Selected Letters of Bertrand Russell* (Routledge, 2001), p. 67.

> Yes! A real, honest spiritual revival was held at the Institute last Thursday … Here were Liberals, Conservatives, Labour men, ILPeers, U.D.C., F.O.R., N.C.F., Socialists and others with no policies at all … to form a Peace Council at Gorseinon. The Chairman … gave a hearty welcome to the visitors from different parts of Wales … One young minister … said he knew men that evening, who were Liberals, and had been staunch Liberals but like himself, had set aside everything to work for Peace. There was no time for politics. What a set-back to the Democracy of the world, this war had been! … It was not an easy thing to be a Pacifist, because it was an uphill fight.[102]

The police raids on NCF officials continued in the autumn of 1916, and during the first week of September twenty-seven homes and offices were searched, including homes in Pontypool, Swansea Valley, Port Talbot, Taibach, Pengam and Cardiff.[103] These included the home of the mother of the Gorseinon NCF secretary, D. J. Williams, in Pontarddulais, where literature was seized, and he was summoned to court.[104] The secretary of the Swansea Valley branch of the NCF, Tom Evans, appeared in Pontardawe before a 'packed court', and was fined £35 for being in possession of certain documents likely to 'prejudice the recruiting, training, discipline or administration of His Majesty's Forces'. The prosecution accused Evans of 'having a hindering effect of the anti-war movement on the Army', and he refused to pay his fine.[105]

The first conventions of the South Wales Division of the NCF were held on the first weekend of November 1916, and followed by a public meeting in which Minnie Pallister presided. Addresses were given by Revd George Neighbour and Fenner Brockway, who drew the disdain of most south Wales newspapers by his statement that if Britain really wished to inaugurate permanent peace after the war, she should 'sink her navy and disband her army'.[106] As conscientious objectors were imprisoned in greater numbers, the NCF continued to attempt to broaden the base of protest

---

[102] *Pioneer,* 29 July 1916, 12 August 1916.
[103] *Tribunal,* 7 September 1916.
[104] *Tribunal,* 11 November 1916.
[105] *Tribunal,* 2 December 1916.
[106] *Tribunal,* 9 November 1916.

against conscription and the treatment of conscientious objectors. In July 1917, protest letters were sent by twenty trades councils and eighty-nine trade union and Labour branches against the ill-treatment of conscientious objectors. The senders included Aberdare, Pontardawe and Treherbert trades councils, the Maesteg and Oswestry branches of the National Union of Railwaymen, the ASLEF branch at Landore, Swansea, four Miners' Federation lodges at Tylorstown, Cwmdu, Abertridwr and Tillery, and two mass meetings of miners in Cwmavon and Afan Valley District, and Llanelli's Labour Association.[107] This attempt to broaden the base of support for the NCF was also reflected in the organisation's close relationship with the National Council of Civil Liberties and its attempts to oppose the extension of conscription into the mining industry, in particular. In the summer of 1917, the NCF's support for workers' and soldiers' 'soviets', or councils, following the Russian Revolution in March, drew the ire of those such as Morgan Jones, who believed that the NCF should confine itself to opposing conscription and preserving the right of conscience, and the majority of the NCF's national committee who decided to be represented in the first workers' and soldiers' conference in Leeds.[108]

As the war progressed, the NCF's attention was increasingly drawn to campaigning against the conditions under which many conscientious objectors were held. In February 1918, East Glamorganshire branches met in Newport and decided to commence a 'vigorous propaganda to secure the release of our tortured comrades',[109] but the organisation suffered its own internal crisis early in 1918. In January 1917, Morgan Jones had returned from prison as the NCF's representative on the national committee, replacing his substitute, 48-year-old Henry (or Harry) Davies, Cwmavon. According to *Llais Llafur*, no socialist in south Wales was better known,[110] and in addition to his role as chair of the Cwmavon branch of

[107] Cumbria Archives, Catherine Marshall Papers, D/MAR/4/21.
[108] Cumbria Archives, Catherine Marshall Papers, D/MAR/4/25, letter to branch secretaries, 17 July 1917.
[109] *Pioneer*, 9 March 1918.
[110] *Llais Llafur*, 26 January 1918.

the ILP and a leader of the NCF in south Wales, Davies was highly regarded in labour circles, had been the county councillor for Cwmavon, and had been selected by the local ILP branches as their nominee as Labour candidate for the new Aberavon division at the General Election to be held at the end of the war. He had been employed as assistant overseer and collector of rates for a local parish for thirteen years, as well as serving as clerk to the Cwmavon Parish Council, and was a member of the Board of Managers for the Port Talbot Group of Schools,[111] but his arrest in January 1918 on charges of embezzling £1,000 caused a seismic shock for the ILP and NCF in south Wales. His supporters compared him to a highwayman who had robbed the rich to give to the poor, and Davies received a sympathetic note from Catherine Marshall, who, even though his disgrace would have been profoundly damaging for the ILP and the NCF locally, hoped they could work together again: 'I have just heard that you have been charged with embezzling money, and have pleaded guilty. I know no more than that – but this I do know, that if it is true you must have been through terrible tortures of mind and spirit.'[112] He was imprisoned for fifteen months in the second division. Surprisingly, and curiously, Davies's main character witness was the arresting police officer, Superintendent Ben Evans, who had previously pursued and prosecuted NCF and ILP activists successfully in Cwmavon and the Briton Ferry area, including Davies. In court he described Davies as a man of 'sober habits and good moral character', but said that his motivation for the embezzlement had been his political activism. In an unhelpful assessment of Davies he concluded:

> to a certain extent it [the money] has gone in propaganda to the Socialist party, of which he is a member, and has taken a very prominent part during the past four years. The prisoner addressed meetings in the district, and he had reason to believe that he had done great harm to the young men of the community.

In mitigation, the defending barrister, Llewelyn Williams KC, MP, gave the more prosaic explanation that Davies had got

---

[111] *Pioneer*, 12, 26 January 1918.
[112] Cumbria Archives, Catherine Marshall Papers, D/MAR/4/16, letter from Marshall to Henry Davies.

into financial trouble and borrowed money to pay his debts. When he failed to borrow more he succumbed to the temptation of using some of the public moneys which he collected, but his political career lay in ruins:[113]

> What he had done in fact was ... given it to some poor bugger in distress and this poor chap couldn't hand it back to him in time to cover it up, you know ... but he went down the drain socially at once when he had.[114]

By the last year of the war, the momentum of the NCF's activity had inevitably slowed and, whilst many branches continued to campaign for the release of imprisoned conscientious objectors, membership declined, and it was 'both physically and psychologically a badly depleted organisation'.[115] Even the Military Service (No. 2) Act of 1918, raising the age limit to 51, and the extension of conscription to Ireland failed to attract new members, and the NCF directed its energy towards the release of the 2,000 conscientious objectors still imprisoned. A campaign was started to release objectors in January, and a memorial signed by 162 prominent people, with Principal Thomas Rees as the sole Welsh signatory.[116] On 8 April 1919, the first absolutists were set free, and it was only finally on 30 July 1919 that the last absolutist conscientious objectors were released, although, ironically, a number of the conscientious objectors who had followed the army's advice and joined the Non-Combatant Corps were not released until late 1919 or 1920.

The NCF was brought to an end in its concluding Convention in November 1919, 'since it had fulfilled its particular work', but it appointed three committees: to guard against conscription, to provide a link for pacifists, and to oppose military training in schools. Its final resolution highlighted its altruistic and utopian hope that it was not through bloodshed that 'freedom could be won or militarism

---

[113] *South Wales Daily News*, 6 March 1918.
[114] Swansea University, South Wales Coalfield Collection, W. H. Gregory interview, Aud. 289.
[115] Kennedy, *Hound of Conscience*, pp. 262–3.
[116] *Tribunal*, 9 January 1919.

destroyed', but that 'through its long and bitter suffering mankind must yet come into the way of love'.[117]

The NCCL in Wales succeeded in bringing together those in the trade union movement and trades councils who feared the imposition of conscription in civilian life, and especially in those industries such as coal, steel and the railways that were essential to the country's war effort. In Wales, its organiser, Ivor Thomas, succeeded in uniting this concern with opposition to the war, and ensured that the voice was amplified to such an extent that the authorities came to view the anti-conscription lobby as a branch of the anti-war movement. Whilst all who opposed the war opposed the extension of conscription, not all who opposed conscription opposed the war. But as the NCCL's meeting in Merthyr Tydfil in December 1916 shows clearly, the two elements could combine to form a powerful lobby that gave government and its intelligence agencies pause for thought. The NCF was rather more directly involved in organising conscientious objectors and giving practical support to them and their dependants. The local organisers of the ILP, the NCCL and NCF were either often closely associated or frequently the same people, as is exemplified by a study of the anti-war movement in Briton Ferry and Merthyr Tydfil. This depth of support provided a reservoir of both passive and active support for anti-war activists that sustained them, even as many were arrested and imprisoned as conscientious objectors from March 1916 onwards.

---

[117] *The No-Conscription Fellowship*, pp. 85, 92.

4

CONSCIENTIOUS OBJECTORS IN WALES

INTRODUCTION

This chapter analyses the extent and nature of conscientious objection in Wales during the Great War and considers how the conscientious objectors (COs) responded to the imperfect and muddled system of exemption from military conscription and coercion created by government. The COs were a diverse group with vastly different backgrounds, views and politics, and their consciences covered a range of motivations, ranging from those Christians who took the commandment prohibiting killing to mean they could take no part in the military, to those who embraced international socialism and refused to fight their fellow workers.[1] A minority of COs, such as the Christadelphians, were 'not conscientiously opposed to bearing arms' as such, but rather were opposed 'to fighting in the armies of the world', and became the only grouping of men to be recognised formally by the army as COs on the basis of their faith.[2] The view of the military and the vast majority of tribunals was that conscientious objection should be limited to religious grounds and that political objections were not permissible. The Labour pro-war newspaper circulating in the Swansea Valley, *Llais Llafur*, for instance, shared this prejudice:

> persons who have a conscientious objection grounded in religion, to military service have a right of total or partial exemption. It is not clear how far the same exemption extends to political objectors. The justification for the indulgence shown to the Quaker is that non-resistance is with him a life-long creed ... The political objector has no such claim as the Quaker on the public indulgence. Local tribunals will have to

---

[1] Lois Bibbings, *Telling Tales About Men: Conceptions of Conscientious Objectors to Military Service during the First World War* (Manchester University Press, 2009), pp. 4, 5.

[2] Frank Jannaway, *Without the Camp* (London: F. G. Jannaway, 1917), pp. 32–5.

use their own judgment as to how far they will exempt political objectors from combatant service, but we hope they will not err on the side of leniency.[3]

Those men who were granted conditional exemption by a tribunal, or had failed in their appeals, were 'deemed ... to have been duly enlisted' by the Military Service Act and were liable for service for the period of the war. If they failed to comply with a notice paper calling them to the colours, they were arrested by the civil police and charged as deserters, then a court of summary jurisdiction fined them and placed them in military custody.[4] Once in military custody, usually in the area headquarters of the army, conscientious objectors would soon make it clear that they were determined to resist all attempts to make them soldiers by refusing to undergo medical examination, to sign documents or put on uniform. In Wales, the main army area headquarters was Maindy Barracks in Cardiff, and most conscientious objectors were transferred to the army camps in Kinmel Park near Rhyl, or Park Hall near Oswestry, where they were court-martialled if they had not been dealt with in Cardiff.

Whilst most soldiers had little sympathy for their plight, there were examples of leading military figures such as Brigadier Owen Thomas, responsible for the army camps in north Wales, who showed compassion to conscientious objectors in army custody. His treatment of COs was reported by George M. Ll. Davies to be 'quite exceptional in its moderation, though some of the sentences have been very severe ones'.[5] Davies also received a letter from Revd John Williams, Brynsiencyn, in which he described Thomas's ready understanding of the conscientious objectors' stance:

> I am now staying with the Brigadier (Owen Thomas) and I had a chat with him last night re the contents of your letter. You have heard I am sure how kind and sympathetic he has been towards the conscientious

[3] *Llais Llafur*, 12 February 1916.

[4] War Office, *Registration and Recruiting*, 21 August 1916, 13–15, cited in John Rae, *Conscience and Politics: British Government and the Conscientious Objector to Military Service 1916–1919* (Oxford: Oxford University Press, 1970), p. 66.

[5] National Library of Wales, E. K. Jones Papers, Box 29, a note from Revd John Williams to George M. Ll. Davies, and enclosed with his letter to Jones, 26 June 1916.

objectors who are in the camp, so much so that they have written to thank him for his great kindness. He says that there will be no objection whatever for ministers and others to visit them.[6]

The creation of the Brace Committee's Home Office Scheme and the Pelham Committee's provision of 'work of national importance' in the summer of 1916 was a belated response to the growing political and moral dilemma for the government and army of what to do with the conscientious objectors. The Home Office Scheme was established under a committee under the chairmanship of William Brace, the south Wales Member of Parliament, former president of the South Wales Miners' Federation (SWMF), and under-secretary of state at the Home Office. This determined the conditions under which conscientious objectors were to be offered work, and created what were considered appropriate work camps. The Pelham Committee was also created to provide advice to tribunals as to 'what service of national importance an applicant for exemption on the ground of conscientious objection should undertake' and attempted to operate as an employment exchange for conscientious objectors, bringing together young men referred by the tribunals and employers who needed labour, especially in agricultural work, and placing men of more mature age and poor physique in clerical employment or light manual labour.[7]

While these alternatives suited many COs, these work camps proved increasingly unpopular with COs in 1917, and those who protested or rebelled were often handed back into military custody and civilian prison. The minority of intransigent absolutists continued to frustrate and refused to compromise in any way with the authorities. Conditional exemption was given to those objectors who expressed a willingness to accept alternative service, on the basis that they undertook work that was deemed to be 'of national importance'. Absolute exemption completely absolved men from

[6] National Library of Wales, E. K. Jones Papers, Box 29, letter from George M. Ll. Davies to Jones, 24 May 1916.

[7] John Williams, 'Brace, William (1865–1947)', *Oxford Dictionary of National Biography* (Oxford: Oxford University Press, 2004).

[7] Friends House Library, T. E. Harvey Papers, Box 9, Pelham Committee Report, 1919.

any military service, but the tribunals were invariably reluctant to grant more than partial exemption, and a number disputed whether conditional exemption or absolute exemption was available in cases of conscience.[8] The Bangor tribunal in February 1916 was a rare exception in granting absolute exemption to eight out of twenty-three students from Bala-Bangor theological college who were in the last year of their studies.[9]

The local tribunals created to enact the Military Service Act and to hear appeals for exemption were organised on the basis of the local government boundaries of town councils, metropolitan borough councils, and urban and rural district councils in England, Scotland and Wales. Their members were 'civilian, middle class and public-minded',[10] and nominated by local authorities. Whilst containing a majority of councillors, tradesmen predominated, particularly in urban areas, whilst in rural areas they were dominated by landowners and farmers, and often included a lawyer and a representative of the labour interest.[11] In theory, the applicant and the military representative had an unrestricted right of appeal against the local tribunal's judgment, if they so wished, but, as Rae points out, the approach of individual appeals tribunals differed wildly, and the interpretation of what constituted conscientious objection varied hugely across the country.[12]

The Local Government Board's early guidance to the tribunals stated clearly that 'the man who honestly and as a matter of conscience objects to combatant service is entitled to exemption', and tribunals were enjoined to interpret the Act in an 'impartial and tolerant spirit'.[13] This provision for exemption was qualified by the statement that every consideration should be given to the man whose 'objection genuinely rests on religious or moral convictions'. But most

[8] Rae, *Conscience and Politics*, pp. 117–20.
[9] Bangor University, Bala-Bangor Papers, f. 3169.
[10] Rae, *Conscience and Politics*, p. 57.
[11] Rae, *Conscience and Politics*, pp. 52–61.
[12] Rae, *Conscience and Politics*, p. 97.
[13] National Archives, Ministry of Health Papers, Class 10, Local Government Board Circular, 'Relating to the Constitution, Functions and Procedure of Local Tribunals', February 1916.

tribunals interpreted this clause as meaning that no exemption should be given to a politically based application for exemption on the grounds of conscientious objection. Neither did many consider that absolute exemption could be granted, and the clerk to the Denbigh appeal tribunal, for instance, wrote that the majority of members were not aware that they had the right to give absolute exemption.[14]

The tribunals' members had difficulty in dealing with their role as arbitrators of conscience, and they invariably included those who had enthusiastically championed the voluntary Derby scheme, which had invited prospective recruits to attest their intention to enlist. Military representatives at the tribunals believed 'almost to the point of obsession', that if they did not take an uncompromising line on claims for exemption, the army would be robbed of their requirement for recruits. The tribunals' role in the military recruiting organisation, the uncompromising policy advocated by the NCF, the pressures of time, and the limitations of the government's provisions, all made it hard for the members to avoid coming to decisions that were unacceptable to many applicants.

ENUMERATING CONSCIENTIOUS OBJECTORS IN WALES

There was no central database or definitive list of named conscientious objectors collated during the Great War, and in 1921, the Ministry of Health, which took over responsibility for tribunal records, ordered that all personal papers relating to exemption on the grounds of conscientious objection, and all minute books, with the exception of those of the Central Tribunal, the Lothian and Peebles tribunal in Scotland and the Middlesex tribunal in England, should be destroyed.[15] However, a number of these local records survive, and in Wales, the records have been retained in local county archives for the Monmouthshire and Cardiganshire appeal tribunals, the Cardiff Rural District tribunal, the Chirk local tribunal in Denbighshire and the Laugharne

---

[14] National Archives, War Office Papers, 32/2051, 3319.
[15] Rae, *Conscience and Politics*, p. 259.

local tribunal in Carmarthenshire. Most appellants appeared in order to be released from being recruited on the basis of their family circumstances or business need, and these local records confirm that there was an extremely small number of appellants who came before them as conscientious objectors. The Cardiganshire appeal tribunal, for example, heard only eight appeals from conscientious objectors amongst the hundreds of appeals it heard in its fifty-nine meetings,[16] but a major difficulty in measuring and assessing the numbers of conscientious objectors is that men could appeal for exemption on numerous grounds, and that individuals who appeared before tribunals were not always named.

The main attempts to quantify the number of conscientious objectors in Britain were initially made by Graham, who estimates the number of COs as 16,100, and Rae, as between 16,000 and 16,500. Graham recognises the difficulty of providing reliable figures for the actual number of conscientious objectors[17] and based his figures for COs primarily on the basis of the reports of the NCF's Conscientious Objector Information Bureau, the Friends Ambulance Unit (FAU), and the Report of the Pelham Committee. He suggests that the number of COs would have been greater if many had not been influenced by their family circumstances: 'It was not uncommon to hear men say that the prospect of leaving mother or wife nearly destitute prevented them taking the stand they would otherwise have taken, and one must admit, if not the validity, at least the force of this plea.'[18] The number was also substantially reduced because of those men employed in trades that were exempted from conscription for most of the war, such as the coal, metal and the railway industries in particular, in which the majority of the Welsh working population were employed.

Rae recognises that the lack of a central method of collating information about conscientious objectors makes it

[16] National Library of Wales, Cardiganshire Appeal Tribunal Records, CTB 2, 3; Hubert H. Vaughan, 'The Cardiganshire Appeal Tribunal March 1916–November 1918', *Wales*, 25 (Spring 1947), 177.

[17] John Graham, *Conscription and Conscience* (Allen and Unwin, 1922), p. 344.

[18] Graham, *Conscription and Conscience*, p. 345.

Arrested	6,261
Pelham Committee cases	3,964
Friends Ambulance Unit	1,200
War Victims' Relief Co.	200
Working directly under tribunals	900
Non-Combatant Corps	3,300
Royal Army Medical Corps	100
Evaded the Act	175
Total	16,100

Table 7: Graham's estimate of conscientious objectors in Britain[19]

difficult to provide a definitive total,[20] but his calculation of the numbers of conscientious objectors was informed by newly available government sources in the 1960s, including the report of the Home Office Scheme's Central Tribunal and its statistical appendices, which were not available to Graham. He suggests that the number of those who were exempted from combatant service is between 1,000 and 1,500 men, and his total therefore is a similar number to Graham's, at between 16,000 and 16,500 (see table 8). This number represents approximately 0.66 per cent of the recruits after January 1916, which demanded a disproportionate amount of the military and the civilian authorities' attention at the time.[21]

Although historians such as Boulton, Moorehead and Hochschild[22] have emphasised the role of the absolutist conscientious objectors, Rae calculates that the tribunals granted conditional exemption to over 80 per cent of conscientious objectors before them. Neither Rae nor Graham attempts to identify individual conscientious objectors, to identify the geographical distribution of objectors in Britain, or to identify the grounds for their conscientious objection. The main differences in their two total figures lie

[19] Graham, *Conscription and Conscience*, p. 349.
[20] Rae, *Conscience and Politics*, p. 70.
[21] Rae, *Conscience and Politics*, p. 71.
[22] David Boulton, *Objection Overruled: Conscription and Conscience in the First World War* (McGibbon and Kee, 1967); Caroline Moorehead, *Troublesome People: Enemies of War 1916–1986* (Hamish Hamilton, 1987); Adam Hochschild, *To End All Wars: A Story of Protest and Patriotism in the First World War* (Macmillan, 2011).

1. Exempt from all military service	
a) Absolutely or conditionally	5,111
b) From combatant service only, conditional on being engaged on work of national importance	1,000–1,500
2. Exempt from combatant service only	
a) Served in the Non-Combatant Corps	2,919
b) Refused to serve and court-martialled	1,969
3. Refused exemption by the tribunal	2,425
Total number of COs subject to tribunal decisions	approx. 13,700
4. Others	2,858
a) Conditionally exempt by the Army Council (Christadelphians)	1,400
b) Did not apply for exemption on the grounds of conscientious objection	1,234
c) Miscellaneous (cases heard after December 1919)	224
Total number of all conscientious objectors	approx. 16,000–16,500

Table 8: Rae's estimate of conscientious objectors in Britain[23]

in the interpretation of the outcome for those who enrolled in the NCC. Graham overestimated the number of COs in the NCC because serving officers were included in his total, but he specifies that a further 1,969 refused to serve and were court-martialled, thus providing more detail than Graham's general description of 'arrested'. Revd E. K. Jones, a visitor on behalf of the NCF who worked in north Wales and the Marches, writing at the end of the war, recognised the difficulty of estimating the correct number of conscientious objectors:

> Some to my knowledge appealed to the Tribunal on more than one ground (including conscientious objection) and got exemption. Many others would not be called up at all. Some escaped the bands that scoured the country for men that had not reported themselves. These bands searched houses and attended public meetings, examining all doubtful persons and arresting many. Some COs would start as absolutists and break down under hard treatment ultimately seeking NCC work. Who, knowing what they had to undergo, can blame them?[24]

[23] Rae, *Conscience and Politics*, p. 132.
[24] National Library of Wales, E. K. Jones papers, Box 29.

The *Pearce Register* has captured the details of over 17,000 anti-war activists in Britain during the First World War, including the majority of conscientious objectors.[25] The database includes not only conscientious objectors, but also those who were arrested as anti-war activists, and includes members of the Welsh company of the RAMC, raised in north Wales, who joined on condition that they would not have to bear arms, and who were for all purposes regarded as conscientious objectors. However, the definition of a conscientious objector on the basis of the Military Service Act excludes these individuals from the recognised list of objectors, and the definition of a conscientious objector deployed in this study is the official one described in the Military Service Act and deployed by Rae and Graham.

The total number of men identified as conscientious objectors in Wales during the Great War is 901, and this analysis of conscientious objectors in Wales is primarily based on the *Pearce Register* of anti-war activists in Britain in the war, but also on the records of the Brace Committee's Central Tribunal,[26] reports of military court martials,[27] local newspapers and conscientious objectors' archives. In Wales, the primary sources are the reports of the most prominent anti-war newspaper in Wales, the *Pioneer*, and other archive collections, including the contemporary reports of the NCF's Conscientious Objector Information Bureau, the NCF's weekly paper, the *Tribunal* and individual archive collections, such as those of Revd E. K. Jones, Cefnmawr. Many of Wales's recruits, including at least a sixth of all conscientious objectors from Wales, were held in army camps, and his records detail information of the 159 objectors from Wales.[28] The Pelham Committee's final report also provides information about the 207 conscientious objectors from Wales who were employed to do 'work of national importance' as part of the Scheme, including a total of 151 Christadelphians, although

---

[25] Cyril Pearce, *Pearce Register of Anti-War Activists in Wales* (Wales for Peace, 2016). Available at *http://www.wcia.org.uk/wfp/pearceregister.html.* Accessed November 2016.

[26] National Archives, Ministry of Health Papers, 47/1, Records of the Brace Committee's Central Tribunal.

[27] National Archives, War Office Papers, 363, Reports of Military Court Martials.

[28] National Library of Wales, E. K. Jones Papers, Box 2.

most are not identified by name.[29] The personnel files of the FAU also reveal another twenty-eight COs from Wales, of whom half were Quakers and the other half were Nonconformists,[30] whilst the Friends War Volunteer Relief organisation included eight members from Wales.

This total of 901 represents approximately 5.6 per cent of the total number of British conscientious objectors. In comparison with the 127,609 conscripted into the armed forces from Wales from January 1916 onwards, it represents 0.7 per cent of the total of men available to be recruited in that period, and their average age was 26. Over half declared an allegiance to a political or religious organisation, and thirty-five per cent were members of the NCF. Of that total, almost a third declared their allegiance to both the NCF and the ILP, and another thirty-five declared their allegiance to both the NCF and either a religious denomination or the FoR. The NCF essentially provided the organisational framework for conscientious objectors, and its members pledged allegiance to a myriad of causes. An example of the breadth of allegiance was the objector who defined himself as an ILP-er, a Socialist, Congregationalist and member of the NCF, and another who declared his allegiance to the NCF, FoR and the UDC, and described himself as both a Baptist and Quaker.[31]

Of those identifiable conscientious objectors in Wales, slightly over half, representing a total of at least 407 conscientious objectors, professed a religious allegiance when they appeared before military tribunals, and this number reflected a wide range of attitudes amongst religious groups towards the war. These conscientious objectors included at least thirty theological students who succeeded in gaining exemption from military service by pleading that they were in the process of being trained for the ministry and were due to be ordained. Whilst the majority of theological students gained exemption, there were isolated exceptions, such as the case of Ben Meyrick, a Baptist minister in Anglesey and a

---

[29] Friends House Library, T. E. Harvey Papers, MSS 835/9.
[30] Friends House Library, Friends Ambulance Unit Papers, Personnel records, 588–601 POS.
[31] *Pearce Register.*

member of the FoR, who was refused exemption and, despite a series of appeals and campaigns led by Revd E. K. Jones and others, was sentenced in October 1917 to two years' imprisonment with hard labour.[32]

Of those who declared an organisational allegiance in their tribunal, or in information provided to the NCF, approximately half of COs in Wales declared an allegiance to a particular religious or political organisation, and of those who declared an allegiance, over seventy per cent did so in relation to a religious organisation (see Table 9).

Christadelphians	155
Quakers	51
Baptists	46
Congregationalists	58
Fellowship of Reconciliation	31
Methodists	21
Jehovah's Witnesses	7
Plymouth Brethren	17
Wesleyan	7
Church of England	8
Jewish	7
Unitarian	1
Church of Christ	1
Catholic	1
Salvation Army	1
Total	**412**

Table 9: Stated religious allegiance of conscientious objectors in Wales

The largest single group of religious conscientious objectors was the Christadelphians, who did not oppose the war so much as oppose the government's attempt to impose its will on the church's members. Of all the religious organisations, only the Christadelphian church succeeded in obtaining a general dispensation that gave exemption to its members of military age, on the basis that they would accept work of

[32] National Library of Wales, E. K. Jones Papers, Box 2, 24 February 1916.

national importance under the control of the Pelham Committee.[33] In Wales, 155 men, or twenty-seven per cent of the total number of objectors from Wales who expressed a religious allegiance, agreed to accept this condition.

Most of those who gave a political organisation as their main allegiance (see Table 10) were members of the ILP, but the statistics that refer to organisational allegiance should be treated with caution, however, and understate the number of political conscientious objectors. For example, no political allegiance is noted beside the names of known members of the ILP such as Mansel Grenfell, David James Jones (Gwenallt) and Evan Parker, Aberdare. The NCF calculated that 1,191 of conscientious objectors in Britain had been 'socialist' (approximately 7.2 per cent of the total).[34]

No-Conscription Fellowship	154
Independent Labour Party	87
Fellowship of Reconciliation	31
British Socialist Party	2
'Christian Socialist'	1
Socialist Labour Party	1
Total	**246**

Table 10: Stated organisational allegiance of conscientious objectors in Wales

Of the Welsh COs who identified any allegiance, eighty-seven of them, or ten per cent, described themselves as members of the ILP. But many conscientious objectors declared multiple loyalties to a religious organisation as well as a political body, and of the ILP members, for example, a number described themselves also as members of the NCF and of Nonconformist denominations.

Some men appealed on more than one basis, and the habit at the tribunals of giving initial temporary exemption and compelling the men to come up again before the tribunal adds to the complication of enumerating the fate of conscientious objectors. According to Graham, the men who were

[33] Jannaway, *Without the Camp*, pp. 198–203.
[34] *The No-Conscription Fellowship: A Souvenir of its Work 1914–1919* (No-Conscription Fellowship, 1919), pp. 37–8.

exempted were nearly all men engaged in religious work but not strictly in holy orders, including secretaries of religious societies, local preachers and a few well-known Quakers. Exemptions were also granted to the members of the FAU whilst working at the front, and these numbered 640 in Britain, including twenty-nine from Wales.[35] A characteristic of the Welsh conscientious objectors is that the occupational profile of this cohort of men tended to be that of the skilled working class or lower middle class. Of the 533 men in Wales who gave their occupation to the tribunals, the most substantial group was that of the fifty-eight coalminers who were conscripted from the end of 1917 onwards, seventy-nine students, including fifty-six theological students, and thirty-nine schoolteachers. There were thirty-five clerks, thirty objectors who had worked in the metal trades of tinplate, iron and steel, twenty grocers, sixteen agricultural workers or farmers, eleven insurance agents, and eight bootmakers or merchants.

The geographical distribution of the conscientious objectors (see Table 11) broadly reflected Wales's distribution of population, with two main exceptions. The number of student conscientious objectors in Bangor inflated the Caernarfonshire total to sixty-five conscientious objectors, and the statistics for Glamorgan and Monmouth mask a concentration of conscientious objectors in areas where the ILP was notably influential, such as the Briton Ferry and Port Talbot area (ninety-six), Merthyr/Aberdare/Mountain Ash (seventy), Cardiff (ninety-six) and Swansea (fifty-three). Newport, the largest town in Monmouthshire, also had the largest concentration of conscientious objectors in the county, with thirty-nine.

Llanelli had the largest concentration of COs in Carmarthenshire, with approximately thirty-eight COs, a third of whom were Christadelphians. Wrexham, the largest town in north Wales, had the comparatively small number of twenty-four conscientious objectors.

---

[35] Graham, *Conscription and Conscience*, p. 346: Friends House Library, Friends Ambulance Unit Papers, Personnel Records 588–601 POS.

County	Number of COs	As percentage of COs in Wales	As percentage of total male population in Wales
Anglesey	5	0.6%	2%
Breconshire	16	2%	2.4%
Cardiganshire	31	4%	2.18%
Carmarthenshire	64	8%	6.49%
Carnarfonshire	65	8%	4.8%
Denbighshire	33	4%	6%
Flintshire	15	2%	3.7%
Glamorgan	448	55%	47.26%
Merionethshire	13	1.6%	1.7%
Monmouthshire	114	14%	17%
Pembrokeshire	9	1%	3.5%
Radnorshire	9	1%	1%
Montgomeryshire	4	0.5%	2%
Total of identifiable COs in Wales	810		

Table 11: Geographical distribution of identifiable COs in Wales by county[36]

HOW THE STATE DEALT WITH THE CONSCIENTIOUS OBJECTOR IN WALES

By the beginning of May 1916, the number of conscientious objectors in Britain had already reached 100 and increased rapidly to almost 700 by 26 May 1916.[37] This sharp increase caused Lord Kitchener to warn the Cabinet that conscientious objectors within the army could only be treated in the same way as all other soldiers were treated: 'it is the clear duty of every commanding officer to do his best with the legitimate means at his disposal to make every man who is handed over to him an efficient soldier'.[38] The detention barracks and military prison had been designed to 'deter the brute elements of a regular army',[39] and since COs refused to cooperate they accumulated punishments and existed on

[36] *Pearce Register.*
[37] *Tribunal,* 4 May, 1 June 1916.
[38] National Archives, Cabinet Papers, CAB 37/147/35.
[39] Rae, *Conscience and Politics,* p. 148.

poor food. After his court martial, Ithel Davies, from Mallwyd in Merionethshire, was moved from the military camp in Kinmel Park to the camp at Park Hall near Oswestry, and then transferred to Mold Military Prison in north Wales where, on his first day, he refused to work sewing mailbags, and was assaulted and placed in a straitjacket for six hours. The following day, when he refused to dig a hole, he was assaulted twice, punched and beaten with the head of a pickaxe and had his nose broken. Davies's case was raised by the Member of Parliament, Llewelyn Williams,[40] and parliamentary scrutiny of Ithel Davies's ill-treatment contributed to the decision to send objectors to civil prisons only, from that autumn.

A reflection of how little the position of the CO had been considered was that they were subject to military law, which included the death penalty for disobedience. Asquith and his Liberal colleagues had wanted to place conscientious objectors under civilian control, whilst Conservative ministers, such as the Local Government Minister, Walter Long, opposed this concession.[41] The army also wished to be rid of its responsibility to deal with conscientious objectors, and proposed that the government should establish a civilian organisation to employ conscientious objectors 'under conditions as severe as those of soldiers at the front'.[42] Major-General Sir Wyndham Childs's main role in the War Office in 1916 was to deal with the time-consuming issue of the conscientious objector:

> it is sad to recall that at least fifty per cent of my own time and energy, and that of a fairly extensive staff, was expended in securing justice in accordance with the Law for people whose sole object seemed to be to desert their country in its time of peril.

Childs found himself torn between his contempt for the conscientious objector in the main, and 'intense sympathy which I could not keep within bounds when I came across specific cases of conscientious objectors who were brutally treated'.[43] He formed an unlikely liaison with the NCF to

---

[40] Ithel Davies, *Bwrlwm Byw* (Llandysul: Gwasg Gomer, 1984), pp. 62–7.
[41] Parliamentary Debates (Commons), 5 HC 82, cols 94–5, 3 May 1916.
[42] National Archives, Cabinet Papers, CAB 37/147/35.
[43] Major-General Wyndham Childs, *Episodes and Reflections* (Cassell and Co.,1930), p. 149.

take action when cases of brutality came to his attention, and there is little doubt that the military detention centres and military prisons were ill-suited to dealing with conscientious objectors. Many of the conscientious objectors were sorely mistreated, and the NCF's assessment was that the military prisons, whilst more lax in rules concerning visits, letters and food, were much more brutal than their civilian counterparts.[44] By the end of May 1916, the army persuaded the government to place the genuine conscientious objector under the civil power,[45] and subsequent Army Orders directed that a conscientious objector found guilty of an offence against discipline should be sentenced to imprisonment and not detention, and that after court martial he should be committed to the nearest civil prison.[46] The men would not be formally discharged from the army, but transferred to section W of the Army Reserve, which was created for 'all soldiers whose service is deemed to be more valuable to the country in civil than military employment'.[47] Asquith agreed that the case of all conscientious objectors committed to civil prison should be reviewed by the Central Tribunal and those deemed to be genuine should do work of national importance under the Home Office. But in a decision that presaged the difficulties of the Brace Committee in accommodating those who opposed the war on political grounds, Childs drew a sharp distinction between the treatment of men who were inspired by 'religious sincerity' and those who, in his view, were not genuine, as they expressed political objections to the war.[48]

Most Welsh COs accepted the alternative options provided by the state, and accepted employment under either the Home Office Scheme, the Pelham Committee or the Army's Non-Combatant Corps, or in a small minority of cases accepted service with the Royal Army Medical Corps (RAMC) or the FAU (see Table 12).

[44] *The No-Conscription Fellowship*, p. 53.
[45] Parliamentary Debates (Commons), 5 HC 22, col. 14, 22 May 1916
[46] National Archives, War Office, Army Order 179, 1916.
[47] National Archives, War Office, Army Order 203, 1916; Rae, *Conscience and Politics*, pp. 155–8.
[48] Childs, *Episodes and Reflections*, p. 148.

Scheme	Number of conscientious objectors	Percentage of total
Pelham Committee[55]	207	23%
Friends Ambulance Unit	28	3%
Friends War Volunteer Relief[56]	8	1%
Non-Combatant Corps[57] (of whom 74 court-martialled)	201	22%
Home Office Scheme[58]	258	28%
'Absolutists'	70	8%
RAMC	5	1%
YMCA	2	0.0022%
Others (including absolute exemption)[59]	122	14%
Total	901	100%

Table 12: Conscientious objectors in Wales

The 201 conscientious objectors from Wales who served in the NCC form a lower percentage of the Welsh COs compared with the British percentage of 29.5 per cent of the total of 16,500. The 207 COs from Wales who joined the Pelham Committee scheme constituted the same percentage of the British total, at 24 per cent. The 258 who joined the Home Office Scheme constituted 30 per cent of the Welsh total, in contrast with the slightly lower British percentage of 27 per cent. The most extreme of conscientious objectors were the 'absolutists', who totalled approximately 1,350, representing 8 per cent of the CO population throughout Britain,[49] and Wales's seventy 'absolutists' are an equivalent percentage of the total.

Most members of the Home Office Scheme experienced at least one term of imprisonment before appearing before the Central Tribunal and being allowed to progress to a work centre. Of those in Wales who eventually accepted the Home Office Scheme, 224 were imprisoned once, sixty-five twice, and twenty were imprisoned three times. The only other significant difference in the comparison with the British-wide statistics is the lower percentage of conscientious objectors in Wales who joined the FAU and the Friends War

[49] Graham, *Conscription and Conscience*, p. 351.

Voluntary Relief, and this may reflect the comparatively weak Quaker tradition in Wales.

THE NON-COMBATANT CORPS

The War Office had already created an alternative for conscientious objectors within the army as early as March 1916, with the creation of the Non-Combatant Corps (NCC). Although these men wore khaki uniform, they were not armed and were employed in road-making, timber-cutting, loading and unloading ships,[50] stretcher-bearing and hospital portering.[51] Although it became popularly known as the 'No-Courage Corps',[52] its members attracted admiration from unlikely sources such as the *Times*, whose description of their work in France categorised them as 'men who are rendering what service they conscientiously can to their country in her need, just like any other patriotic Britons'.[53] Significantly, Graham hardly mentions their role in his otherwise detailed volume,[54] and this may reflect his and the NCF's view that the experience of absolutists and imprisoned members was more deserving of attention. The NCC provided an unsatisfactory answer to the moral dilemmas of many conscientious objectors, and was rejected by the NCF and the Quakers when its creation was announced: 'the men for whom we speak can, under no circumstances, become part of this corps, which we observe will be under the control of the War Office, and in every sense part of the military machine'.[55]

However, the NCF's review published at the end of the war described many of the conscientious objectors in the NCC as showing great courage and 'withstanding most brutal efforts to make them perform services to which they were

---

[50] Childs, *Episodes and Reflections*, p. 149.
[51] National Archives, War Office, WO293, Army Council Instruction No. 456, 4 March 1916; *The Times*, 14 March 1916.
[52] Philip Snowden, *British Prussianism: The Scandal of the Tribunals* (Manchester: Manchester National Labour Press, 1916), p. 8.
[53] *The Times*, 19 May 1916.
[54] Graham, *Conscription and Conscience*, p. 349.
[55] *Tribunal*, 16 March 1916, letter from NCF and the Quakers to Asquith.

opposed'.[56] The training for the NCC was carefully prescribed, and men were trained in squad drill without arms and in the use of various forms of tools used in field engineering. Once trained, the companies were posted to camps in England and France, where they could not be employed in the firing line and were normally confined to army chores, such as building roads, erecting hutted camps, loading and unloading ships and railway wagons, and burning excreta.[57] But confusion as to the meaning of 'non-combatant' caused great difficulty when objectors were occasionally asked to handle munitions or other military supplies, and many found it an unsatisfactory option and refused to take further orders. In the instance of Welsh COs, the slightly higher proportion of forty-five per cent of the 201 who joined the NCC were court-martialled.[62] This high level of rejection reflects the extent to which this option failed to satisfy the requirements of the COs, although Childs alleged that this rarely led to much trouble: 'sometimes we used to get sporadic outbreaks of disobedience, such as once occurred when some of them were required to load barbed wire. The disobedience was confined to a few, however, who were punished in the ordinary way, and obtained no sympathy.'[58]

Conscientious objectors within the NCC did protest when they were asked to manhandle munitions of war, and in a number of instances, their protests led to court martials and subsequent imprisonment. The earliest and most serious instance was the transfer of thirty-seven men from the Eastern NCC who had refused to obey orders and who, on being shipped to France, had thirty of their number condemned to death. The army's intention was to frighten the men, and on 9 June 1916 the death sentences were formally read out to the men, but were commuted to ten years' penal servitude. The numbers of COs in the NCC rose quickly, from 700 in May 1916 to 3,181 by the end of the year,[59] and many of those who joined were members of religious sects such as the

[56] *The No-Conscription Fellowship*, p. 78.
[57] Rae, *Conscience and Politics*, p. 192.
[58] Childs, *Episodes and Reflections*, p. 150.
[59] *Statistics of the Military Effort of the British Empire in the Great War 1914–1920* (HMSO, War Office, 1922), p. 226.

Seventh Day Adventists and Plymouth Brethren.[60] Many objectors had difficulty in coming to terms with the discipline of the NCC. For example, T. J. Gwilym, a Bangor theological student, opposed the war on religious grounds and was given conditional exemption by the local tribunal in May 1917 on condition that he performed work with the RAMC, but he found it to be inappropriate to his needs:

> being of a profoundly sympathetic disposition, I could not stand aloof, while the cream of the country's youth shed their blood ... on the request of the tribunal I joined the RAMC at Cardiff, but was informed by the officer in command that every member of the RAMC was now expected to bear arms for the purpose of protecting themselves and the wounded, if necessary.

In consequence, he declined to join the RAMC and was sent to the NCC at Henlle, which was part of the Park Hall complex of military camps near Oswestry, where he was instructed to engage in sanitary work and the general tidying up of the camp. However, on 6 December 1917, with fourteen other COs, he refused an order to repair training trenches.[61] In spite of representations by the MP for East Denbighshire, E. T. John, they were subsequently court-martialled, and Gwilym was sentenced to six months with hard labour in Wormwood Scrubs prison. Another conscientious objector on religious grounds, William Griffiths from Tirydail, near Ammanford, sought advice from E. K. Jones and how he could accommodate his conscience as Christian pacifist with military service in the NCC:

> nid oes busnes ar un cyfrif i ladd neb naill yn uniongyrchol neu yn anuniongyrchol; ac fel mae yn wybyddus i chwi fod yma rywrai am ein gorfodi i wneuthur peth felly yn y dyddiau nesaf yma, carwn yn fawr pe buasech yn rhoddi i mi gair o gyfarwyddyd. Mae fy nghariad i at Grist a'i egwyddorion yn ddigon i farw drostynt. Mae hyn yn beth mawr i ddywedyd, ond credaf yn cydwybod y caf nerth yn ôl yr achos.[62]

> (it is not acceptable on any grounds to kill anyone directly or indirectly: and as you know there are those who will make us do so in the

---

[60] Childs, *Episodes and Reflections*, pp. 149–50.
[61] National Library of Wales, E. K. Jones Papers, Box 29, undated letter T. J. Gwilym to Jones, 1918.
[62] National Library of Wales, E. K. Jones Papers, Box 29, letter from William Griffiths to Jones, 26 February 1916.

next few days, I would be very grateful if you could give me a word of advice. My love for Christ and his principles are enough to die for. This is a big statement but I believe in my conscience that I will get the strength to do so.)

Having joined the NCC in north Wales, Griffiths could not come to terms with its requirements, and wrote to his commanding officer to declare that he could not remain in it any longer.[63] He was court-martialled on 20 February 1917, and sentenced to two years' hard labour. A month later, his father wrote that William's brother, John, had been killed on active service in France, but that, in spite of his deep sorrow and grief, he supported his son's stand as a conscientious objector:

> yr ydym yn llawenychu yn y ffaith mae carcharor dros egwyddorion crefydd Crist Iesu ydyw. Mae duwolion yr oesau wedi bod yno o'i flaen.[64]

> (We rejoice in the fact that he is a prisoner for the religious principles of Jesus Christ. The god-fearing people of the ages have been there before him.)

It is ironic that although the conscientious objectors within the NCC had compromised most with the requirements of the military, they were also the last to be released from military control. Whilst all the objectors in the Home Office camps were released by April 1919, and all absolutist objectors freed by July 1919, it was not until the beginning of 1920 that those conscientious objectors in the NCC, many of whom were still stationed in France, were finally allowed to return home.[65]

---

[63] National Library of Wales, E. K. Jones Papers, Box 29, letter from William Griffiths to his commanding officer, 5 February 1917.

[64] National Library of Wales, E. K. Jones Papers, Box 29, letter from father of William Griffiths to Jones, 13 August 1917.

[65] *Tribunal*, 24 April 1919; Parliamentary Debates (Commons), 5 HC col. 118, 2001–2, 30 July 1919.

THE BRACE COMMITTEE'S HOME OFFICE SCHEME

The Brace Committee's Home Office Scheme was created only because of the failure of the government's initial provisions for COs, and probably caused more frustration for those involved than any other aspect of their treatment.

By June 1916, many hundreds of COs were wilfully disobeying orders and had entered military detention barracks and prisons. In order to implement the work of the Brace Committee, they were ordered to appear before a Central Tribunal to assess whether they might be ready to undertake an alternative to prison and engage in what was termed 'work of national importance'. From 27 July 1916 onwards, the Central Tribunal met in Wormwood Scrubs Prison at least twice a week for the duration of the war, and personally interviewed every conscientious objector serving a sentence of imprisonment or detention for refusing to obey orders. Most men dealt with by the Committee were then released from prison, transferred to the Army Reserve and distributed to work centres set up throughout the United Kingdom. The majority of COs were thus accommodated, although the 'absolutists' remained as an intractable problem for the authorities.[66] Those COs who continued to disobey appeared before a court martial, and received sentences ranging from a short period of confinement in barracks to hard labour for two years, which was invariably commuted to 112 days by the Army Council. The majority of COs faced a 'net' sentence of between 28 and 112 days, usually in a military detention barracks or military prison.[67]

The army's policy was that whilst this provision should act as a deterrent to those who saw conscientious objection as a safe alternative to active service, at the same time it wished to be relieved of the thankless task of trying to make soldiers of men who did not wish to cooperate with the authorities. The Central Tribunal took the advice to heart that it should not adopt the same standard as applied to the statutory appeals for exemption, with the result that the extraordinarily high

---

[66] Rae, *Conscience and Politics*, pp. 162–7.
[67] Rae, *Conscience and Politics*, p. 148.

proportion of ninety per cent of those reviewed cases were recommended for release from prison, in the belief that 'many of the men were of no use to the Army; their presence in military units was a hindrance to the performance of military duties at a time when all officers were fully employed in training new levies'.[68]

The scheme's Central Tribunal categorically rejected any conscientious objection that was based on socialist or overtly political grounds under the terms of the Military Service Act, although it allowed for the broader nature of a moral objection to war to be sympathetically considered.[69] It interviewed a total of 5,944 applicants who were consequently allocated into five categories. Categories A and B included the ninety per cent of the men who either should be treated as having a conscientious objection to all military service or whose convictions appeared to be so uncertain as not to warrant a distinct finding, and these men were allowed to join the Home Office Scheme. Men in Categories C and D tended to have a strong objection to war in general, but would fight in a war for a purpose of which they approved, and they were returned to prison. The men classified in Category E were absolutists, who either refused absolutely to appear before the Central Tribunal or refused to accept the conditions of the Tribunal's enquiry.[70] The number of Welsh COs who accepted the Home Office Scheme was approximately 258, or thirty-five per cent of the total number of Welsh COs, which was slightly more than the twenty-five per cent of COs throughout Britain who had accepted the Home Office Scheme.[71] The total number of absolutist COs in Britain was 985, or 6 per cent of the total, and of that number there were seventy in Wales, at 8 per cent a slightly higher proportion of the Welsh population of conscientious objectors.

Bertrand Russell, the chairman of the No-Conscription Fellowship, excoriated the new scheme:

[68] National Archives, Ministry of Health Papers, 47/1, 'Report of the Central Tribunal', 23.
[69] National Archives, Ministry of Health Papers, 47/1, 'Minutes of the Central Tribunal, 24 July 1916'.
[70] National Archives, Ministry of Health Papers, 47/3, 'Report of the Central Tribunal', 24.
[71] Rae, *Conscience and Politics*, p. 190.

it was launched with the usual flavour of good intention, and was sincerely intended as a relief, but it was baffled by lack of comprehension of the minds of the men dealt with and by the dull penal instruments employed, incited, always by the baying of newspapers, and relying on an abnormal inflammation of public opinion.[72]

But in spite of his protestations, the high level of acceptance for the 'Home Office' scheme was a fatal blow to the NCF's attempts to destroy the Military Service Act through a policy of uncompromising non-cooperation. The principal achievement of the Central Tribunal was not to separate the sincere and the humbug, but to separate those prepared to accept the HO scheme, and those who refused to make any compromise. The Brace Committee subsequently not only agreed that men should be employed in large groups, but also set as a matter of principle that the conditions of employment 'should not be appreciably better than those applying to non-Combatants on Home Service',[73] and that those who were granted exemption on the grounds of taking up work of national importance were required to make some sacrifice, such as not remaining within the neighbourhood of their own homes.[74]

The number of appellants interviewed by the Central Tribunal fell from 2,288 in 1916 to 1,165 in 1918, and the changing composition in the population of conscientious objectors during the last year of the war reflected the 'combing out' from those industries of those who had wished to avoid military service, and the increased understanding amongst younger recruits of the advantages of the government's schemes to accommodate objectors. Over a fifth of the men who appeared before the Central Tribunal had not appeared before a lower tribunal, often because they had been protected by various authorities, such as Colliery Recruiting Courts, War Agricultural Executive Committees

[72] *Tribunal*, 17 August 1916.
[73] National Archives, Ministry of Health Papers, 47/3, 'The Home Office and Conscientious Objectors: a Report prepared for the Committee for Imperial Defence, 1919; Part I The Brace Committee', p. 3.
[74] National Archives, Ministry of Health Papers, 47/3, 'Report of the Central Tribunal', p. 12.

and Munitions Area Recruiting Courts. Whereas in 1916 the proportion of men before the Tribunal who had not made any application to any other tribunal on the grounds of conscientious objection was only four per cent, in 1918 it had increased to thirty per cent. This change illustrated the impact of 'combing out' in key industries, where men delayed making applications for exemptions until it was too late and they were arrested. Of the remainder, a number escaped to Ireland to escape military service.

The Central Tribunal's final report highlighted that after May 1918, conscientious objectors from areas where peace organisations were known to be extremely active, such as the south Wales coalfield and Lanarkshire, did not apply to the local tribunal for exemption but elected either to be taken into custody and imprisoned or to accept work of national importance. The proportion of men from Glamorgan who appeared before the Central Tribunal in 1916 was four per cent, but increased to six per cent in 1918, after the commencement of the 'combing out' of the coal industry, metal trades and agriculture. This, in the opinion of the Tribunal, was explained by a greater knowledge of the tribunal system, 'with the result that 50 per cent of the men seen from these areas did not apply to Tribunal for exemption on the ground of conscientious objection, but preferred to serve a term of imprisonment'.[75]

The Home Office Scheme was based on a fundamental contradiction that in law those who joined it were technically soldiers for the period of the war, whilst on the scheme they were classified as conscientious objectors.[76]

In March 1917, Morgan Jones, the Welsh representative on the NCF's national committee, rejected 'absolutism' as 'not useful', and defended the scheme:

> The Home Office scheme suffers deplorably by comparison with conditions in a trade like mining – as far as pay is concerned. But in so far as helping the war is concerned I am prepared to state categorically that the Home Office seems to be extraordinarily free from it. This scheme does not constitute the kind of alternative service which appeals to me.

[75] National Archives, Ministry of Health Papers, 47/3, 'Report of the Central Tribunal', p. 27.
[76] Rae, *Conscience and Politics*, p. 190.

But then, what is one to do when he has to choose between two kinds
of alternative service? The one is performed in prison and might,
and does help to make material directly for the war under conditions
of perpetual silence and repression, and where no useful service is
done for the community. The other is performed outside prison with
complete immunity from military service, outside army control, and
under conditions of greater freedom. It should be evidence of 'human
frailty' that I should have chosen the latter, particularly as I found the
principle of 'Absolutism' logically untenable.[77]

The first conscientious objectors in the scheme started
work on 12 August 1916, and most of the men released for
employment were transferred to work centres where they
were employed in the repair of main roads, in quarrying,
timber-felling and agriculture.[78] The Road Board had been
persuaded to employ up to 1,000 objectors on road-making
and quarrying, and the government's sponsored Home
Grown Timber Committee agreed to occupy gangs of thirty
to forty men on felling trees. In addition, the Board of Inland
Revenue and Llanelli Rural District Council offered to take
some men, the former for clerical work and the latter for
the repair and maintenance of the waterworks in Llannon,
near Tumble.[79] The first camps for men who accepted the
scheme were set up in August 1916 at Haverhill in Suffolk,
at Newhaven in Sussex, at Dyce, near Aberdeen, in Scotland,
and at Llanddeusant in Wales. The work involved was chiefly
navvying work on roads, quarries and waterworks, or timber-
cutting, and from the end of 1916 the Home Office took over
Wakefield, Warwick, Dartmoor and Knutsford Prisons.[80]

The Dyce camp, near Aberdeen, was opened in high
summer, yet within three months the camp was closed and
abandoned because 'the results as regards discipline and
return for labour had been so bad'.[81] Work consisted of back-
breaking labour in the stone quarries, and the men managed
to negotiate a reduction in working hours. They were forced

[77] *Pioneer*, 10 March 1917.
[78] National Archives, Ministry of Health Papers, 47/3, 'Report of the Central
Tribunal', p. 23.
[79] Rae, *Conscience and Politics*, p. 171.
[80] *The No-Conscription Fellowship*, p. 69.
[81] National Archives, Ministry of Health Papers, 47/3, 'The Home Office and
Conscientious Objectors', p. 5.

to live in old army tents that were not waterproof, and the squalid living conditions led to unsuccessful protests to Parliament. In September, one of their number, Walter Roberts, a conscientious objector originally from Hawarden in Flintshire, died after a short illness. Dyce became 'unmanageable': the men were in revolt against the work offered to them, and rules were widely ignored.[82] Dyce was closed as a result at the end of October and its conscientious objectors given a week's leave, and ordered to return to work centres in Wakefield and Warwick prisons.

By April 1917, there were twenty-eight camps run as part of the Home Office Scheme, containing over 2,000 conscientious objectors, and the largest number were placed in Wakefield (579) and Dartmoor Work Centre (582). Wakefield Prison was transformed, with locks taken from the doors of the cells, as warders acted as instructors, the work of sewing mailbags stopped at five in the evening, and the 600 men could spend their evening in or out till 9.30pm. This state of affairs lasted until Whitsun 1918, when objectors were attacked by a local crowd, and the work centre was closed.[83] W. I. Thomas, from Gorseinon, described the atmosphere as one that resembled an university rather than a place of confinement:

> Here we find hundreds of COs talking and arguing as COs always did. Just inside the reception hall we find stalls where the revolutionary Communist would be selling his literature, likewise the Anarchist, ILP and another stall with its religious tracts. Each section zealously pushing what it had to sell. I could hardly believe my eyes. Was it all a dream? I soon found that the whole prison was run by the COs with only one or two warders acting as instructors. To crown everything I found that it was a sympathetic Quaker who, having offered his services, was the Governor who acted as the Home Office Agent.[84]

The new work centre was opened in Dartmoor Prison in March 1917 and renamed the Princetown Work Centre. It took rather less than one-third of the total number of

---

[82] Graham, *Conscription and Conscience*, pp. 232–3.
[83] Graham, *Conscription and Conscience*, p. 233.
[84] David Cleaver, 'Conscientious Objection in the Swansea Area', in *Morgannwg*, 28 (1984), 52.

men under the Home Office Scheme,[85] and between April and autumn 1917 the number grew to 1,200 men. The work involved quarrying, reclaiming land for the Duchy of Cornwall, gardening, carpentry, blacksmithing and ordinary prison industries.[86] Such a concentration of conscientious objectors also highlighted the range and variety of their religious and political views, which often came into conflict. George M. Ll. Davies, a Christian pacifist, described this as a Babel of political and religious beliefs:

> Er Corinth ni bu erioed gymaint o gymysgedd credoau ac opiniyniau – Eglwyswyr, Pabyddion, Presbyteriaid, Methodistiaid, Christadelffiaid, 'Plymouth Brethren', Marxian Socialist, Anarchists, Gwyddelod, Saeson, Scotiaid, Cymry, Iddewon, Rwsiaid, arlunwyr.[87]

> (Since Corinth, never was there such a mixture of creeds and opinions – Church people, Catholics, Presbyterians, Methodists, Christadelphians, Plymouth Brethren, Marxist Socialists, Anarchists, Irishmen, Englishmen, Scots, Welsh, Jewish, Russians, painters.)

Objectors sang the 'Red Flag', walked out of church when the National Anthem was played, and distributed subversive leaflets.[88] There was constant unrest in the camp, and when an inmate, Harry Firth, died of diabetes in February 1918, his friends accused the prison doctor of negligence and called for a public inquiry into the circumstances of his death.[89] Welsh conscientious objectors were in the vanguard of the protests, and the Anglesey inmate Percy Ogwen Jones complained publicly that in spite of Firth's diabetes and poor health, he had been given heavy work to break stones in the quarry. A general meeting of the men decided to strike in protest against the treatment of Firth and against the ill-treatment of conscientious objectors in prisons and camps,[90] and its so-called 'ringleaders', the chairman of the men's committee, Dan Griffiths from Llanelli, and Ieuan

[85] Graham, *Conscription and Conscience*, p. 240.
[86] National Archives, Ministry of Health Papers, 47/3, 'The Home Office and Conscientious Objectors', p. 5.
[87] *Y Dinesydd*, 5 May 1918.
[88] *Daily Mail*, 23–30 April 1917.
[89] *Pioneer*, 1 March 1918.
[90] National Library of Wales, Morgan Humphreys Papers, A/16196, letter from Percy Ogwen Jones.

P. Hughes, its secretary and former secretary of the NCF in Wales, were taken to Exeter to be court-martialled and returned to prison.[91]

The Brace Committee's inquiry considered that 'on the very smallest foundation they build a superstructure of oppression and improper conduct on the part of officials'.[92] But an indication of the government's frustration with the working of this committee was the replacement of most of its members in July 1917 by new members who had a military or penal background.[93] George M. Ll Davies described the deep divisions between political objectors of various persuasions in Dartmoor:

> Y mae'r Sosialwyr wedi rannu'n gyffelyb: un ysgol a blediant y Rhyfel Dosbarth – Gweithiwr yn erbyn Meistr – yn gwawdio a chondemnio Sosialwyr yr ILP y rhai a gredent nad yw ennill y feistrolaeth ar gyfalaf yn Alpha ac Omega pob ymgais llafurawl. Y mae yr Anneddfwr (Anarchist) yn ysgwyd ei ben arnynt ill eu dau ac yn gofyn paham y talent y fath wrogaeth i lywodraeth a cheisio ennill a defnyddio ei awdurdod, yn lle argyhoeddi y werin mai mewn Llywodraethau – a'r gallu a roddir iddynt ormesu gwerin gan y werin – y mae'r drwg gwrei-ddiol yn dechreu.[94]

> (The Socialists are divided similarly: one school favours the Class War – Worker against Master – that ridicules and condemns the ILP Socialists, who believe that winning mastery over capital is not the Alpha and Omega of every effort by labour. The Anarchist shakes his head at both and asks why they pay such fealty to Government and try and win and use its authority, instead of convincing the people that it is in Governments – and the ability given to them to oppress people by people – that the original evil starts.)

The overwhelming mentality of Princetown was one that challenged authority, and the effect of prison was to stiffen the inmates' resolve. Davies detected an intolerance in 'Atheistic Socialists', who held hellfire religionists in contempt, and who condemned and resented other socialists who had wider

---

[91] Rae, *Conscience and Politics*, p. 188.

[92] Parliamentary Debates (Commons), 5 HC vol. 103, cols 1628–31, 28 February 1918.

[93] Rae, *Conscience and Politics*, pp. 186–7.

[94] *Y Dinesydd*, 5 May 1918.

loyalties than their love for the working class.[95] The Brace Committee was openly contemptuous of the beliefs and physical character of the men who came before them: 'Many of the men were feeble in physique, weak of will or unstable of character. Nearly all were cranks, incapable of sustained collective effort, and cohering only to air their grievances or to promote queer and unusual ends.'[96] By the end of 1916 the Committee had exercised its power to recommend a return to prison for ninety-two of the worst offenders, and after objectors were attacked in the village of Princetown, they were confined to the prison grounds.[97] From April 1917 the Brace Committee attempted to impose stricter discipline and there was a sharp increase in the number of men sent back to prison for breaking the rules. By the autumn of 1917, however, new rules were brought in that gave men the opportunity to have 'exceptional employment', which allowed men who had shown 'industry and good conduct' for twelve months to work for a private employer. But this also implied that most of those left in Princetown were 'neither industrious or well-behaved'.[98]

As part of the Home Office Scheme, four work camps were created in Wales, namely Llanddeusant near Llangadog, which held eighty-five men, and which involved vegetable growing, painting and whitewashing; Llannon reservoir, Tumble, near Llanelli, which employed thirty-two men in repair work and closed in August 1917; Penderyn waterworks, near Mountain Ash, which employed twenty-three men; and Talgarth, in Breconshire, where a small group of men worked in the hospital grounds.[99]

Llannon and Llanddeusant work camps
The first Home Office work camp in Wales was created by Llanelli Rural District waterworks, who required labour to

[95] *Y Dinesydd,* 5 May 1918.
[96] National Archives, Ministry of Health Papers, 47/3, 'The Home Office and Conscientious Objectors', p. 9.
[97] National Archives, Ministry of Health Papers, 47/3, 'The Home Office and Conscientious Objectors', pp. 5, 6.
[98] *Committee on the Employment of Conscientious Objectors: Additional Rules,* Command Paper 8884, HMSO, cited in Rae, *Conscience and Politics,* p. 188.
[99] *Tribunal,* 5 April 1917.

work on the building of a reservoir above Llannon, since its contractors had had difficulty in attracting sufficient men to work on the site. Work on the reservoir had progressed very slowly, and conscientious objectors from Llanelli and Cardiff Prison were brought to work at the reservoir and spend their time 'on the bleak top of the hill'.[100] The local newspaper considered it to be a fit use for conscientious objectors:

> there is no reason why they should not serve their country in some other way, and this way seems to me to be excellent, as they are helping to supply the great want of good water which prevails in Carmarthenshire and thereby making the people much healthier than they were before.[101]

The work of the men at Llanddeusant was at the waterworks at Llyn-y-fan near Llangadog in the east of Carmarthenshire. A visiting journalist from the Liberal *South Wales Daily News* waxed lyrical about the work camp at Llanddeusant: 'The scheme seems to have been an unqualified success, for the men under expert supervision, have brought about a complete transformation of the sense of desolation and disaster, which met their eyes on their first arrival.'[102] He reported that most in the camp were from Lancashire and the Midlands, but it included no Welshmen:

> presumably the policy is to send men right away from the districts with which they were familiar. There seemed to be almost as many professions and trades represented as men in the camp. I found many religious denominations represented in the camp ... A considerable section of the men are Socialists, and their objection to war is moral and economic rather than religious.[103]

This slightly rose-tinted perspective contrasted with complaints of 'slacking and malingering' against the conscientious objectors in the Llannon and Llanddeusant camps. Two NCF representatives, W. J. Roberts and E. E. Hunter, visited the camps in March 1917 and reported Llanddeusant as being a 'sea of mud' and so isolated that visitors, such as the Gorseinon members of the NCF who came to hold

---

[100] *Llanelly Chronicle*, 7 December 1916.
[101] *Llanelly Chronicle*, 7 December 1916.
[102] *Pioneer*, 21 October 1916.
[103] *Llais Llafur*, 24 March 1917.

a concert, had to abandon their car and walk the last two miles, and then obtain a permit to remain, so the concert had to be held two and a half miles away in the church hall in Llanddeusant.[104] The small number of Jehovah's Witnesses there were allowed out only to attend their closest meetings, twenty-two miles distant in Clydach, with no transport available.[105] The inspection by Roberts and Hunter highlighted the halving of the camp's rations, and the effect of new regulations which reduced the opportunities for rail travel from such a remote location. During their inspection of the camp, the same issues of alleged slacking, agitation and substitution were raised with them, together with the men's concern about low rates of pay for overtime, which they worked in order to make up for time lost through bad weather. The works inspector was complimentary of the men: 'of course, the work was strange to the boys at first, and one could hardly expect any more from them and there was a tremendous difference between the Pen and the Pick. But now he could make no complaint.'[106]

The local villagers of Tumble gave a warm welcome to the men of the Llannon camp:

> I was extremely gratified to learn that the boys are highly respected by the whole of the villagers. Invitations to tea, etc., are freely given, and freely accepted. Industrially it is a mining village, and the miners who support by weekly contributions, the local Institute and library, decided on a referendum, with only four dissentients, that both institute and library be placed at the disposal of the C.O.'s.[107]

This impression was reinforced by one of those objectors, E. P. Jones, Pontypridd:

> oedd y Tumble yma yn neilltuol, yn neilltuol fel 'na. Oe chi'n cael mynd i de efo nhw ar ddydd Sul a phopeth, i bobman, pob enwad ac yn garedig, efo popeth, menthyg y library a chwbwl, oedd ma library yma y pryd hynny. Wel fedre chi ddim cael mwy o garedigrwydd.[108]

---

[104] *Pioneer*, 21 October 1916.

[105] *Pioneer*, 21 October 1916.

[106] McMaster University Archive, Bertrand Russell Papers, W. J. Roberts, 'Report to the National Committee on South Wales Home Office Camps', COIB Report 45.

[107] McMaster University Archive, Bertrand Russell Papers, MX-3801-N, undated letter to the National Committee of the NCF, McMaster University Papers, Ontario.

[108] Swansea University Archive, South Wales Coalfield Collection, interview with E. p. Jones, Aud. 82.

(the Tumble was special like that. You would go for tea with them on
Sunday, and everyone, everywhere, every denomination, were kind
with everything; they let us borrow books from the library and all.
There was a library here then. You could not get more kindness.)

As for allegations of slacking in Llannon, Roberts highlighted
a recent incident, when a policeman came to the camp,
armed with a warrant for the arrest of two COs, Charles H.
Pett for 'slacking', and Selwyn Jones, Port Talbot, for 'slacking
and insolence'. Neither had the opportunity to defend themselves and they were taken to Cardiff Prison. Whilst Roberts
accepted that in Jones's case there may have been just a 'little
room' for the charge of slacking, the charge of insolence was
said to be totally unfounded. A letter from one of the men
in the camp, Gwilym Rees to Revd E. K. Jones, who was also
Selwyn Jones's uncle, gave a more detailed explanation for
his arrest.[109] Jones had been taken ill in November 1916 and,
although confined to his bed, was reported by the agent for
insolence and unsatisfactory workmanship. He was given two
days to respond, in which he denied the allegation, and he
and Pett were arrested and taken to Cardiff prison on the
basis that he had refused work. Rees described a 'rousing
send-off' by the people of the village, 'whose sympathy has
now been commanded', and on the following Monday the
men went on strike and left the settlement in protest against
the management.

But their biggest concern was the arrests of nineteen men
in the camp before March 1917 who were then returned to
prison.[110] One objector, Frank Davenport from Rochdale,
was sent back to prison for refusing to go to his work during a
snowstorm, and another returned to prison because of the
'callous neglect' he had suffered in the Llannon camp, after
he had suffered a serious illness.[111]

---

[109] National Library of Wales, E. K. Jones Papers, Box 29, letter from Gwilym Rees,
10 March 1917.
[110] Macmaster University Archive, Bertrand Russell Papers, MX 3801.
[111] Graham, *Conscience and Conscription*, p. 16.

Penderyn

The third camp in south Wales was in Penderyn, near Hirwaun, where sixty-one conscientious objectors worked to build a reservoir for Mountain Ash local authority. While most similar projects came to an end in 1915 because of a lack of labour, this scheme was continued by the COs, quartered nearby, who worked 'at a lethargic rate'. Sometime during the war the contractor relinquished the contract and the council administered it direct.[112] The daily routine of working with puddle clay to build the foundations of the dam disillusioned many of the men, and a number left the scheme in protest. R.T. Holloway was sent to Penderyn from Dartmoor in March 1917:

> I may say that the work here is very hard indeed being navvying at a Reservoir and the hours are very long from 6.30 am to 5.30 pm with half an hour for breakfast and half an hour for dinner. We are trying to obtain an 8 hour day if possible. As things develop I will let you know from time to time ... We are in all 60 and about 30 or 40 being Welshmen living near here.[113]

The camp resolved in August 1917 to protest against their treatment:

> We regard the rules issued by the H.O.C. [Home Office Committee] as being penal, unnecessary, and in their nature petty; designed to make the position of men working under the scheme unbearable, and we hereby call upon all members of H.O. camps to link up and unitedly repudiate them.[114]

This disillusionment increased as more men entered the camps, and even the mildest and most quietist conscientious objectors who attempted to make the scheme work became disenchanted:

> the lack of purpose and the sense of frustration it engendered encouraged some to return voluntarily to prison and drove others to

[112] Harold D. Bowtell and Geoffrey Hill, *Reservoir Builders of South Wales: Dam Builders in the Age of Steam* (Malvern: The Industrial Locomotive, 2006), p. 64.
[113] National Library of Wales, E. K. Jones Papers, Box 29, letter from R. T. Holloway.
[114] *Committee on the Employment of Conscientious Objectors: Additional Rules*, Command Paper 8884, HMSO.

sympathise with the methods of the militant Marxists and anarchists who had never had any intention of cooperating with the (Brace) Committee'. Only the quietist Jehovah's Witnesses, and Plymouth Brethren stood to one side as the protests mounted.[115]

Whilst a number were returned to prison, the scheme's administrator, the Home Office agent, Sammy Heap, turned a blind eye to those local COs who disappeared home on their bikes over the weekends to the Swansea area and the Amman Valley, and some of the Welsh COs hosted the English and Scottish COs in the camp 'on a sort of rota' for an occasional weekend.[116]

Talgarth

The fourth camp to be opened in south Wales in July 1917 was in Talgarth, near Brecon, and contained sixty men, who were involved in helping to supply water and drainage to a new sanatorium erected by the Welsh National Memorial Association. Their work lay in digging trenches of various depths to lay a water main, for the purpose of carrying water from a stream some one and a half miles away to the sanatorium. This hard, laborious work meant working for ten hours per day in two five-hour shifts, and the food was considered to be 'quite inadequate' for the nature of the work. After a letter-writing campaign and protests, some small improvement were gained:

> On Saturdays they are expected to work six hours without rest or food. This is a physical impossibility, and after the agent fining the men two weeks' pay on two occasions for ceasing work at twelve o'clock (the usual dinner hour), the H.O. allowed the men 8 ozs of cake for Saturday mornings only. The agent by his actions appears to be making things as uncomfortable and unpleasant as he possibly can. The men are very unhappy and discouraged.[117]

Their accommodation was often 'hopelessly inadequate', and the men slept in tents, old cottages and disused barns.[118]

---

[115] Rae, *Conscience and Politics*, p. 175.

[116] Albert Davies, 'Wanderings' (unpublished autobiography, undated).

[117] *NCF News sheet for the Home Office Centres and Camps*, Acc. 13388 (Autumn 1917), National Library of Scotland.

[118] *NCF News sheet for the Home Office Centres and Camps*.

A number of objectors ran away from the Home Office work camps and flouted the scheme's rules, although many were caught and recalled to the army. The prominent Marxist and lecturer Nun Nicholas was granted four days' leave by authorities at Wakefield work centre, but extended his leave to six weeks' duration and continued his propaganda before being arrested:

> He received a warning commanding him to return otherwise he would be arrested. He ignored the warning and ten days later he was arrested and taken to Cardiff Prison, where he now is. Whilst at home he was not inactive in the Labour movement. He delivered two brilliant lectures before the Swansea Industrial History Class on 'The Tribal System in Wales'. He also spoke at the inaugural meeting of the Clydach Trades Council. Also he delivered the opening lecture for the Clydach Industrial History Class. At Glais he gave a most humorous account of his experiences at Kinmel Park and Wormwood Scrubs.[119]

The escapees from the Home Office scheme tended to be socialist COs who had utter contempt for the system, and amongst those who went on the run was Ness Edwards, an 'advanced' man, a firebrand member of the ILP and future MP for Caerphilly. He absconded to the home of a Russian count in Hammersmith, and later hid in a cave above his home town of Abertillery before giving himself up because of the tough wintry conditions.[120] Approximately twenty-two of the Welsh conscientious objectors became fugitives from either the army or the Home Office schemes, and Henry Riding, for example, an ILP member from Newport who was a council clerk, escaped from Princetown to Bristol and southern Ireland, working there as a farm hand before travelling to Liverpool and onwards to Huddersfield, where he found work until the end of the war.[121] William Duncan, from Cardiff, went absent without leave from Princetown in March 1918 and was only recalled to his military unit in January 1919. When he refused to return, he was declared a deserter, but the authorities failed to trace him. Prominent

---

[119] *Pioneer*, 24 February 1917.
[120] Wayne David, *Remaining True – A Biography of Ness Edwards* (Caerphilly: Caerphilly History Society, 2006), pp. 4–6.
[121] *Pearce Register.*

union activists, such as Arthur Horner, avoided the 'comb-out' in the mining industry by escaping to Ireland, where Horner lived under an assumed name under the protection of the Irish Citizens' Army. When he was caught in Holyhead on his return, he was accompanied by two brothers who were also deserters, George and Frank Phippen, both ILP members from Pentre, Rhondda.[122] Tom Gale, from Penygraig in the Rhondda, escaped from custody on his way to Princetown from Cardiff prison, and reached southern Ireland, where he was also given shelter by the Irish Citizens' Army. Together with a number of other Welsh fugitives he trained with them in the Wicklow hills outside Dublin, before departing to New Jersey in the United States, where he engaged in socialist propaganda against the war.[123] Bryn Roberts, a miner and ILPer from the Swansea Valley, escaped from prison in Northumberland.[124] Even after the end of the war, the authorities pursued the recalcitrant objectors. The unconventional 40-year-old Alfred Goodman Dunn, Merthyr, escaped in 1917 and went to live in disguise as a woman in Bristol.[125]

The Central Tribunal continued its work until April 1919, at which point the government authorised the discharge of all conscientious objectors on the Home Office Scheme. On 19 April 1919, the last man was released officially and the Scheme ceased to exist, but those who had absented themselves from the scheme, and who had therefore been recalled to the army, were still pursued. A Swansea Valley CO, William Howells, a coal merchant from Trebanos, went absent without leave from the work camp in Knutsford, alleging that he had been posted to a work centre in south Wales. In March 1919 he was deemed to have deserted. He was arrested at home in August 1919 and subsequently given a six-month prison sentence, but had his sentence remitted and was dishonourably discharged for misconduct.[126] When the

[122] Nina Fishman, *Arthur Horner: A Political Biography. Vol I. 1894 to 1944* (Lawrence and Wishart, 2010), pp. 58–61.
[123] Swansea University Archive, South Wales Coalfield Collection, interview with Tom Gale, Aud. 49.
[124] *Pearce Register.*
[125] *Pearce Register.*
[126] *Pearce Register.*

Armistice was announced, Albert Davies from Pontardawe abandoned his work in the Home Office camp in Penderyn and went on the run, joining a 'band of CO fugitives', who changed their names and worked on tree-felling in the Brecon Beacons, where the forest owners knew but did not reveal their identities.[127]

THE PELHAM COMMITTEE

The Pelham Committee was appointed in March 1916 by the Board of Trade to 'provide advice as to what service of national importance an applicant for exemption on the ground of conscientious objection should undertake', under the chairmanship of the Hon. T. H. W. Pelham, an Assistant Secretary at the Board of Trade. The majority of those referred to the scheme were married, and half were over 30, and so were much more likely than their younger comrades to provide little trouble. Of the 4,000 conscientious objectors who came under the Pelham Scheme, 1,400 were Christadelphians who had been granted certificates of exemption by the Army Council, many of whom went to work in munition factories and for government contractors. Others were assigned to welfare work with the YMCA, the Red Cross and the General Service Section of the FAU, to hospitals, asylums, to the railways, the docks, the mines, and to the manufacture and distribution of food.[128] The Committee attempted to ensure that it responded to the differing views of tribunals about where objectors should be offered work, either in the immediate vicinity of the tribunal's district, or whether they should be employed at a distance from their home.[129] The total number of men from Wales coming under the Pelham Scheme was 207 (see Table 13), of whom 155 were Christadelphians. The percentage of those Christadelphians as a proportion of those who came under the Committee in Wales, at 75 per cent, is a much larger percentage of the total

[127] Albert Davies, 'Wanderings', p. 30.
[128] Friends House Library, T. E. Harvey Papers, Box 9, Pelham Committee Report, Appendix H.
[129] Friends House Library, T. E. Harvey Papers, Box 9, Pelham Committee Report, p. 4.

than the equivalent for England, at 42 per cent. Of the total number of 3,964 who came under the Pelham Committee, 5.2 per cent of the total came from Wales. The Christadelphians were primarily based in Glamorgan, Monmouthshire and in the Llanelli and Ammanford areas of Carmarthenshire.

County	Others	Christadelphians	Total
Glamorgan	28	71	99
Monmouthshire	3	58	61
Carmarthenshire	2	24	26
Cardiganshire	6	____	6
Caernarfonshire	6	____	6
Denbighshire	5	____	5
Brecknock	2	____	2
Pembroke	____	2	2
Total	52	155	207

Table 13: Conscientious objectors in Wales under the Pelham Committee[130]

The Christadelphians were a millenarian Christian group with an unique alternativist position, in that they were prepared to work directly for the prosecution of the war, even in a munitions factory, and they secured exemption from military service by the Army Council in August 1916, when they were brought under the Pelham Committee's scheme.[131] They were customarily greeted with respect in tribunal hearings. Writing about his experience of serving on the Cardiganshire Appeal Tribunal, Herbert Vaughan only dealt with a small number of CO cases:

> we were fortunate in having remarkably few of such cases brought before us ... one of these applicants interested me greatly ... he described himself as a Christadelphian, and he was the only member of that religious sect I have come across. He was a nice young fellow, and I am sure his abhorrence at the mere notion of having to kill his fellow-men, even his enemies, was deep rooted and genuine ... after some arguments we offered to have him allocated to a labour battalion at the front, which would only be equipped with spades and other

---

[130] Friends House Library, T. E. Harvey Papers, Box 9, Pelham Committee Report, 'Schedule of Counties and Outstanding Localities'.
[131] Jannaway, *Without the Camp*, pp. v–vi, 198–203.

trenching tools, and with this decision on our own part this young objector seemed fully satisfied.[132]

The next biggest religious groups of COs under the Pelham Committee were the Plymouth Brethren (145) and Quakers (140),[133] and those from Wales were varied in their background and skills. An analysis of those who came under the authority of the Pelham Committee included a total of 124 who were university students, of whom ten came from the University of Wales. The son of a prominent Conservative industrial family who owned quarries in Caernarvonshire, H. C. Darbishire, was transferred away to a farm in Benson in Oxfordshire; but work was found for a John Davey of Swansea, who had been a mariner, to work as circular sawyer with a local company. W. A. W. Pope, a coal trimmer, was found work with Tharsis Sulphur and Copper Co., but a Tredegar collier, Evan R. Price, had disappeared and was untraceable.

The Committee's attempt to ensure that conscientious objectors were not given work within travelling time of their homes was reflected in the experience of an R. Morgan, who had appeared before Gelligaer local tribunal and was employed by a local company of timber merchants in Bargoed. The committee directed that he should find work on a farm or in a controlled establishment away from the town. Commercial companies were asked if they were prepared to keep men who were conscientious objectors, and Powell Duffryn agreed, for instance, to retain the service of an I. J. Powell, Pontlottyn, as a miner.[134] John Thomas, a well-known teacher in Aberdare, a member of the ILP and secretary of the local NCF branch, an anti-war activist and prominent in the Workers' Education Association, was granted exemption from service in May 1916, provided he was engaged in work of national importance. He was required to obtain market garden work at least fifty miles from his home, and he wrote to one of the committee's members, the

---

[132] Vaughan, 'The Cardiganshire Appeal Tribunal', 177.
[133] Friends House Library, T. E. Harvey Papers, Box 9, Pelham Report Schedule.
[134] Friends House Library, T. E. Harvey Papers, Box 9, Pelham Committee minutes, 1 February–1 March 1917.

Quaker T. E. Harvey, alleging that this would be 'no more than deportation'. He felt victimised both by the Pelham Committee's attitude and by his local tribunal, who he felt had 'prejudiced' his case and who were biased against him because of his political activities:

> the Clerk and the chairman of the local tribunal have done their best to prejudice my case – that is evident or they would have mentioned that I am the only son at home helping a widowed mother and a little brother 12 years old. I stated all these facts of domestic responsibility to them in my original appeal ... They are anxious to penalise me for the uncompromising attitude I have taken up on the Militant question on platforms, and in the press ...

> I hate this insidious way the Local Tribunal hope to exile or deport me ... I am not prepared to go fifty miles from home merely to satisfy the spite and retaliatory spirit of a Chairman and clerk of a Local tribunal who think that as a CO and a secretary of the N.C.F. branch and a Public speaker against Militarism I ought to be hounded out of the place. I'll go the whole hog and face the trials of prison before I'll do that. You can rely upon my keeping absolutely confidential all you have told me in your last letter.[135]

This letter suggests a degree of collusion and sympathy between the two correspondents. On 4 June, he wrote to Harvey again to thank him for the Committee's agreement for him to accept the offer of agricultural work in the Cowbridge area within the permitted radius.[136] Thomas later moved to the Swansea area, and was publicly active in the ILP and anti-war movement throughout the rest of the war.

The Pelham Committee considered that whilst a number of conscientious objectors had caused 'an extraordinary amount of trouble', in the main they had worked with 'some fair degree of discipline' and in 'a considerable amount of cases they received the commendation of their employers'. The Committee viewed its task as keeping the conscientious objectors at work, under supervision, and preventing as far as possible any harm to recruiting or to the efficient prosecution of the war. The Committee's view of the character of the

---

[135] Friends House Library, T. E. Harvey Papers, Temp MSS 835/T1, letter from Thomas to Harvey, 28 May 1916.
[136] Friends House Library, T. E. Harvey Papers, Temp MSS 835/T1, letter from Thomas to Harvey, 4 June 1916.

conscientious objector, however, was so uncharitable that the Committee's Quaker member, T. E. Harvey, insisted on withdrawing his signature from a paragraph of the final report because he could not agree with its malevolent sentiment that 'taken as a whole COs seemed to be abnormal in their general outlook on life, as well as in the matter of military service, and a substantial number of them were found to suffer from some form of physical disability'.[137] By February 1919, all those under the authority of the Pelham Committee had been allowed to go home.

THE 'ABSOLUTISTS'

The 'absolutists' believed that any kind of service that was an alternative either to military service or to their ordinary employment was unacceptable. In their opinion any compromise would only help in the organisation of the country for war and therefore they refused to accept anything but absolute exemption.[138] A divisive debate arose within the No-Conscription Fellowship between 'alternativists', such as Morgan Jones, the south Wales representative, who believed that the alternative schemes such as the Home Office scheme should be accepted, and 'absolutists', such as the NCF's chairman, Clifford Allen, its founder, Fenner Brockway, and individuals, such as Mansel Grenfell, Gorseinon, who believed that no conscientious objectors should compromise with the state. This discussion was conducted mainly through the pages of the *Tribunal*, where Fenner Brockway argued that the Home Office scheme served the military machine:

> it is in reality a form of slavery the acceptance of which is a denial of that sense of the worth of human personality which is the foundation of all we are doing. The positive contribution which the NCF is making is its insistence on the value of individual liberty. What will history say of us if we only resist military service to fasten upon ourselves and our successors a vicious scheme of indentured labour?[139]

[137] Friends House Library, T. E. Harvey Papers, Box 9, Pelham Committee Report, p. 7.
[138] *The No-Conscription Fellowship*, p. 65.
[139] *Tribunal*, 7 September 1916.

The absolutists argued that by doing work of national importance, one was doing work considered important for war, and
thereby liberating others to go to the front.[140] Ithel Davies
described his sense of betrayal towards those who accepted
alternative service:

> teimlem ni a wrthododd fod y lleill wedi ein bradychu braidd ac wedi
> ei gwneud yn haws i'r llywodraeth ein cadw yng ngharchar. Teimlem,
> petai pawb wedi gwrthod ac wedi hawlio rhyddid diamodol, y byddai'n
> anos i'r llywodraeth ein cadw yng ngharchar.[141]

> (We felt as those who had refused alternative service that the rest had
> betrayed us somewhat and that it made it easier for the government
> to keep us in prison. We felt that if everyone had refused and had
> demanded unconditional freedom, it would have been more difficult
> for the government to keep us in prison.)

This debate was conducted in the pages of the *Pioneer*
between the alternativist position, represented by Morgan
Jones, and the absolutist position, represented by Emrys
Hughes and Mansell Grenfell, and proved the main point of
conflict between Jones and Hughes in the election for the
Wales representative on the NCF's national committee in the
autumn of 1916. Jones was imprisoned initially in May 1916,
then re-imprisoned in July 1916, and although initially an
absolutist, accepted the Home Office scheme, but his experience in prison convinced him of the pointlessness of the
absolutist position:

> most absolutists like myself went into gaol in the early days under the
> spell of that wondrous dictum that we must do the work there because
> we were not fighting the civil authorities but the military only! We did
> the work – some made mailbags; some (absolutists and alternativists)
> have actually been making ship's fenders for the Admiralty, others
> of us more fortunate than the rest got some fresh air working in the
> gardens … To my mind the whole pitch was queered for the absolutist
> immediately.[142]

He withdrew his acceptance of the Home Office Scheme and
returned to prison before apparently suffering a nervous
breakdown. In Wormwood Scrubs, he felt he was:

[140] Graham, *Conscription and Conscience*, p. 214.
[141] Davies, *Bwrlwm Byw*, pp. 72, 73.
[142] *Pioneer*, 3 February 1917.

imposing unnecessary worry upon those most dear to me and possibly by ruining my physical and mental powers, I might be prejudicing my future usefulness in the great fight that would have to be fought later when Europe returned to sanity. I therefore re-accepted the scheme with the same proviso as before so long as my conscientious convictions were not violated.[143]

Ironically Morgan Jones again fell foul of the recruiting authorities. On furlough because of poor health, he recommenced his anti-war activity, and was re-arrested in April 1919, accused of being a deserter, which he vehemently denied, and he was imprisoned until August 1919.[144] The authorities also had to deal with the shifting population of men returned to prison for disobeying the rules of the Home Office scheme. These different groups presented the prison authorities with a particularly difficult problem, for the absolutists refused to obey some prison rules, on the grounds of conscience, and the militants who had left the Home Office scheme often set out to undermine the system by calculated disobedience and contempt for authority.[145] Of the conscientious objectors from Wales, seventy men, representing eight per cent of the total of Welsh conscientious objectors, were absolutists. Of the Welsh COs, Emrys Hughes received the greatest number of court martials and imprisonments, and was amongst the handful of COs in Britain who were imprisoned on five separate occasions for a total of three years. Another five conscientious objectors from Wales were court-martialled four times, and another fifteen COs were court-martialled three times.[146]

Whilst an analysis of these objectors suggest a wide range of reasons for their absolutism, membership of the ILP was an important motivating force. Emrys Hughes was the son of a minister of religion and a schoolteacher from Abercynon who had trained in Leeds Technical College and was one of the most prominent leaders of the ILP in south Wales. He

[143] *Pioneer*, 10 February 1917.
[144] John Sheaff, 'Morgan Jones, educationalist and Labour politician: a biographical study', CO/051, Liddle Collection, Leeds University; Dylan Rees, 'Morgan Jones, educationalist and Labour politician', *Morgannwg*, 31 (1987), 66–83.
[145] Rae, *Conscience and Politics*, p. 202.
[146] *Pearce Register*.

was a friend and disciple of Keir Hardie, and would later marry Hardie's daughter, Agnes. He was one of the founding members of the NCF and active in the anti-conscription movement. He disliked the term 'conscientious objector', and preferred to describe himself as a socialist, an anti-militarist or as anti-war.

His experience as an absolutist conscientious objector is the most extreme of the Welsh conscientious objectors in terms of the number of prison terms he served, and his treatment reflects the difficulty the military and civil authorities had in dealing with uncompromising objectors. His first incarceration was in Devizes Military Prison, after he had been court-martialled and sentenced to two years' hard labour, commuted to nine months' detention. Taken there in handcuffs and forcibly dressed in a soldier's uniform, he was 'knocked about' by non-commissioned officers and fed at various intervals on bread and water for refusing to do work of a military nature. After seven weeks, he was again court-martialled for refusing to drill, sentenced to a further twenty-one months' hard labour (commuted to nine months' detention) and transferred to Shepton Mallet Civil Prison. From there he was taken in chains to Cardiff, from where he was transferred to Wormwood Scrubs to appear, briefly, before the Central Tribunal, which came to the conclusion that Hughes could not possibly possess any conscientious scruples to military service.[147]

Hughes's absolutism was anathema to the Central Tribunal and he was sent back to complete his sentence of nine months in Cardiff prison. He was released from Cardiff Prison in March 1917 and immediately returned to the Kinmel Park barracks, court-martialled again, and sentenced to hard labour for another two years, to Caernarfon prison.[148] Released on 9 January 1918, he was escorted to join the 3rd Welsh Regiment in Redcar and sentenced to another six months' hard labour at North Allerton prison in North Yorkshire. After four months he was sent back to the regiment in Redcar and was there when the war ended, after

[147] *Pioneer*, 10 March 1917.
[148] National Archives, Ministry of Health Papers, 47/3, Central Tribunal minutes, 25 August 1916.

which he was sentenced to two years' hard labour and returned to North Allerton prison. He was eventually released in 1919 more than three years from the day of his first arrest.[149]

At his fifth court martial at Redcar in July 1918, having described himself as an 'abandoned and unrepentant criminal', he set out his principles as an absolutist:

> I am (also) opposed to taking part in any alternative war service or in any of the industrial efforts to solve the problem of the conscientious objectors, by first of all compelling them to work under degrading conditions in penal settlements, and then allowing them to find other work if they promise to agree from propagating their opinions ...

> I think the greatest service I can render to the people of this country is to oppose the military institutions which have been introduced and established during a time of panic and terror and by which thousands of men have been forced to submit to a loathsome routine of military discipline and then sent to be miserably butchered in a bloody, futile and foolish war, in which their rulers have involved them. The greatest menace to the liberty of the people is the Conscription Law; the greatest duty of the intelligent citizen is to oppose it at all costs and to continue such opposition and defiance until it is overthrown.[150] </q>

In contrast, Ithel Davies was brought up in rural Montgomeryshire and became one of a small number of conscientious objectors in Britain who were court-martialled four times. Already a well-known writer and poet at the beginning of the war, Davies was a socialist and a farmer's son, whose elderly father farmed an upland farm, with 1,500 sheep, with the aid of his two sons. He had been raised in a Nonconformist and radical tradition, and influenced by the ILP and socialist newspapers such as the *New Leader*, which his father received at home. He was an active NCF member and mentored a number of young men locally to apply for exemption from the tribunal, to the extent that he believed that the authorities had targeted him because of his anti-war activity.[151] After his beating in Mold Military Prison, the

---

[149] National Library of Scotland, Keir Hardie and Emrys Hughes Papers, Dep. 176, Box 8(1), 'Welsh Rebel', pp. 102–213.

[150] *Pioneer*, 3 August 1918.

[151] Davies, *Bwrlwm Byw*, p. 61.

ensuing public outcry ensured from the late summer of 1916 that all conscientious objectors were henceforth placed in civilian prisons.[152]

Ithel Davies was gaoled in another three prisons following his period in Mold Military Prison, in Shrewsbury, Winson Green in Birmingham, and Armleigh in Leeds.[153] The other Welsh COs who were court-martialled four times reflected the extent to which the religious, moral and political attitudes of individual conscientious objectors were fused together. John Christopher Morgan from Hendy, near Pontarddulais, was an active trade unionist in the Transport Union and described himself as a Congregationalist and a member of the NCF. He was first arrested in May 1916, and remained in prison until January 1919. Pryce Brown, from Guildsfield near Welshpool in Montgomeryshire, aged 29 in 1916, described as a student and a cowman on a farm, was first court-martialled in May 1916, and was not released until the summer of 1919. E. D. Mort, a well-known political activist and trade unionist in the Dockers' Union in Taibach, near Port Talbot, had agreed initially to join the Home Office scheme on the Llannon reservoir scheme before he was 'rejected' by managers and returned to prison. Philemon James Edwards, from Tongwynlais, was a coalminer, a member of the ILP, a Baptist, a Quaker and a member of the NCF. He was arrested in June 1916, and although he was given conditional exemption by the Central Tribunal and required to join the NCC, he was charged as an absentee and imprisoned for the first time in September 1916, before being released after his fourth imprisonment on medical grounds in June 1918. Edgar Davies from Abergavenny described himself as a member of the Fellowship of Reconciliation, a Baptist and an attender in Quaker meetings. He was also a member of the NCF and the UDC, and had been employed as a bank clerk and as a teacher in a Quaker school in Greater Malvern.[154]

The War Office was content for the civilian prison system to have everyday care for the men, although they were still

---

[152] Davies, *Bwrlwm Byw*, p. 68.
[153] Davies, *Bwrlwm Byw*, pp. 64–79.
[154] *Pearce Register.*

military prisoners.[155] In common with the general population of imprisoned objectors, those from Wales tended to be
distributed anywhere in England or Wales to serve their
prison sentences. Men court-martialled in Kinmel Park
tended to be imprisoned in Walton gaol in Liverpool, or in
other prisons in the north of England and the Midlands.
Those from mid-Wales who were court-martialled at Park
Hall, near Welshpool, could be taken to Shrewsbury Prison,
and Ithel Davies recalled a group of Welsh conscientious
objectors there that included Harold Watkins from Llanfyllin,
the Marxist propagandist Nun Nicholas from the Swansea
Valley, two brothers from Briton Ferry, Hwyrnos and
Cynwawrddydd Jones, and Jimmy Hudson, the future
Scottish MP.[156] The prisons used in Wales to accommodate
conscientious objectors were Cardiff and smaller local
prisons in Carmarthen and Caernarfon. There is no evidence
that conscientious objectors were accommodated in Swansea
or Brecon prisons.

Carmarthen was an exceptionally small prison and held a
total of thirty-one conscientious objectors as prisoners
between June 1916 and July 1919, whilst Caernarfon held no
more than ten conscientious objectors at any one time. In
prison conscientious objectors were subject to the rules of
the 'Third Division', in which they were sentenced to imprisonment with 'hard labour', which meant that prisoners were
kept in isolation for twenty-eight days, then worked in association, and after two months were allowed to receive visits
from relatives and 'respectable friends'. By the end of 1917,
the government agreed to release objectors because of their
poor state of health,[157] and in the next eighteen months, over
300 absolutists were released under this War Office concession.[158] The Home Office's final attempt to resolve the
problem of the absolutists was in August 1918, when they
created a special establishment in an empty Wakefield prison
where the men would be granted the maximum freedom

---

[155] Rae, *Conscience and Politics*, p. 203.
[156] Davies, *Bwrlwm Byw*, p. 73.
[157] Parliamentary Debates (Commons) 5 HL, vol. 27, cols 53–6, 4 December 1917;
Tribunal, 8 January 1920.
[158] *Tribunal*, 8 January 1920.

consistent with their status as prisoners. Between 200 and 300 of those who had been in prison for more than two years were brought there, and they were given freedom to wander anywhere within the prison complex, and the cells were left unlocked. They were allowed to wear their own clothes, mix and smoke freely after working hours, and enjoy generous privileges with regard to letters and visits.[159] But the absolutists were dubious of the government's motives, and refused to cooperate, which led to the abandonment of the experiment in September 1918.[160]

The delay in the release of conscientious objectors after the Armistice led to a succession of hunger strikes in the first three months of 1919. The authorities attempted to deal with the 'die-hards' who were hunger-strikers under the 'Cat and Mouse' Act, namely the 'Prisoners Temporarily Discharged for Ill Health Act' of 1913, which had been introduced initially to deal with the suffragette movement.[161] One hundred and thirty conscientious objectors were temporarily released under the Act after periods of forced feeding. The only example of this policy operating in Wales was in Carmarthen, when Arthur Horner, together with another half a dozen objectors, was released after conducting a hunger strike in May 1919,[162] and the Home Office issued instructions that forcible feeding should be abandoned. The militants amongst the conscientious objectors promoted unrest and disruption and Wandsworth prison became the centre of activity, where there were over 100 conscientious objectors, described as 'extreme anti-authoritarians', who had been turned down by the Central Tribunal or had been sent back to prison from the Home Office scheme. On 3 April 1919 the Secretary of State for War, Winston Churchill, agreed to release all objectors who had served twenty months, with time spent in military custody or on the Home Office scheme being allowed to count towards the total.[163] This enabled the Home Office to release the majority of

[159] Davies, *Bwrlwm Byw*, pp. 74–5.
[160] *The Friend*, 20 September 1918.
[161] Childs, *Episodes and Recollections*, p. 151.
[162] Fishman, *Arthur Horner*, p. 66.
[163] National Archives, Cabinet Papers, CAB 23/10/553(I), 3 April 1919.

conscientious objectors from prison by the end of May, and the remainder by the end of August 1919. The absolutists were discharged for 'misconduct', and other conscientious objectors still within the army were discharged on demobilisation: 'none of them received any bounty on discharge, and that was about the only difference we made between the fighting man and the "conchy".'[164]

THE 'ULTIMATE PRICE': THE DEATHS
OF CONSCIENTIOUS OBJECTORS

In 1921, the Conscientious Objector Information Bureau published a final list of seventy-three men who had died as a direct result of the treatment they had received in prison or at military hands, of whom ten had died in prison, twenty-four in the Home Office work centres, six in military custody and the rest shortly after release.[165]

The NCF alleged that these men died as a result of their treatment by the military or in the conditions of the prisons or the Home Office scheme. Graham asserts that these men's deaths were characterised by emaciation caused by want of exercise and nourishment, and by mental and physical suffering, so that they were unable to resist the 1919 influenza epidemic or related illnesses, such as bronchitis, pneumonia or consumption.[166] Rae disputes this interpretation and argues that many of these deaths were caused by illnesses contracted before conscription or by illnesses contracted while working on the scheme.[167] It is undoubtedly the case that many conscientious objectors were either physically unsuited to or incapable of hard manual work in the inhospitable climate of work camps such as Llanddeusant or Llannon, and the scars of their experiences affected the health of many conscientious objectors for many years. Morgan Jones's health broke in prison, for instance, and was never fully restored,[168] and numerous conscientious

---

[164] Childs, *Episodes and Recollections*, p. 154.
[165] Boulton, *Objection Overruled*, p. 266.
[166] Graham, *Conscription and Conscience*, p. 313.
[167] Rae, *Conscience and Politics*, p. 190.
[168] Sheaff, *Morgan Jones M.P. 1885–1939*, p. 16.

objectors, such as Alfred Major, Pontypridd, and George Neale, Blackwood, were released early on medical grounds because of their ill-health. Others such as Maurice Andrews, Aberaman, were released on grounds of ill-health after suffering brutal treatment, in his case for refusing an order to put on an uniform:

> He was forcibly stripped and left in a cold cell in singlet and pants for eight days. The military authorities refused to return his civvies, forced him into khaki, and put him into a padded cell, and in addition to this strapped his hands behind his back for four hours every day, a proceeding which caused him unspeakable agony.[169]

The first conscientious objector to die as result of his experiences was Walter Roberts from Flintshire, who contracted high fever from being constantly wet and sodden in the rotten and condemned tents on the muddy hillside at the first work centre in Dyce, near Aberdeen.[170] A total of six other Welsh objectors are thought to have died as a result of their experiences – Hal Beynon from Swansea, George Dardis from Risca, Albert Rudall from Newport, Alfred Ernest Statton from Wrexham, Glyn Evans from Pontardawe and John Evans from Cardiff.

John Evans's death highlighted how ill-suited he was for the work given to him as part of the Home Office scheme. A 24-year-old former clerk and a student who was studying for the ministry, he was not politically inclined. He refused to join the NCC and during his initial imprisonment at Cardiff prison he was offered and accepted the Home Office scheme, but his health was affected by the prison diet, and the work camp in Newhaven, where he worked as a navvy on road-making, the winter conditions and his accommodation in a tent without heating apparatus were hardly likely to suit a man who had become emaciated from prison life. Evans's health gradually declined and, after six months at Newhaven, he was sent to Wakefield centre, where the medical officer certified him to be in an advanced stage of consumption, as tuberculosis was commonly called.

[169] National Library of Wales, E. K. Jones Papers, Box 2.
[170] Graham, *Conscription and Conscience*, p. 312.

In Easter 1917, his mother came to know for the first time of his serious condition, and her application to the Home Office resulted in permission being given to him to return home and he was discharged. He died on Whit Sunday 1917. The *Tribunal* castigated those authorities who had let him decline so rapidly:

> those who are left behind may be pardoned for a less saint-like attitude towards certain authorities – the men who have maladministered the Military Service Acts, and those who under the pretence of furnishing work of national importance, have imposed injurious and penalising conditions of labour.[171]

Albert Rudall of Newport died in October 1918 after a few days' illness. He had been a prominent 'Socialist with a strong belief in internationalism' and had left Dartmoor two months previously for Newport on the promise of 'exceptional employment' in tree-felling. This work did not materialise, and in order to get employment within the time limit imposed by him by the Home Office scheme, he undertook work on the blast furnaces at the Dos steelworks, Newport. Previous to his arrest in 1916 he had had bouts of rheumatic fever and he was far from robust, and to the *Tribunal* it seemed clear that his death has been caused by the unsuitability of his work.[172] George Dardis, a schoolteacher from Risca, a member of the ILP and the local branch secretary of the NCF, died at home after his release from Wakefield prison in the autumn of 1917. Twenty-year-old Hal Beynon of Swansea succumbed to a severe bout of pneumonia at Gloucester in October 1918, where he worked under the Home Office scheme. He had been arrested in Swansea in January 1918 and, after serving part of his sentence in Wormwood Scrubs, he accepted the Home Office scheme and was transferred to Dartmoor and then to Gloucester, where he died.[173] Glyn Evans of Cross Inn, Pontardawe, was arrested in the summer of 1916, and was one of the first group of men to be sent to Dyce Camp, in August 1916. In early 1918 he went from the Princetown work camp to Swansea, where he had obtained work as a

---

[171] *Tribunal*, 27 June 1917.
[172] *Tribunal*, 17 October 1918.
[173] *Tribunal*, 7 November 1918.

dentist under the Exceptional Employment Scheme, but he died of pneumonia in October 1918. A friend wrote of him:

> He was a quiet and unassuming man and he was twenty-eight years of age. He called to see me and I noticed then that he had suffered from physical and mental exhaustion and I have no doubt that his sufferings in prison and in the Home Office camps are responsible for his death.[174]

Alfred Statton from Cardiff, a married wood sawyer and machinist, and member of the NCF, had joined the Home Office scheme in the Wakefield work centre. He was reported to be suffering from mental illness and delusions, and he was taken to Wakefield asylum, and then to Shrewsbury prison, being removed to Hereford County asylum in July 1917, where he eventually died in 1919.[175] Statton was only one of a number of objectors who became mentally ill and physically ill as a result of their experiences. The COIB gave the final number of those who had 'lost their reason' as thirty-one, although it is impossible to verify that figure.[176] Aneurin Morgan, for example, a young draper and hosier from Cwmavon, who had been in Walton prison, was taken to Rainhill asylum in Liverpool, where he was reported to be suffering from 'delusional insanity' and believed he was Jesus Christ. He had to be fed through a tube, and his case was taken up by Catherine Marshall and the NCF's Wales organiser, Henry Davies, Cwmavon.[177] A letter from one of the NCF's prison visitors to Aneurin's father described his solitary and obsessively religious demeanour, and his brother Tal wrote, following a visit to Aneurin in the hospital:

> I found him to be quite normal in conversation, in manner and behaviour; in short I saw no trace of insanity in him. He was however, piteously reduced physically, being extremely thin and weak as a result of his policy of hunger-striking. He adopted this plan of refusing food and work in Walton, he told me, so that he might precipitate matters

---

[174] *Tribunal,* 7 November 1918.

[175] *Pearce Register.*

[176] Boulton, *Objection Overruled,* p. 258.

[177] Cumbria Archives, Catherine Marshall Papers, D/MAR/4/53 file on Aneurin Morgan, letter from Superintendent of County Asylum to Henry Davies, 9 February 1917.

towards his re-trial by the Central Tribunal ... I saw no trace of his suffering from religious mania ... I was keenly on the lookout for any sign of mental aberration in him, and I together with an elder brother who accompanied me failed to find anything wrong with him.[178]

Catherine Marshall was pressed to see General Childs and secure Morgan's discharge from the army or to appear before the Central Tribunal,[179] and Davies echoed the brother's fear that if Morgan was returned to Walton gaol, he would resume his policy of hunger-striking, in which case a second breakdown was almost inevitable and might have more serious consequences. Morgan was discharged from the army in June 1917 as no longer physically fit for service.[180]

THE LEGACY OF THE CONSCIENTIOUS OBJECTORS

The concluding convention of the NCF was held in November 1919, and it considered its success to have been to break the spell of the 'military machine' and to bring together the two main wings of the conscientious objectors – those pacifists who believed all war to be evil, and those who, whilst believing that war was necessary in certain circumstances, also believed that engaging in war should be left to the individual conscience.[181]

At the end of the war, the Christian pacifist E. K. Jones idealised the experiences of the conscientious objectors as a 'golden chapter' in his recollection of three years of persecution:

The prayer meeting in that locked cell: the spiritual talk (or chat), the verses of scripture written upon that wall of iron: the sorrow over that fine soldier that had been sacrificed in vain, the gentle conduct of our men at the Court Martial, the courage shown in the face of collapsed health and when reason was failing, and the cheerful readiness to die for the faith. It was delightful to witness the tenderness of many ordinary soldiers and of officers and doctors towards the prisoners. It is

[178] Cumbria Archives, Catherine Marshall Papers, D/MAR/4/53 file on Aneurin Morgan, letter from Tal Morgan to Henry Davies, 13 April 1917.
[179] Cumbria Archives, Catherine Marshall Papers, D/MAR/4/53 file on Aneurin Morgan, letter from Henry Davies to Catherine Marshall, Spring 1917.
[180] *Pearce Register.*
[181] *The No-Conscription Fellowship*, pp. 88–95.

true that we were brought face to face with incredible cases of malice and utterly uncalled for cruelty. May God forgive these ignorant and hard-hearted men.[182]

The stigma of being a 'conchie' stayed with conscientious objectors for many years and made employment difficult for many. But the observance of the ban on voting imposed on COs under the Representation of the People Act (1918) was kept more in the breach than the observance. Indeed, the Caerphilly by-election was won in 1921 by the former conscientious objector and NCF leader, Morgan Jones, and this event indicated how far public opinion had moved since the end of the war. Of the Welsh conscientious objectors, at least five – Morgan Jones, Emrys Hughes, T. W. Jones, Wrexham, Ness Edwards and G. M. Ll. Davies – became Members of Parliament. Others, such as Arthur Horner, David Thomas, Nun Nicholas and Mark Starr, became prominent trade unionists, educationalists and labour activists, either within the Labour or Communist parties. A number of these young men went on to play active roles as pacifists in the Nonconformist denominations, and within the Labour Party, the trade union movement and the growing anti-war movement of the 1920s and 1930s.

The experience of the government in dealing with the thorny problem of conscientious objection during the Great War informed its thinking in the Second World War, and those who could recall the unhappy policy that led to the re-arrest and consecutive imprisonment of the absolutist conscientious objectors, in particular, attempted to avoid these circumstances again. When the re-introduction of conscription was considered in 1939, the government did not wish to revive hostility towards conscientious objectors, and it ensured that civilian control was granted over both civilian and military manpower, and semi-professional tribunals were appointed by ministers. The opportunity was afforded to objectors to have a range of options for exemption, including 'work of national importance' that was strictly under civilian control, and to have tribunals that were

---

[182] *Y Deyrnas*, April 1919 (E. K. Jones's own translation).

appointed on the basis of the principle of impartiality.[183] The Prime Minister, Winston Churchill, emphasised the importance of respecting the principle of conscientious objection and deplored any tendency 'in the nature of persecution, victimisation, or man-hunting' towards the conscientious objector, which he believed was 'odious to the British people'.[184]

---

[183] Rae, *Conscience and Politics*, pp. 241–5.
[184] Parliamentary Debates (Commons), 5 HC 370, col. 284, 20 March 1941.

CONCLUSION

The Great War marked an 'immense break with the past, in social and in political terms' and, as Morgan suggests, 'in no part of the British Isles was the contrast between pre- and post-war conditions more pronounced'.[1]

The war was the major fissure in Welsh life in the twentieth century, marking the political turning point from Liberalism to Labour, the growing ferment of revolutionary thought that sought the overthrow of capitalism, the fault-line between religious and areligious Wales, and the consolidation of the state. The history of the opposition to the Great War in Wales has invariably been written in the context of these transformational changes, but this book emphasises how attitudes toward the war varied throughout this period, and how dissent towards the war found support in certain areas of the country and amongst groups of political activists within the ILP, the FoR, and the 'advanced men' of the labour movement. Wales's response to the course of the war was not always coherent and uniform, as the initial high level of support for war in the early autumn of 1914 fell away and was replaced by a greater awareness of the human cost of warfare by the end of 1915, with increased support for the anti-war movement in response to the introduction of conscription in January 1916. The anti-war movement was buoyed by growing war-weariness, the impact of the Russian Revolution, and the pressure for a peace settlement in the summer of 1917, before enthusiasm was rekindled by the British Army's successes on the Western Front from the late spring of 1918 onwards.

A more nuanced local and regional analysis of the nature of the response to the course of the war, including the

---

[1] K. O. Morgan, *Re-birth of a Nation: Wales 1880–1980* (Oxford: Oxford University Press, 1982), p. 177.

changing nature of the anti-war movement, is necessary to comprehend how attitudes towards the war varied between different areas of Wales and during the different stages of the war.

This study of the anti-war movement tells a hitherto untold story that has been largely obscured or minimised in our histories of Wales. Much anti-war activity was only captured contemporaneously in a very small number of newspapers and journals, and subsequently in the biographies, autobiographies and archives of those who took part in the movement opposed to the war. The latter tended to frame opposition to the war within the realms of Christian pacifism or political principle and, whilst concentrating on the plight of individual conscientious objectors, gave rather less attention to the diverse nature of the anti-war movement, whether it took political form in the Independent Labour Party and the 'advanced men' within the South Wales Miners' Federation, or religious form through the Fellowship of Reconciliation and the pages of *Y Deyrnas*. Local studies, such as Weller's study of north London, Pearce's study of the anti-war movement in Huddersfield,[2] and Duncan's and Kenefick's studies of anti-war protest in Scotland,[3] reflect very diverse responses to the war in other parts of Britain. This study builds on the pioneering Welsh local studies of Adams's granular and impassioned accounts of the anti-war movement in Briton Ferry and Port Talbot,[4] and considers communities such as these and Merthyr Tydfil, whose anti-war movements were integrated within the context of the vigorous politics of the ILP, local trade unions and trades and labour councils, with the involvement of a small number of supportive local chapels and ministers. This was especially so in those localities where the ILP was most influential, including

[2] Cyril Pearce, *Comrades and Conscience* (Francis Boutle Publishers, 2001).

[3] Robert Duncan, *Objectors and Resisters* (Glasgow: Common Print, 2015); William Kenefick, 'War Resisters and Anti-Conscription in Scotland: An ILP Perspective', in Catriona Macdonald and E. W. MacFarland (eds), *Scotland and the Great War* (Edinburgh: Tuckwell Press, 1998).

[4] Philip Adams, *Not in My Name: War Dissent in a Welsh Town* (Ludlow: Briton Ferry Press, 2015); Philip Adams, *Daring to Defy: Port Talbot's War Resistance 1914–1918* (Ludlow: Briton Ferry Press, 2017).

Wales's main towns – Swansea,[5] Cardiff, Newport and Wrexham – the Swansea and Amman Valleys,[6] Briton Ferry and the Afan Valley, Bargoed, Tredegar, Merthyr Tydfil and Aberdare.

The religious opposition to the war was composed of a small minority, but its main effect was to provide the moral underpinning for the beliefs of many conscientious objectors. Whilst the numbers of conscientious objectors in Wales were proportionally comparable to those in England, what gave the anti-war movement its unique quality was the Welsh language as an element of its anti-war armoury, as embodied in the journal *Y Deyrnas*, which remarkably achieved the same readership in Wales as the FoR's *The Venturer* throughout the whole of Britain. Its intellectual energy was provided by the group of activists that surrounded Principal Thomas Rees of Bala-Bangor theological college, and the Fellowship of Reconciliation provided the organisational framework for Christian witness against war.

The political opposition to the war was underpinned by the organisation of the ILP, and a study of areas such as Briton Ferry and Merthyr Tydfil provides a more detailed understanding of those networks that enabled the ILP to work symbiotically with other anti-war organisations, such as the NCF and the NCCL, in order to broaden its influence. In the 'new communities' of the coalfield, such as the Rhondda and Monmouthshire's eastern valleys, the vanguard of the anti-war movement was the grouping of 'advanced men' who propagated industrial unionism and workers' control. This study focuses on the agitation against the 'comb-out' within the mining industry as a barometer of attitudes towards the war, marks the influence of the Russian Revolution on political thought in the south Wales coalfield, and measures the achievement of the Unofficial Reform Committee (URC) in postponing the 'combing-out' of men in the mining industry until December 1917.

---

[5] Thomas McCarry, 'Labour and Society in Swansea, 1887–1918' (unpublished PhD thesis, Swansea University, 1986).

[6] Aled Eirug, 'Gwrthwynebu'r Rhyfel mawr yng Nghwm Tawe', *Llafur*, 12/1 (2016), 25–42.

This study also highlights the NCCL's effectiveness in bridging the anti-war movement and the trade union movement and trades and labour councils. It stoked the fear of the further extension of military conscription and the creation of civilian conscription within vital industries such as coal, steel, tinplate and transport. Its success in south Wales, as in London, lay in its ability to gain wider support from trade unions and trade councils to campaign against the extension of conscription. The personal connections and influence of its organiser, Ivor Thomas, embodied the symbiotic relationship between the NCCL, the local trades and labour councils, and the anti-war movement, and ensured that their voice was amplified to such an extent that the authorities came to view the anti-conscription lobby as a branch of the anti-war movement. As the NCCL's conference in Merthyr Tydfil in December 1916 suggested, the two elements could combine to form a powerful lobby that gave government and its intelligence agencies pause for thought.

The number of conscientious objectors in Wales, at about 900, is similar to the proportion of men in England who followed the same path. Most opposed on religious grounds, and many did so on grounds of morality as well, in which a belief in the pacifism of Christ's Sermon on the Mount was as much an article of faith as a belief in the efficacy of political change. A smaller proportion of conscientious objectors described themselves as 'political' objectors, although the NCF was run invariably by members of the ILP. Tension continued amongst these conscientious objectors between the 'absolutists', who refused to compromise with the state, and the 'alternativists', who accepted the government's work schemes in the majority of cases. Contrary to popular myth promulgated by histories that concentrate on the plight and sacrifice of individual objectors, only a minority were absolutists and therefore served imprisonment without accepting alternative work. Seven of their number from Wales died as a result of their treatment, yet most accepted alternative work, albeit in unsatisfactory circumstances, in former prisons and work camps. As this study suggests, the primacy of the individual conscience made it difficult to mould this group of men into an effective political weapon against conscription, and they were weakened by the absence of a 'common commander'.[7] The journalist and conscientious objector Percy Ogwen Jones echoed this view, believing that the anti-war movement's greatest weakness was its lack of unity and that its only shared focus was its challenge to military conscription. A substantial minority of objectors, such as the Christadelphians and Jehovah's Witnesses, objected to compulsory military service under the authority of the state, rather than to the war in principle.

For many, the conscientious objectors represented the anti-war movement, and these men were often labelled 'traitors' and 'shirkers' who did not deserve respect or recognition. But even those who supported the war effort, such as the Member of Parliament for East Carmarthenshire, W. Llewelyn Williams, who also served as Recorder of Cardiff, became increasingly sympathetic towards them because of the mistreatment many received, and Williams decried the persecution of COs such as Ithel Davies:

> He knew of a young Welsh poet who was doing hard labour for the fourth time. As Recorder he had never given two years' hard labour to the most hardened criminal who had come before him. 'Are we living really in the twentieth century in the era of Christ?' he asked. 'Are people who profess to be Christians so lost to all sense of shame that these things are going to be allowed to go on? I protest against it myself, and I care nothing what the consequences may be.'[8]

As a prominent barrister in south Wales, Williams appeared on behalf of conscientious objectors and anti-war activists in the local courts, and his comments reflect an increased grudging respect towards objectors. A portrayal of their self-sacrifice and suffering was presented often in biographies and autobiographies of COs, or in thinly disguised novels by former conscientious objectors, such as Gwenallt. But one sensitive objector, Thomas W. Jones (later Lord Maelor and MP for Wrexham), reflected that whilst his experience as a CO had instilled a hermit's attitude in him, which he compared to the greatest bereavement that he could

---

[7] Keith Robbins, *The Abolition of War* (University of Wales Press, 1970), p. 96.
[8] *Llanelly Star*, 12 January 1918.

experience, he acknowledged that much of the inevitable bitterness against conscientious objectors was engendered by the loss of a loved one in the war and that it was 'difficult for these families to understand my standpoint'.[9]

The significance of the stand taken by the conscientious objectors was that the British state, for the first time, was forced to face substantial civil dissent, described as 'flat disobedience, followed up by a weighty weapon of passive endurance'.[10] The anti-war movement in Wales, as in parts of the north of England and central Scotland, succeeded in developing opposition to conscription through the local activism of the ILP in those areas of south Wales where the party had its deepest roots. The NCCL and the NCF bridged the anti-war element of the labour movement and brought in that part of the trade union movement that was concerned about the extension of military conscription into civilian life. Allied to the increasingly assertive and class-conscious 'advanced men' of the SWMF, this made for a potent mix of revolutionary fervour and political radicalism.

The fruit of this alliance was not reflected immediately in the 1918 'Khaki' Election, held only weeks after the Armistice, which underlined the unpopularity of unsuccessful anti-war candidates, such as T. E. Nicholas, Labour's candidate in the Merthyr Boroughs.[11] Yet, in 1921, the Caerphilly by-election saw Morgan Jones returned as the first conscientious objector to become a Member of Parliament after the war. The changing attitudes towards conscientious objectors may have reflected a growing disillusionment with the social and economic conditions that soldiers suffered on their return from the war. James Griffiths reflected that the onset of conscription in 1916 had been the 'first break' in the unity between Nonconformists and the Liberal Party, and felt it was the beginning of the dissolution of the traditional alliance, creating the opportunity for Labour to win the Nonconformist vote.[12] Together with the response to Lloyd

---

[9] Lord Maelor, *Fel Hyn y Bu* (Denbigh: Gwasg Gee, 1970), p. 88.

[10] John W. Graham, *Conscription and Conscience* (Allen and Unwin, 1922), p. 343.

[11] David Howell, *Nicholas of Glais: The People's Champion* (Clydach Historical Society, 1991), p. 25.

[12] James Griffiths, *Pages from Memory* (J. M. Dent, 1969), pp. 22–3.

George's refusal to implement the Sankey Commission's majority recommendation to maintain ownership of the coal industry in public hands, it ensured that Labour in Wales grew from ten parliamentary seats in 1918 to eighteen seats in 1922, and became the majority party in Wales.[13] At least five Labour MPs for Welsh constituencies had been anti-war activists: Ramsay MacDonald (Aberavon), David Williams (Swansea East), Morgan Jones (Caerphilly), Dr J. H. Williams (Llanelli) and R. C. Wallhead (Merthyr Tydfil).[14] The election of the prominent peace activist and conscientious objector G. M. Ll. Davies as a Member of Parliament for the University of Wales in the 1923 General Election symbolised the post-war mood. He stood as an independent Christian Pacifist, supported by the University's Labour club, and although he only won by ten votes, his victory suggested that 'the ideals of war and militarism were thought to be in the past'.[15]

In Wales, the passion for a strong peace movement increased throughout the 1920s and 1930s. David Davies, the Liberal MP for Montgomeryshire, created the League of Free Nations Association in 1917 and founded the chair of International Politics at University College of Wales in Aberystwyth in 1919. Following the creation of the League of Nations in 1920, he supported the establishing in January 1922 of the Welsh League of Nations Union, which attracted the support of all political parties, with the exception of the Communist Party, and had a membership of over 20,000 in Wales by 1924.[16] The youth organisation Urdd Gobaith Cymru (the Welsh League of Youth) was established in 1922 and launched its annual message of peace aimed at the youth of the world. In 1923, the Welsh League of Nations launched a petition to the women of the United States, asking them to use their influence to persuade their country to become full

---

[13] J. Beverley Smith, *James Griffiths and His Times* (Ferndale: W. T. Maddock, 1969), p. 21.
[14] Beti Jones, *Etholiadau Seneddol yng Nghymru* (Talybont: Y Lolfa, 1977), pp. 59–64.
[15] Barlow, *Wales and World War One*, p. 233.
[16] Huw L. Williams, 'Segurdod yw Clod y Cledd; David Davies a'r Helfa am Heddwch Wedi'r Rhyfel Mawr', in Gethin Matthews, *Creithiau* (Cardiff: University of Wales Press, 2016), p. 187.

members of the League of Nations, which was signed by the remarkable number of almost 400,000 women throughout Wales. In May 1926, 2,000 women from villages in the Nantlle Valley near Caernarfon began a Peace Pilgrimage and held fifteen public meetings in north Wales before marching on Hyde Park in London, where over 10,000 women gathered to urge the government to agree to international arbitration and to support the forthcoming Disarmament Conference of the League of Nations.

This Peace Pilgrimage led to the formation of the North Wales Women's Peace Council and the Women's International League for Peace and Freedom. In 1935, a 'Peace Ballot' to support Britain remaining as a member of the League of Nations was signed by the remarkable number of over a million Welsh electors, representing sixty-two per cent of the Welsh electorate, the largest percentage of any part of Britain. But as Fascism achieved ascendancy in Spain, Italy and Germany by 1936, the League of Nations faltered fatally, and by 1938, the opening of the Temple of Peace and the establishing of the Centre for the Study of International Affairs in Cardiff presaged the failure of collective international action.[17]

The political campaign against the Great War had an obvious influence on Britain throughout the 1920s and 1930s, as the ILP's foreign policy of ensuring arbitration between countries through the League of Nations became the Labour Party's foreign policy. After the Great War, hopes for a genuinely different international order, based on the surrender of some sovereignty to an international body, were frustrated by the 1919 Paris Peace Conference, and only gradually did Labour, for instance, accept the League of Nations as a viable organisation. But those policies quickly faltered in the face of the Great Depression and the emergence of challenges to the international order in Nazi Germany, Fascist Italy and the militarily resurgent Japan. A gradual recognition of the weakness of the League of Nations led many of those ILP-ers who had opposed the Great War to

---

[17] Goronwy J. Jones, *Wales and the Quest for Peace* (Cardiff: University of Wales Press, 1970), p. 140.

conclude by the mid-1930s that the case for Britain's re-armament was unanswerable. Hugh Dalton was one of the party's
leaders who questioned the belief that force could not be
justified, and in spite of the views of the party leader, George
Lansbury, and his adherence to pacifism, figures such as
Morgan Jones, Aneurin Bevan and James Griffiths, who had
been prominent in the anti-war movement, supported
re-armament in terms that might have been inconceivable
twenty years earlier. In a speech in November 1933, Morgan
Jones suggested that the League of Nations ought to take
'violent action' against a nation which showed aggression
against another nation. This shift in his attitudes coincided
with the growing aggression of Italy and Germany, but for
him and others on the left, it was the Spanish Civil War that
occasioned them to press for military intervention, and after
the bombing of the Basque village of Guernica, he urged the
government to allow volunteers from Britain to join the
Republican cause.[18] Aneurin Bevan accepted the general
Marxist belief that imperial rivalries led to war, and while the
peace movement and the League of Nations Peace Ballot in
1935 marked the zenith of the anti-war movement, it was the
Spanish Civil War in 1936 that persuaded him and other anti-
war activists for the first time of the efficacy of armed
intervention.[19] By 1938, the majority of Welsh MPs, by twenty
to thirteen, voted against Chamberlain's Munich agreement
and went on to support re-armament.[20]

George M. Ll. Davies, like other Christian pacifists,
condemned the Guernica bombing, but he opposed intervention and poured his considerable energy into the Peace
Pledge Union, established in 1934, which became the vehicle
for a purer non-violent renunciation of war than the emphasis
of the League of Nations on collective security. He became
the British chairman of the PPU after the Second World War.
In Wales, it was established at the National Eisteddfod in
August 1937, and in an echo of the distinctive nature of the
group of activists that coalesced around *Y Deyrnas* in 1916, a
Welsh and Welsh-speaking wing of the PPU, named

---

[18] Wayne David, *Morgan Jones* (forthcoming, 2018).
[19] Michael Foot, *Aneurin Bevan* (Victor Gollancz, 1997), p. 109.
[20] John Davies, *Hanes Cymru* (Allen Lane, 1990), p. 572.

Heddychwyr Cymru (Welsh Pacifists), was created in April 1938, with George M. Ll. Davies as its first president, and with Gwynfor Evans, one of the most prominent leaders of the Blaid Genedlaethol (the Welsh Nationalist Party) as its main organiser.[21]

By the Second World War, the authorities had learnt the lesson from its experience during the Great War of dealing with an intransigent and uncooperative cadre of war resisters. When the government prepared its legislation for conscription at the beginning of the Second World War, the claim for exemption on conscientious grounds was included, but the tribunals in the Second World War were appointed semi-professional bodies and dealt exclusively with applications from conscientious objectors. The legislation also provided for more categories of exemption on grounds of conscientious objection, as it was regarded, in the words of the Prime Minister, Neville Chamberlain, as an 'useless and exasperating waste of time and effort'[22] to persuade absolutists to behave in a manner that was contrary to their principles, whilst they had no objection to doing work that was non-military in nature. The spectre of repeated prison sentences imposed on the absolutists was prevented by the government's acceptance of the use of civilian legal machinery to discharge from the army a soldier who had committed an offence for conscientious reasons. These provisions were placed in the Military Training Act 1940 and, as Rae states, they 'enabled those affected by the Act to exercise freedom of conscience to a degree unequalled in any other country'.[23]

Studies such as Adams's study of Briton Ferry and Port Talbot, and Barlow's study of rural Carmarthenshire[24] suggest a wide diversity of responses that reflect changing attitudes towards the Great War, from the reaction to the introduction of military conscription, and the industrial and social unrest that concerned the government in the summer

---

[21] Jen Llywelyn, *Pilgrim of Peace: A Life of George M. Ll. Davies* (Talybont: Y Lolfa, 2016).

[22] Parliamentary Debates (Commons), 5 HC, cols 2097–8, 4 May 1940, cited in John Rae, *Conscience and Politics* (Oxford: Oxford University Press, 1970), p. 242.

[23] Rae, *Conscience and Politics*, p. 245.

[24] Robin Barlow, 'Aspects of the First World War in Carmarthenshire 1914–1918' (unpublished PhD thesis, University of Wales, 1991).

of 1917, and which led to a more receptive attitude towards the anti-war movement. The task of assessing the strength of the anti-war movement in Wales has been aided by the *Pearce Register* online database[25] which, for the first time, provides the opportunity to follow the stories of hundreds of individuals who became conscientious objectors, and the further investigation of personal archives provides the opportunity for revelatory illumination of a period that marks a watershed in Wales's history.

Although the resistance to war was always a minority response, the changes in attitudes in this period have seldom been captured by sweeping, general 'national' histories. The conscientious objectors were not simply 'heroic or misguided individuals', but also 'groups and individuals expressing a broader community consciousness'.[26] Since anti-war activity was such a profoundly controversial matter at a time when newspapers and even individual conduct were subject to unprecedented government control, it is inevitable that surviving contemporary sources, such as newspapers that describe the anti-war movement in a comparatively cool and rational manner, are relatively scarce. For many conscientious objectors, their experiences of resistance to militarism was viewed as one of the great adventures of their lives. As Emrys Hughes declared to Bertrand Russell:

> When I think of my life before I was arrested, of trying to fit into the environment of one of those soul-killing schools in the Rhondda valley, of disheartening little encounters with the headmasters of the old regime and all the dismal shabbiness of life in a South Wales village, I feel a thrill to think of how we have challenged it all, refused to fight for the foul old ideas and tried to show the way to a better world.[27]

---

[25] Cyril Pearce, *Pearce Register of Anti-War Activists in Wales* (Wales for Peace, 2016). Available at *http://www.wcia.org.uk/wfp/pearceregister.html*. Accessed November 2016.

[26] Pearce, *Comrades in Conscience*, p. 27.

[27] McMaster University Archive, Bertrand Russell Papers, Emrys Hughes to Russell, 4 March 1917.

BIBLIOGRAPHY

1 PRIMARY SOURCES

i) Manuscripts
Bodleian Library, Oxford
Addison Papers
Milner Papers

British Library of Political and Economic Science, London School of Economics
Fellowship of Reconciliation Papers
Independent Labour Party Papers

Cumbria Archives, Carlisle
Catherine Marshall Papers

Friends House Library, London
Friends Ambulance Unit Papers
T. E. Harvey Papers (including Pelham Committee papers)
Arnold Rowntree Papers

House of Lords Record Office
Lloyd George Papers

Imperial War Museum, London
William Knott Diary
Percy Wall Papers

National Archives
Cabinet Office papers, Class 23
Home Office Papers, Class 45
Military Intelligence Reports, Air 1
Ministry of Health Papers, Classes 10 and 47
Security Service Papers, Class KV1–3
War Office Papers, Class 32

National Library of Scotland
Keir Hardie and Emrys Hughes Papers

National Library of Wales
Cardiganshire Appeal Tribunal Papers
Edgar Chappell Papers
E. K. Jones Papers
Thomas Jones Papers

McMaster University, Ontario, Canada
Bertrand Russell Papers

Liverpool University
J. Bruce Glaiser Papers

Bangor University
Bala-Bangor Papers
Bangor Golf Club Papers
Morgan Humphreys Papers
Thomas Jones Papers
Thomas Rees Papers
David Thomas Papers

Leeds University
Liddle Collection

Swansea University
South Wales Coalfield Collection

Online sources
National Library of Wales, 'Y Rhyfel Byd Cyntaf a'r profiad Cymreig/The Welsh experience of World War One', *http://cymruww1.llgc.org.uk*
Digital database of Welsh newspapers of the Great War period, *www.welsh-journals.llgc.org.uk*
Pearce Register (Wales for Peace, 2016): database of anti-war activists during the Great War in Wales compiled by Cyril Pearce and hosted by the 'Wales for Peace' heritage lottery project, *http://www.wcia.org.uk/wfp/pearceregister.html*

Unpublished manuscripts in their families' possession
Albert Davies Papers
D. J. Davies Papers
Percy Ogwen Jones Papers

ii) Newspapers and journals
Y Beirniad
Brecon and Radnor Express

Cambria Daily Leader
Y Darian
Y Deyrnas
Y Dinesydd
The Friend
Y Goleuad
Y Gwyliedydd Newydd
Labour Leader
Llais Llafur
Y Llan
Llanelly Chronicle
Llangollen Advertiser
North Wales Chronicle
The Pioneer (Merthyr)
Plebs Magazine
South Wales Daily News
South Wales Daily Post
The Times
The Tribunal
Y Tyst
The Venturer
Wales
Welsh Outlook
Western Mail

iii) Books and pamphlets

Annual Conference Report of the Union of Welsh Independents, Brynaman, 13–16 June 1916 (Swansea: Y Llyfrfa)

Annual Conference Report of the Union of Welsh Independents, Merthyr Tydfil, 19–22 July 1915 (Merthyr: Williams and Son)

Census of England and Wales 1911, County Report on Glamorgan (London: HMSO, 1914)

Centenary of the Baptist Cause in Briton Ferry 1837–1937, Souvenir Programme (Neath, 1938)

Commission of Enquiry into Industrial Unrest, No. 7 Division, *Report of the Commissioners for Wales, including Monmouthshire*, Command 8668 (London: HMSO, 1917)

Committee on the Employment of Conscientious Objectors, *Additional Rules*, Command Paper 8884 (London: HMSO, 1916)

Hay, W. F., *WAR! And the Welsh Miner* (Tonypandy, 1914)

Independent Labour Party, *Souvenir ILP 20th Annual Conference Easter 1912* (Merthyr: ILP, 1912)

Independent Labour Party, *Reports of Annual Conferences, 1914–1919* (Harvester Microfilms)

The No-Conscription Fellowship: A Souvenir of its Work during the Years 1914–1919 (London, 1919)

Peace among the Nations (London: Friends House, 1915)

Snowden, Philip, *British Prussianism: The Scandal of the Tribunals* (Manchester: National Labour Press, 1916)

Statistics of the Military Effort of the British Empire during the Great War (London: HMSO, 1922)

Stevenson, F. L., *Through Terror to Triumph. Speeches and Pronouncements of the Right Hon. David Lloyd George, M.P. Since the Beginning of the War* (London: Hodder and Stoughton, 1915)

Unofficial Reform Committee, *The Miners' Next Step* (Tonypandy, 1912)

What Happened at Leeds (Council of Workers and Soldiers Delegates, Pelican Press, 1917)

2 SECONDARY SOURCES

i) Works of reference

Williams, L. J. (ed.), *Digest of Historical Statistics*, 2 vols (Cardiff: Welsh Office, 1985)

Dictionary of Labour Biography

Dictionary of Welsh Biography

Oxford Dictionary of National Biography

The Labour Who's Who, 1927: A biographical directory to the national and local leaders in the labour and co-operative movement (London: Labour Publishing Company, 1927)

Who's Who in Wales (3rd edn; London: Belgravia Publications, 1937)

ii) Interviews and unpublished materials

David, Wayne, 'Biography of Morgan Jones' (forthcoming, 2018)

Davies, Albert, 'Wanderings' (unpublished autobiography in private hands, undated)

Evans, Owain Gethin, 'Quakers in Wales and the First World War' (unpublished article provided by the author)

Freeman, Michael, 'Conscientious Objectors in Cardiganshire', Aberystwyth (published privately, 2015)

Jones, Percy Ogwen, 'Ceinciau Cymysg', BBC Cymru radio talk, 6 November 1964

Ivor John, Cwmavon (interview by author, March 1978)

Ivor Jones, Briton Ferry (interview by author, March 1978)

Swansea University, South Wales Miners' Library: transcriptions of interviews (South Wales Coalfield Collection)

Aud. 339 Will Cockrill

Aud. 289 W. H. Gregory

Aud. 82 E. P. Jones

Aud. 309 George Protheroe
Aud. 282 Len Williams

iii) Books and articles

Adams, Philip, *A Most Industrious Town* (Ludlow: Briton Ferry Books, 2014)

Adams, Philip, *Daring to Defy: Port Talbot's War Resistance 1914–1918* (Ludlow: Briton Ferry Books, 2016)

Adams, Philip, *Not in Our Name: War Dissent in a Welsh Town* (Ludlow: Briton Ferry Books, 2015)

Arnot, R. Page, *South Wales Miners: A History of the South Wales Miners' Federation (1914–1926)* (Pontypridd: Cymric Press, 1975)

Awbery, Stan, *Labour's Early Struggles in Swansea* (Swansea Printers Ltd., 1949)

Barlow, Robin, 'Military Tribunals in Carmarthenshire 1916–1917', in Nick Mansfield and Craig Horner, *The Great War* (Newcastle upon Tyne: Cambridge Scholars Publishing, 2014), pp. 7–27

Barlow, Robin, *Wales and World War One* (Llandysul: Gomer Press, 2014)

Bartlett, Thomas, and Jeffery, Keith (eds), *A Military History of Ireland* (Cambridge: Cambridge University Press, 1996)

Bassett, T. M., *The Welsh Baptists* (Swansea: Ilston House, 1977)

Beddoe, Deirdre, *Out of the Shadows: A History of Women in Twentieth Century Wales* (Cardiff: University of Wales Press, 2000)

Bibbings, Lois B., *Telling Tales About Men: Conceptions of Conscientious Objectors to Military Service During the First World War* (Manchester: Manchester University Press, 2009)

Botten, John, *The Captive Conscience* (Birmingham: Christadelphian Military Service Committee, 2002)

Boulton, David, *Objection Overruled* (MacGibbon and Kee, 1967)

Bowtell, Harold D., and Hill, Geoffrey, *Reservoir Builders of South Wales: Dam Builders in the Age of Steam* (Malvern: Industrial Locomotive Society, 2006)

Braybon, Gail, *Evidence, History and the Great War* (New York, Oxford: Berghahn Books, 2003)

Brock, Peter, *Pacifism Since 1914: An Annotated Reading List* (University of Toronto Press, 2000)

Brock, Peter, *Twentieth-Century Pacifism* (New York: Syracuse University Press, 1970)

Brockway, Archibald Fenner, *Inside the Left: Thirty Years of Platform, Press and Parliament* (Hart-Davis McGibbon, 1977)

Burge, Alun, 'Labour, Class and Conflict', in Chris Williams, Andy Croll and Ralph A. Griffiths (eds), *Gwent County History. Volume 5: The Twentieth Century* (Cardiff: University of Wales Press, 2013), pp. 320–40

Bussey, Gertrude, and Tims, Margaret, *Pioneers for Peace: Women's*

International League for Peace and Freedom 1915–1965 (WILPF British section, 1965, re-issued 1980)

Ceadel, Martin, *Pacifism in Britain, 1914–1945: The Defining of a Faith* (Oxford: Clarendon Press, 1980)

Challinor, Raymond, *The Origins of British Bolshevism* (Croom Helm, 1977)

Childs, Major-General Wyndham, *Episodes and Reflections* (Cassell and Co., 1930)

Cleaver, David, 'Conscientious Objection in the Swansea Area', *Morgannwg*, 28 (1984), 48–54

Cragoe, Matthew, and Williams, Chris (eds), *Wales and War: Society, Politics and Religion in the Nineteenth and Twentieth Centuries* (Cardiff: University of Wales Press, 2007)

Crick, Martin, *The History of the Social Democratic Federation* (Birmingham: Keele University Press, 1994)

David, Wayne, *Remaining True – a biography of Ness Edwards* (Caerphilly History Society, 2006)

Davies, Dewi Eirug, *Byddin y Brenin: Cymru a'i Chrefydd yn y Rhyfel Mawr* (Swansea: Tŷ John Penry, 1988)

Davies, Ithel, *Bwrlwm Byw* (Llandysul: Gwasg Gomer, 1984)

Davies, John, *Hanes Cymru* (Allen Lane, 1990)

Davies, Paul, *A. J. Cook* (Manchester: Manchester University Press, 1987)

Davies, Paul, 'The Making of A. J. Cook: His Development within the South Wales Labour Movement, 1900–1924', *Llafur*, 2/3 (1978), 43–63

Davies, Russell, *Hope and Heartbreak: A Social History of Wales and the Welsh, 1776–1871* (Cardiff: University of Wales Press, 2005)

Davies, Russell, *People, Places and Passions: 'Pain and Pleasure': A Social History of Wales and the Welsh 1870–1945* (Cardiff: University of Wales Press, 2015)

Davies, Thomas Eirug, *Y Prifathro Thomas Rees: ei Fywyd a'i Waith* (Llandysul: Gwasg Gomer, 1939)

Donahaye, Jasmine, *The Greatest Need* (Dinas Powys: Honno, 2015)

Dowse, R. E., *Left in the Centre* (Longmans, 1966)

Duncan, Robert, *Objectors and Resisters* (Glasgow: Common Print, 2015)

Edwards, W. J., *From the Valley I Came* (Angus and Robinson, 1956)

Egan, David, 'Noah Ablett 1883–1935', *Llafur*, 4/3 (1986), 19–30

Egan, David, 'The Swansea Conference of the British Council of Soldiers and Workers Delegates, July, 1917: Reactions to the Russian Revolution of February, 1917, and the Anti-War Movement in South Wales', *Llafur*, 1/4 (1975), 12–37

Egan, David, 'The Unofficial Reform Committee and the Miners' Next Step: Documents from the W. H. Mainwaring Papers, with an introduction and notes', *Llafur*, 2/3 (1978), 64–80

Eirug, Aled, 'Agweddau ar y Gwrthwynebiad i'r Rhyfel Byd Cyntaf yng Nghymru', *Llafur*, 4/4 (1987), 58–68

Evans, Neil, 'Writing the Social History of Modern Wales: Approaches, Achievements and Problems', *Social History*, 17/3 (1992), 479–92

Evans, Owain Gethin, *Benign Neglect: Quakers and Wales circa 1860–1918* (Wrexham: Bridge Books, 2014)

Evans, Rhys, *Gwynfor Evans: Rhag Pob Brad* (Talybont: Y Lolfa, 2005)

Fell, Alison, and Sharp, Ingrid, *The Women's Movement in Wartime: International Perspectives, 1914–1919* (Basingstoke: Palgrave Macmillan, 2007)

Finch, Harold, *Memoirs of a Bedwellty M.P.* (Risca: Starling Press, 1972)

Fishman, Nina, *Arthur Horner* (Lawrence and Wishart, 2010)

Foot, Michael, *Aneurin Bevan* (London: Victor Gollancz, 1997)

Francis, Hywel and Smith, David, *The Fed: A History of the South Wales Miners in the Twentieth Century* (Lawrence and Wishart, 1980)

Gibbard, Noel, *Tarian Tywi* (Caernarfon: Gwasg y Bwthyn, 2011)

Graham, John W., *Conscription and Conscience: A History 1916–1919* (London: Allen and Unwin, 1922)

Gregory, Adrian, 'British "War Enthusiasm" in 1914: A Reassessment', in Gail Braybon (ed.), *Evidence, History and the Great War: Historians and the Impact of 1914–18* (Berghahn Press, 2003), pp. 67–85.

Griffiths, E. H., *Heddychwr Mawr Cymru: George M.Ll. Davies* (Caernarfon: Llyfrfa'r Methodistiaid Calfinaidd,1967)

Griffin, Nicholas, *The Selected Letters of Bertrand Russell – The Public Years 1914–1970* (Routledge, 2001)

Griffiths, James, *Pages from Memory* (J. M. Dent and Sons, 1969)

Griffiths, Robert, *S. O. Davies – A Socialist Faith* (Llandysul: Gomer Press, 1983)

Griffiths, Robert H., *The Story of Kinmel Park Military Training Camp 1914 to 1918* (Llanrwst: Gwasg Carreg Gwalch, 2014)

Grigg, Russell, 'Jehovah's Witnesses', in Richard C. Allen, David Ceri Jones and Trystan O. Hughes (eds), *The Religious History of Wales* (Cardiff: Welsh Academic Press, 2014)

Hayes, Dennis, *Conscription Conflict: The Conflict of Ideas in the Struggle for and against Military Conscription in Britain Between the Years 1916 and 1919* (Sheppard Press, 1949)

Hinton, James, *The First Shop Stewards' Movements* (London: Allen and Unwin, 1973)

Hochschild, Adam, *To End All Wars: A Story of Protest and Patriotism in the First World War* (Pan Books, 2012)

Hopkin, Deian, 'A. J. Cook in 1916–1918', *Llafur*, 2/3 (1978), 81–3

Hopkin, Deian , 'The Membership of the Independent Labour Party, 1904–10: a spatial analysis', *International Review of Social History*, 20 (1975), 175–92

Hopkin, Deian, 'The Merthyr Pioneer 1911–1922', *Llafur*, 2/4 (1979), 54–64

Hopkin, Deian, 'Patriots and Pacifists in Wales 1914–1918', *Llafur*, 1/3 (1974), 27–41

Hopkin, Deian, 'The Rise of Labour in Wales, 1890–1914', *Llafur*, 6/3 (1994), 120–41

Horne, John N., *Labour at War: France and Britain 1914–1918* (Oxford: Clarendon Press, 1991)

Horner, Arthur, *Incorrigible Rebel* (MacGibbon and Kee, 1960)

Howard, Chris, 'The Focus of the Mute Hopes of a Whole Class – Ramsay Macdonald and Aberavon, 1922–1929', *Llafur*, 7/1 (1996), 68–77

Howell, David, *British Workers and the Independent Labour Party, 1888–1906* (Manchester: Manchester University Press, 1983)

Howell, David, *Nicholas of Glais: The People's Champion* (Clydach Historical Society, 1991)

Hughes, Clive, *I'r Fyddin, Fechgyn Gwalia: Recriwtio I'r Fyddin yng Ngogledd-Orllewin Cymru 1914–1918* (Llanrwst: Gwasg Carreg Gwalch, 2014)

Hughes, Emrys, *Keir Hardie* (London: Allen and Unwin, 1956)

Hughes, R. R., *John Williams, Brynsiencyn* (Caernarfon: Llyfrfa Cyfundeb y Methodistiaid Calfinaidd, 1929)

Hughes, Steve, and Reynolds, Paul, *A Guide to the Industrial Archaeology of the Swansea Region* (Aberystwyth: Royal Commission on the Ancient and Historical Monuments of Wales, 1988)

James, Gerwyn, *Y Rhwyg: Hanes y Rhyfel Mawr yn Ardal Llanfair Pwllgwyngyll 1914–1932* (Llanrwst: Gwasg Carreg Gwalch, 2013)

Jannaway, Frank G., *Without the Camp* (London: F. G. Jannaway, 1917)

Jeffery, Keith, *Ireland and the Great War* (Cambridge: Cambridge University Press, 2000)

Jenkins, Geraint H., and Smith, J. Beverley, *Politics and Society in Wales 1840–1922* (Cardiff: University of Wales Press, 1988)

Johnes, Martin, 'For Class and Nation: Dominant Trends in the Historiography of Twentieth Century Wales', *History Compass*, 8/11 (2010), 1257–74

Jones, Beti, *Etholiadau Seneddol yng Nghymru* (Talybont: Y Lolfa, 1977)

Jones, Gareth Elwyn, *Modern Wales, A Concise History, 1485–1979* (Cambridge: Cambridge University Press, 1984)

Jones, J. Graham, *David Lloyd George and Welsh Liberalism* (Aberystwyth: Welsh Political Archive, The National Library of Wales 2010)

Jones, J. Graham, *The History of Wales* (Cardiff: University of Wales Press, 1990)

Jones, Goronwy J., *The Quest for Peace* (Cardiff: University of Wales Press, 1969).

Jenkins, Gwyn, *Cymry'r Rhyfel Byd Cyntaf* (Talybont: Y Lolfa, 2014)

Jones, R. J., *Troi'r Dail* (Swansea: Tŷ John Penry, 1961)

Jones, R. Tudur, *Hanes Annibynwyr Cymru* (Swansea: Welsh Union of Independents, 1966)

Jones, R. Tudur, *Yr Undeb* (Swansea: John Penry Press, 1975)

Jones, Simon B., and Evans, E. Lewis (eds), *Ffordd Tangnefedd: Pregethau a Barddoniaeth* (Llandysul: Gwasg Gomer, 1943)

Jenkins, Philip, *The History of Modern Wales 1536–1990* (London: Longmans, 1992)

Kendall, Walter, *The Revolutionary Movement in Britain, 1900–1921: The Origins of British Communism* (London: Littlehampton Book Services, 1969)

Kenefick, William, 'War Resisters and Anti-Conscription in Scotland: An ILP Perspective', in Catriona Macdonald and E. W. McFarland (eds), *Scotland and the Great War* (Edinburgh: Tuckwell Press, 1998), pp. 59–80

Kennedy, Thomas C., *British Quakerism: The Transformation of a Religious Community 1860–1920* (Oxford: Oxford University Press, 2001)

Kennedy, Thomas C., *The Hound of Conscience: A History of the No-Conscription Fellowship* (Fayetteville: University of Arkansas, 1981)

Kennedy, Thomas C., 'Public Opinion and the Conscientious Objector, 1915–1919', *Journal of British Studies*, 12/2 (1973), 105–19

Koss, Stephen, *Nonconformity in Modern British Politics* (B. T. Batsford, 1975)

Laybourn, Keith, and James, David (eds), *The Centennial History of the I.L.P.* (Bradford: Bradford Libraries and Archive Service, 1987)

Liddington, Jill, *The Life and Times of a Respectable Radical: Selina Cooper 1864–1946* (London, 1984)

Llwyd, Alan, and Edwards, Elwyn, *Y Bardd a Gollwyd: Cofiant David Ellis* (Barddas,1992)

Llywelyn, Jen, *Pilgrim of Peace; A Life of George M. Ll. Davies, Pacifist, Conscientious Objector, and Peace-maker* (Talybont: Y Lolfa, 2016)

Maelor, Lord, *Fel Hyn y Bu* (Denbigh: Gwasg Gee, 1970)

Mansfield, Nicholas, and Horner, Craig (eds), *The Great War: Localities and Regional Identities* (Newcastle upon Tyne: Cambridge Scholars Publishing, 2014)

Marquand, David, *Ramsay MacDonald* (Jonathan Cape, 1977)

Marwick, Arthur, *Clifford Allen: Open Conspirator* (Edinburgh and London: Oliver and Boyd, 1964)

Marwick, William H., 'Conscientious Objection in Scotland in the First World War', *Scottish Journal of Science*, 1/3 (1972), 157–64

McDermott, James, *British Military Service Tribunals 1916–1918: 'A very much abused body of men'* (Manchester: Manchester University Press, 2011)

McNair, John, *James Maxton: The Beloved Rebel* (London: Allen and Unwin, 1955)

Miles, Gareth, 'Review of "Cofiant David Elis"', *Taliesin*, 81 (1993),106–10

Merthyr Tydfil Teachers' Centre, *Merthyr Tydfil: A Valley Community* (Merthyr, 1981)

Millman, Brock, *Managing Domestic Dissent in Britain* (Frank Cass and Co., 2000)

Minchinton, W. E. (ed.), *Industrial South Wales 1750–1914* (Frank Cass and Co., 1969)

Moorehead, Caroline, *Troublesome People: Enemies of War 1916–1986* (Hamish Hamilton, 1987)

Mor-O'Brien, Anthony, 'Keir Hardie, C.B. Stanton, and the First World War', *Llafur*, 4/3 (1986)

Mor-O'Brien, Anthony, 'Patriotism on Trial: The Strike of the South Wales Miners, July 1915', *Welsh History Review*, 12 (1984), 76–104

Mor-O'Brien, Anthony, 'The Merthyr Boroughs Election, November 1915', *Welsh History Review*, 12 (1985), 538–66

Morgan, D. Densil, *The Span of the Cross: Religion and Society in Wales 1914–2000* (Cardiff: University of Wales Press, 1999)

Morgan, Jane, 'Police and Labour in the Age of Lindsay, 1910–1936', *Llafur*, 5/1 (1988), 15–20

Morgan, K. O., *Keir Hardie, Radical and Socialist* (Weidenfeld and Nicolson, 1975)

Morgan, K. O., *Labour People* (Oxford: Oxford University Press, 1987)

Morgan, K. O., 'Peace Movements in Wales, 1889–1945', *Welsh History Review*, 10/3 (1981), 398–430

Morgan, K. O., *Re-birth of a Nation* (Cardiff and Oxford: University of Wales Press and Clarendon Press, 1981)

Morgan, K. O., *Revolution to Devolution; Reflections on Welsh Democracy* (Cardiff: University of Wales Press, 2014)

Morgan, K. O., *Wales in British Politics* (Cardiff: University of Wales Press, 1963, repr. 1970)

Morris, A. J. A., 'Book review of *Abolition of War: The Peace Movements in Britain, 1914–1919*, by Keith Robbins', *Welsh History Review*, 9/1 (1978), 108–12

Nicholson, Ivor, and Williams, Lloyd (eds), *Wales: Its Part in the War* (Hodder and Stoughton, 1919)

No-Conscription Fellowship, *The No-Conscription Fellowship: A Souvenir of its Work during the Years 1914–1919* (London: No-Conscription Fellowship, 1919)

Pamffledi Heddychwyr Cymru (Denbigh: Gwasg Gee, 1943)

Parri, Harri, *Gwn Glan a Beibl Budr* (Caernarfon: Gwasg y Bwthyn, 2014)

Parry, Cyril, 'Gwynedd and the Great War, 1914–1918', *Welsh History Review*, 14/1 (1988), 78–117

Pearce, Cyril, *Comrades and Conscience* (Francis Boutle Publishers, 2001)

Peate, Iorwerth, *Y Traddodiad Heddwch yng Nghymru, Pamffledi Heddychwyr Cymru* (Denbigh: Gwasg Gee, 1944)

Pennell, Catriona, *A Kingdom United: Popular Responses to the Outbreak of the First World War in Britain and Ireland* (Oxford: Oxford University Press, 2012)

Pope, Robert, *Building Jerusalem: Nonconformity, Labour and the Social Question in Wales 1906–1939* (Cardiff: University of Wales Press, 1997)

Pope, Robert, 'Facing the Dawn: Socialists, Nonconformists and *Llais Llafur*', *Llafur*, 7/3 (1999), 77–87

Pretty, David A., *Farmer, Soldier and Politician. The Life of Brigadier-General Owen Thomas MP: Father of the Welsh Army Corps* (Wrexham: Bridge Books, 2011)

Rae, John, *Conscience and Politics: the British Government and the Conscientious Objector to Military Service 1916–1919* (Oxford: Oxford University Press, 1970)

Rees, D. Ben, *Herio'r Byd* (Liverpool: Cyhoeddiadau Modern Cymreig, 1980)

Rees, D. Ben, *Dal i Herio'r Byd* (Liverpool: Cyhoeddiadau Modern Cymreig, 1983)

Rees, Dylan, 'Morgan Jones, educationalist and Labour politician', *Morgannwg*, 31 (1987), 66–83

Rees, Harding, 'Rhai Atgofion Gwrthwynebydd Cydwybodol o'r Rhyfel Byd Cyntaf', *Trafodion Hanes y Bedyddwyr* (2001), 19–26

Rees, Ivor Thomas, 'Thomas Evan Nicholas 1879–1971', *National Library of Wales Journal*, 35 (2010), 1–15

Robbins, Keith, *The Abolition of War: The Peace Movement in Britain, 1914–1919* (Cardiff: University of Wales Press, 1976)

Ronan, Alison, *A Small Vital Flame: Anti-War Women in North West England, 1914–1918* (Scholars Press, 2014)

Smith, Dai, *Aneurin Bevan and the World of South Wales* (Cardiff: University of Wales Press, 1993)

Smith, J. Beverley (ed.), *James Griffiths and his Times* (Ferndale: W. T. Maddock, 1977)

Spiers, Edward M., Crang, Jeremy, and Strickland, Matthew (eds), *A Military History of Scotland* (Edinburgh: Edinburgh University Press, 2012)

Supple, Barry, *The History of the British Coal Industry, 1914–1946: The Political Economy of Decline*, 4 (Oxford: Oxford University Press, 1987)

Swartz, Marvin, *The Union of Democratic Control in British Politics during the First World War* (Oxford: Clarendon Press, 1971)

Tanner, Duncan, Williams, Chris, and Hopkin, Deian (eds), *The Labour Party in Wales 1900–2000* (Cardiff: University of Wales Press, 2000)

Tanner, Duncan, *Political Change and the Labour Party 1900–1918* (Cambridge: Cambridge University Press, 1990)

Tatham, M., and Miles, J. E., *The Friends Ambulance Unit 1914–1919* (Swarthmore Press, 1920)

Tiltman, H. Hessell, *James Ramsay MacDonald* (Plymouth: Mayflower Press, 1928)

Tobias, Lily, *Eunice Fleet*, introduction by Jasmine Donahaye (Dinas Powys: Honno Classics, 2004)

Tomos, Angharad, *Hiraeth am Yfory* (Llandysul: Gwasg Gomer, 1995)

Vaughan, Hubert H., 'The Cardiganshire Appeal Tribunal March 1916–November 1918', *Wales*, 25 (1947), 171–80

Vellacott Newberry, Jo, 'Anti-War Suffragists', *History*, 62 (1977), 411–25

Vellacott, Jo, 'Review of Thomas C. Kennedy, *The Hound of Conscience*', *Russell: The Journal of Bertrand Russell Studies*, 1/2 (1981), 158–61

Vellacott Newberry, Jo, 'Review of Keith Robbins, *Abolition of War*', *Russell: The Journal of Bertrand Russell Studies*, 23/34 (1976), 52–60

Vellacott Newberry, Jo, *Bertrand Russell and the Pacifists in the First World War* (Brighton: The Harvester Press, 1980)

Vellacott Newberry, Jo, *Pacifists, Patriots and the Vote: The Erosion of Democratic Suffragism in Britain During the First World War* (Basingstoke: Palgrave Macmillan, 2007)

Wallace, Ryland, *The Women's Suffrage Movement in Wales 1866–1928* (Cardiff: University of Wales Press, 2003)

Wallis, Jill, *Valiant for Peace: A History of the Fellowship of Reconciliation 1914 to 1989* (Fellowship of Reconciliation, 1991)

Watkins, Harold, *Life Has Kept Me Young* (Watts and Co., 1952)

Weller, Ken, *Don't Be a Soldier: The Radical Anti-War Movement in North London 1914–1918* (Journeyman Press, 1985)

White, Stephen, 'Soviets in Britain: The Leeds Convention of 1917', *International Review of Social History*, 19 (1974), 165–93

Wilcox, F. McL., *Seventh Day Adventists in Time of War* (Washington DC, 1936)

Williams, Chris, *Democratic Rhondda: Politics and Society 1885–1951* (Cardiff: University of Wales, 1996)

Williams, David, *The History of Modern Wales* (John Murray, 1950)

Williams, Glanmor (ed.), *Merthyr Politics: The Making of a Working Class Tradition* (Cardiff: University of Wales Press, 1966)

Williams, Gwyn A., *When Was Wales?* (Penguin Books, 1985)

Williams, Huw L., '"Segurdod yw Clod y Cledd"; David Davies a'r Helfa am Heddwch Wedi'r Rhyfel Mawr', in Gethin Matthews, *Creithiau* (Cardiff: University of Wales Press, 2016), pp. 183–203

Winter, J. M., *Socialism and the Challenge of War: Ideas and Politics in Britain 1912–1918* (Routledge and Kegan Paul, 1974)

Williams, R. R. *Breuddwyd Cymro mewn Dillad Benthyg* (Liverpool: Gwasg y Brython, 1964)

Wilkinson, Alan, *The Church of England and the First World War* (SPCK, 1978)

Wrigley, Chris, *David Lloyd George and the British Labour Movement: Peace and War* (Aldershot: Gregg Revivals, 1976)

iv) Theses and dissertations

Barlow, Robin, 'Aspects of the First World War in Carmarthenshire 1914–1918' (unpublished PhD, University of Wales, 1991)

Davies, David Keith, 'The Influence of Syndicalism and Industrial Unionism on the South Wales Coalfield 1898–1921: A Study in Ideology and Practice' (unpublished PhD, University of Wales, 1991)

Demont, Susan E., 'Tredegar and Aneurin Bevan: A Society and its Political Articulation' (unpublished PhD, University of Wales, 1990)

Hughes, Clive, 'Army Recruitment in Gwynedd' (unpublished MA, University of Wales, 1983)

Marwick, Arthur, 'The Independent Labour Party 1918–1932' (unpublished BLitt, University of Oxford, 1960)

Matthews, Ioan A., 'The World of the Anthracite Miner' (unpublished PhD, University of Wales, 1995)

May, Edward, 'Social and Industrial Relations in the South Wales Coalfield' (unpublished PhD, University of Wales, 1995)

McCarry, Thomas, 'Labour and Society in Swansea, 1887–1918' (unpublished PhD, University of Wales, 1986)

Phillips, Rob, 'Gorfodaeth Filwrol yn Sir Gaerfyrddin yn ystod y Rhyfel Mawr' (unpublished MPhil, University of Wales, 1992)

Price, Mark David, 'The Labour Movement and Patriotism in the South Wales Coalfield during the First World War' (unpublished MA, University of Wales, 1999)

Quinn, Desmond Francis, 'Voluntary recruitment in Glamorgan 1914–1916' (unpublished MA, University of Wales, 1994)

Thomas, John, 'The South Wales Coalfield under Government Control 1914–1921' (unpublished MA, University of Wales, 1925)

Williams, Chris, 'Democratic Rhondda: Politics and Society 1885–1951' (unpublished PhD, University of Wales, 1991)

Wright, Martin, 'Wales and Socialism: Political Culture and National Identity *c.*1880–1914' (unpublished PhD, Cardiff University, 2011)

INDEX